Portrait of a Profession

Portrait of a Profession

A History of the Solicitor's Profession, 1100 to the Present Day

By

HARRY KIRK

Solicitor, sometime Scholar, Oriel College, Oxford

LONDON

Oyez Publishing

1976

OYEZ HOUSE, 237 LONG LANE
LONDON SE1 4PU
1976

ISBN 85120 289 6

Published December 1976

PRINTED IN GREAT BRITAIN BY
BUTLER & TANNER LIMITED
FROME AND LONDON

FOREWORD BY THE PRESIDENT OF THE LAW SOCIETY

When it was realised that no recent authoritative account of the history of the solicitor's branch of the legal profession existed, consideration had to be given as to who was best fitted to undertake the task of writing one. The name of Harry Kirk virtually suggested itself. Besides his wide experience as a practising solicitor he had sat as a member of the Council of The Law Society for nineteen years and had performed, with distinction, the arduous task, amongst many others, of Chairman of the Council's Professional Purposes Committee. That the choice was, in the event, a wise one is evident from the talent for research and clear exposition which this work clearly manifests.

Mr Kirk's book is published whilst a Royal Commission is enquiring widely into the provision of legal services. Its publication is therefore timely, since those who read it will see that the rise of the profession to its present status has involved strenuous endeavours on the part of solicitors dedicated to the interests of the profession and the public over long periods of time. Those who believe great institutions are the better for slow development under which each stage is tried and tested, rather than a revolutionary approach aimed at instant perfection, will follow in these pages the achievements which have been gradually wrought and which continue to be effected with the passage of each year.

The legal profession and those who are interested in it will glean much benefit and understanding from a careful study of Mr Kirk's work and there is no doubt that it will provide a ready source of authoritative reference for many years to come.

The Law Society's Hall DAVID NAPLEY

PREFACE

This book has been written at the invitation of The Law Society, but I have been left a completely free hand as to form, contents and opinions. It is not intended as an apologia and indeed none is necessary. It is an attempt to paint a true-to-life portrait of the solicitor's profession and at the same time to show how its features have developed over the past eight hundred years or so. Every man has his own mental picture of the profession and even that varies according to the circumstances of the moment. The solicitor is to one man his best friend and to another his worst enemy; to the one he is shrewd and resourceful and to the other the same qualities make him appear devious and tricky. One nineteenth-century writer on the professions in general said of this one that 'from the world it receives every deference when in need and every ingratitude when not required'. It is natural that critics and observers should seek to delineate and define an average solicitor, primarily for the purpose of comparing him with other professional men, but it is a futile search, for there is no such thing and solicitors are as varied in their attributes as the people they serve. A professional portrait is therefore necessarily a group picture.

Until the eighteenth century the reliable material is really rather scarce and there is a danger that one tries to read too much into what there is. The material becomes increasingly substantial after that date and from the beginning of the nineteenth century onwards the day-to-day events were recorded and discussed in detail by a numerous legal press representing different points of view. That too was the period in which the profession in the fullest sense of that term came into being, mainly due to the establishment of The Law Society in 1825. The picture one can paint now is mellower than it would have been one hundred and fifty years ago. Using the word in the mid-Victorian sense, more of the group look more gentlemanly; more are much better educated; although the enormously rich men of the earlier period have faded out of the picture the present group is generally much more prosperous. All in all it is much more pleasing. I have not tried to make it so; when I have seen blemishes I have not painted them out. One has to say that in spite of this better aspect there inevitably remain people who do not like it and want to change it. My readers will see that this has been a constant theme and the present-day critics are but sucking doves compared with those of earlier times. The every-man-his-own-lawyer objective has been entertained not only by revolutionaries like Jack Cade but by men of the calibre of Sir Thomas More, Cromwell and Napoleon; for more than three hundred years English Parliaments showed their dislike of litigants having professional assistance. The arguments have never changed much in their essentials and it is not likely that they will do so in the future. A profession which has withstood all the criticisms and accusations levelled at it for so many centuries and which can today present the picture as I have painted it is entitled to be proud of itself and confident of its future.

I have received considerable help in the libraries which so readily placed their resources at my disposal and I gladly and gratefully acknowledge it. In particular I mention Mr Paul Richardson, The Law Society's Librarian, and his assistant Mr Alfred Darby, now, alas, retired; Miss Marshallsay and Miss Hoyle at the Southampton University Library; and the staff at the Bodleian and University Law Library at Oxford. All showed me great kindness and patience as well as giving me the benefit of their knowledge and experience. I have inevitably drawn heavily on the work of other writers and I hope that I have acknowledged in my footnotes each occasion when I have done so. To them I am also deeply grateful.

Wareham, Dorset
October 1976

H KIRK

CONTENTS

CHAPTER 1

Origins and Evolution

A solicitor is an officer of the court appointed by members of the public to act for them, generally for a fee, in their legal business or in other matters which require the skill and knowledge usually possessed by a member of a court of law.[1] In that sense there have been solicitors, then called attorneys, in England and Wales since the twelfth century, but it was not until the Supreme Court of Judicature Act 1873 was passed that the solicitor of the Supreme Court was created as an amalgam of the attorney, the solicitor, the proctor and the court official, each of whom had performed his own part in the complicated system of law agency which had developed over a period of some six hundred years to meet changing needs and conditions. Antiquity is generally reckoned to confer virtue on those institutions which possess it and none esteem it so highly on that account as lawyers. It is therefore tempting in looking at the early formative years to read into documents, words and events intentions and meanings not intended or contemplated at the time by their authors and actors. But 'when we consider the emergence and development of attorneys ... it is imperative we should first of all remove from our minds the unwarranted assumptions and misleading anachronisms by which the matter is so greatly obscured. Few subjects in the history of the Law have stood in such need of rescue from their friends.'[2] Medieval kings and administrators tended to be pragmatic; they dealt with specific problems of immediate concern and generally did not work out long-term policies. One of their problems was the adaptation of court procedures to meet new situations; frequently judges, officials and litigants had made their own attempts at a solution and then the problem became one of regularising or controlling what had already happened in practice. One important instance was the representation of a litigant by an agent.

The fundamental rule of the Anglo-Norman legal system was that disputes had to be settled by personal confrontation between the parties in battle. 'To make the parties fight it out under the supervision of the court was an obvious and easy means of discovering the judgment of God and

[1] Maugham, Treatise on the Law of Attorneys and Solicitors (1825), p 4. Although a solicitor is frequently referred to as an officer of the court, he is, strictly speaking, an officer of the Supreme Court.

[2] Selden Society, vol 76, p xxix.

was used all over Europe in early times.'[3] Queen Elizabeth I intervened in 1571 to stop a trial by this method, and it survived in England until 1819, when it was abolished by statute following a decision that it was still legal.[4] The Church and the courts gradually caused it to fall into disuse in practice, and in 1179 the Grand Assize entitled a defendant in a possession action to elect to have the issue tried by the assize rather than by battle.[5] But the personal attendance of the parties was still required. The concept of a party being represented by an agent was completely alien to the system; each must appear to face his adversary even if physical combat were not involved. This presented little difficulty when men were static and justice was local, but as these conditions changed motives of convenience if not of necessity led to a relaxation of the strict rule of personal attendance. One practical difficulty after the Conquest was that the language of the courts was Norman-French and so remained until 1373; this made some arrangement necessary for the native Englishman. By the time that Glanvill was writing his Treatise[6] in 1181 it was common practice for a party to appear personally in court and there to nominate somebody to answer for him—a *'responsalis ad lucrandum vel perdendum'*. At first the appointment was a matter of grace by the King's writ, but as the practice became more widely adopted the appointment was made as a matter of course by the court. When this stage was reached is not known, but it was probably by the end of the twelfth century. Another type of representative known as an essoiner was also permitted. An essoin was an excuse for non-attendance and the man who tendered it to the court was an essoiner. A skilful use of essoins could enable a defendant to defer judgment interminably and the device was widely used. The concept of personal attendance had therefore been breached by the early thirteenth century, and from that point it was only a short step to the acceptance of a representative who had full power to do all that his principal might do if he were present in person. That was given statutory recognition in 1236 by the Statute of Merton, which authorised every freeman to appoint an attorney in counties, hundreds and wapentakes without seeking a royal writ on each occasion.[7] The Statute is the first appearance of the title 'attorney' in relation to a legal representative in a court and an attorney was said by Bracton, writing at the time, to be very different from the *responsalis*, though he did not specify what the difference was. Clearly, however, one was the forerunner of the other. In any event it is fruitless to attempt now to give to these titles—*responsalis*, essoiner or attorney—any precise

[3] Harding, Law Courts of Medieval England, p 39.

[4] 59 Geo 3 c 46; *Ashford* v *Thornton* (1818), 1 Barn & Ald 405; Inderwick, The King's Peace, pp 62–67.

[5] See J H Round, *The Athenaeum*, 28th January 1899.

[6] Treatise on the Laws and Customs of the Realm of England.

[7] The date is often given as 1235, but the numeration is 20 Hen 3 c 10 and Pollock and Maitland, History of English Law, vol I, p 179, give 1236 and the occasion the Queen's Coronation.

definition, and every attempt to do so breaks down in the face of instances which are inconsistent with each other.[8] The courts at the time were grappling with the problem of adapting and indeed creating a legal system to meet the changing requirements of society and they gradually allowed to *responsales* and essoiners functions which earlier they would have refused. By the time that statutory recognition was given to their practice by the Statute of Merton it was appropriate to give a generic title to the men who represented litigants. The term chosen was not unnaturally attorney, for 'attournee' was a word which had been used in the Grand Coustumier de Normandie of a man who attorns to defend or prosecute a suit. The Statute was not creating a new form of legal representative: it was applying a traditional title to existing ones.

The transition to the acceptance of the attorney, the *alter ego* of the litigant, was accelerated by the centralisation of the Court of Common Pleas at Westminster as part of the reforms embodied in Magna Carta in 1215. For the barons who had exacted this concession it was manifestly an advantage to know where the court was to be found rather than to have to follow it to wherever the King happened to be, but for lesser men seeking justice it must have been a considerable burden to go to Westminster to get it. Accordingly, starting in 1256 with the Statute of Merton and ending with a statute of 1587, the right to appoint attorneys was gradually extended until it became universal.[9] The attorney could probably be any free and lawful person. There were cases where women were appointed, though the Mirror of Justices[10] stated the position to be that 'all who are

[8] Selden Society, vol 76, pp xx–xxi: 'The functions of an essoiner seem sometimes indistinguishable from the functions of an attorney': and Cohen, History of the English Bar, p. 141: 'The pre-attornatus system which Bracton had in mind is not now intelligible.'

[9] 1236 (20 Hen 3)—Statute of Merton, *supra.*

1275 (3 Edw 1)—Statute of Westminster: required a defendant who had 'appeared' to appoint an attorney or to defend in person—if he did neither he was not to be 'essoined' or excused for his absence but might have judgment given in his absence.

1278 (6 Edw 1)—Statute of Gloucester: removed the bar on a defendant in an action 'touching wounds and maims' appointing an attorney and authorised the sheriff to proceed against an unsuccessful defendant personally.

1285 (13 Edw 1)—Statute of Westminster II: enabled a person who owned lands in several shires to appoint one person his general attorney to represent him in all courts on the circuit.

1299 (27 Edw 1): a person unable to travel to the court or who lived abroad should 'have a writ out of Chancery to some sufficient men that shall receive their attornies when need is'.

1318 (12 Edw 2)—Statute of York: authorised defendant in action of novel disseisin to appoint attorney.

1383 (7 Ric 2): power of appointment given to persons going abroad with the King's licence, and in

1405 (7 Hen 4): to persons outlawed by wrong process of law, and in

1407 (9 Hen 4): to everybody until the next Parliament.

1587 (29 Eliz 1): Statute enabling attorneys to be appointed in penal statute cases.

[10] Selden Society ed, p 88. This statement was much canvassed in *Bebb* v *Law Society* [1914] 1 Ch 286 on Miss Bebb's application to be allowed to sit the Society's examinations with a view to becoming a solicitor.

not prohibited by law may be attorneys but the law will not suffer women to be attorneys nor infants nor serfs'. It was of course one thing to have the right to appoint an attorney; it was another to have the right person available to appoint. For the great men and the great monastic houses the problem did not much arise. They had in their establishments bailiffs well able to undertake the task. But lesser men had to find among their relations, friends or neighbours somebody to undertake this difficult and onerous task, and many succeeded in doing so. The attorneys named in the Year Books and Court Rolls down to the end of the fifteenth century are mainly men in this category. Yet the task they were undertaking called more and more for technical knowledge and skill. An admission by an attorney for most purposes bound his principal, and attorneys were frequently asked in court whether they admitted this or that fact, with the decision of the court dependent on their replies. Exclusive rights of audience in the courts had not been established and attorneys could and did argue cases for their principals. The form of appointment even was important. If for safety's sake a litigant appointed two attorneys both had to be present unless he had taken the precaution of appointing them jointly and severally;[11] if both were present they could make conflicting admissions or submissions so that the litigant had to tell them carefully what they should and should not say;[12] and if the attorney did not have the warrant of appointment available he might be imprisoned.[13] The formalities were becoming more complicated. At the beginning of the thirteenth century there were fifty or sixty forms of writ in the Register of Writs; by the end of the century there were 120; and by 1320 there were 890. Moreover the control of procedural matters by the clerks—which eventually almost strangled the common law—meant that strict compliance with form and precedent was essential. The relief from the obligation to attend personally and the right to nominate somebody who was entitled to deal with the whole business greatly increased the amount of litigation,[14] and this pressure of business in the courts must in its turn have made the task of the amateur attorney even more difficult. It must also have increased the length of time which he might have to spend in London or wherever the courts might be sitting. In these circumstances there was a pressing need for some professional assistance.

The guidance and help which the litigant needed were provided in the first instance mainly by the court officials, who acted as attorneys for fees paid by those they assisted. The clerks in Common Pleas up to and including the first prothonotary were dependent entirely on fees for their income, and from the time of Edward I the fees paid by litigants for services rendered as attorneys provided the clerks with a substantial additional

[11] Petition of Mayor etc of Gloucester, Selden Society, vol 16, p 213.
[12] YB (Rolls Series) 20 Edw 3 (I), p 270.
[13] Selden Society, vol 76, p 47.
[14] Coke's Institutes, vol 2, p 249.

and stable income. The Exchequer clerks were also professionally employed on a substantial scale before the end of the twelfth century. This function of the court officer was known and recognised as a perfectly proper one for at least six hundred years. At first the clerks were well fitted to undertake the work because the litigant's chief need was a knowledge of the procedure before and after the actual trial. The idea of the attorney of the litigant being an officer of the court and being primarily concerned with procedural matters was thus early established. But there was a limit to the help which the clerks could give. They could do only what could be transacted in the court offices. Moreover the sheer volume of business was such that they could not tackle anything like all of it. In 1129–1130 the Pipe Rolls recorded only 162 judgments in the King's favour; in 1176–1177 there were 1215. In the 1198 eyre Norfolk litigants alone were involved in more than 200 judgments. The whole period from the end of the reign of Henry II to the latter part of the thirteenth century was a time of upheaval and civil strife in which the acquisition and defence of property and other rights became a major occupation for many people. The solution to the difficulty was found in the appointment of a common attorney—a man open to accept instructions to represent any who would pay his fee, as distinct from the attorney accepting appointment as a favour for a friend or relation. There is no evidence as to the way in which such a man was found or selected, but it is reasonable to suppose that then as ever since there were men who frequented the precincts of the courts ready to help for a consideration those who were palpably at a loss what to do in an unfamiliar atmosphere and place. It is likely that these men worked in close association with the court clerks and earned money for the service of directing clients to them. They would learn the business as they went along and the better of them would be able to obtain appointment as attorneys in preference to or in default of a court clerk. Professionalism of this sort started quite early, and the first complaints about common attorneys were made in the twelfth century.

The litigant had other assistance available to him, particularly when he needed somebody to speak for him before the court itself. How and when the professional advocate first appeared is not known. 'The history of the attorney, obscure as it often is, is lucidity itself when set against all we can learn about the process whereby the friend who gave disinterested advice developed into the stranger serjeant at law who offered his eloquence for hire';[15] 'I prefer to stand on the clear and certain ground that the first official recognition of the counsel or advocate authorised to represent his client in court is to be found in the 3rd year of Edward I' (ie 1275).[16] The professional advocate or counter or narrator had of course emerged before that date; it had by that time become necessary to control him and the other professionals assisting litigants. The counter was so

[15] Selden Society, vol 55, p civ.
[16] Inderwick, op cit, p 89.

called because the count or declaration comprehended the substance of the original writ and was the foundation of the action. The legal scene was described by the author of the Mirror of Justices: 'There are many who know not how to defend their causes in judgment and there are many who do; and therefore pleaders are necessary so that that which the plaintiffs or actors cannot or know not how to do by themselves they may do by their serjeants, attorneys or friends. Counters are serjeants skilful in the laws of the realm who serve the common people to declare and defend actions in judgment for those who have need of them for fees.'[17] Although there were from the outset signs of specialisation and therefore of separation of the functions of the counters from those of the attorneys, that process had by the end of the thirteenth century not gone very far. There was simply an amorphous body of men offering services in legal matters in return for fees. Their titles and their functions were alike indefinite and perhaps interchangeable. Serjeants are to be found 'attorning' and the same man in the same eyre may be called an attorney or a narrator.

The changes which had taken place in the judicial system and the general confusion caused by the political unrest of the period made it necessary to restore some sort of order into the legal organisation. The first formal step was taken in 1275 by the Statute of Westminster,[18] which declared that if any serjeant, counter, or other person did any manner of deceit or collusion in the King's court or consented unto it in deceit of the court or to beguile the court or the party and thereof was attainted he was to be imprisoned for a year and a day and excluded from pleading in future; if the offender was not a pleader he was liable to imprisonment for a year and a day. When Edward I returned from the French wars in 1289 he started a general cleaning-up process and as part of it made the Ordinance of 1292[19] in the following terms:

'De Attornatis et apprenticiis: Dominus Rex injunxit J de Meetingham et sociis suis, quod ipsi per eorum discretionem provident et ordinent certum numerum de quodlibet comitatum de melioribus et dignioribus et libertius addiscentibus, secondum quod intellixerunt quod curiae suoae et populo de regno melius valere potent et majus commodi fuerit et quod ipsi quos ad hoc eligerint, curiam sequantur et se de negotiis in eadem curia intromittent et alii non. Et viderunt Regi et ejus consilio quod septes viginti sufficere poterint; apporant tamen praefiti justiciarii plures si viderunt faciendum vel numerum anticipent. Et de alii per discretionem justiciarorum.'

No piece of medieval legislation has been subjected to so close a scrutiny as this Ordinance and none has been so variously interpreted or had so much read into it. It has been interpreted as applying to the Common Pleas and not to the King's Bench;[20] as applying to the King's Bench and

[17] Selden Society ed, p 47.
[18] c xxix.
[19] Rot Parl 1, p 84.
[20] Selden Society, vol 55, p ci, *n*3.

not to the Common Pleas;[21] as possibly originating 'the staffs of professional attorneys attached to the three common law courts';[22] as not applying to attorneys at all;[23] as possibly not even applying to 'apprentices', who were men studying to become serjeants;[24] as 'the origin of our present system of advocates with exclusive audience in the High Court—of the Bar of England';[25] and as the first official recognition of legal professional education.[26] That it applied to the King's Bench seems more likely from the references to appointments in each county and particularly to the phrase *'curiam sequantur'*. It has been suggested that this means merely being in attendance,[27] but the better view appears to be that the phrase is analogous to that in Magna Carta which fixed the Common Pleas at Westminster—*'Communia Placita non sequantur curiam nostram'*. The Ordinance was an attempt to provide a practical solution to a present problem. It was in the nature of things that lawyers of whatever leaning would prefer to remain stationary at Westminster rather than follow the judges and that it was necessary to ensure so far as possible that litigants who had to appear before the King's court on its travels should have proper and approved assistance available. The Ordinance recognised that the professional lawyer existed, that there was a need for his services and that it was in the public interest that the numbers should be limited, and that the courts should control both numbers and qualifications. Whether it was ever operated in practice is open to doubt; there is little or no evidence that it was. The reality of the problem was further recognised by a petition of the Commons in 1364 based on the difficulty of getting 'wise counsel'[28] and again in 1415 when they asked that judges should have power to appoint attorneys wherever they might be sitting and even that the power should be extended to serjeants.[29]

In the thirteenth century it is possible to get a much clearer picture of the professional attorney. The number of attorneys and apprentices recommended in the 1292 Ordinance was 140 and this underlines how few men were involved outside the court clerks. Between 1272 and 1307 there were not more than twenty or so whose names appear at all regularly on the King's Bench Rolls and certainly until the end of the century the court clerks were doing most of the work. In the Year Books for 1304–1305 only twenty-seven of the parties involved in the 373 cases reported were represented by attorneys and only a proportion of these would be professionals; in 1302–1303 the numbers were nine out of 335 and in 1292–1293 there

[21] Birks, Gentlemen at Law, p 38, and *Law Magazine and Review*, 1857, p 245.
[22] Holdsworth, History of English Law, vol 2, p 317.
[23] Cohen, op cit, p 283.
[24] Barrington, quoted *Law Magazine and Review*, 1857, p 246.
[25] A R Ingpen QC, Inns of Court and Chancery, p 122.
[26] Plunkett, History of English Law, 5th ed, p 217.
[27] Selden Society, vol 76, p lxv.
[28] 2 Rot Parl 286 No 4.
[29] 4 Rot Parl 80 No 11.

were only six attorneys in 261 cases.[30] The numbers did not materially increase during the fourteenth century. In the period 1388–1390 there were only fourteen attorneys whose names appear more than once; the most mentioned were John Sparrowe and John Russell, who appeared in six cases each. Of course, the reported cases were only a small part of the total litigation, but one would have expected professional attorneys to have been involved in a higher number of the reported cases, which presumably were the most important. In any case one has a yardstick from the cases in which serjeants or pleaders appear. The Year Books for 1389–1390 are typical of the others and they show that there were nine serjeants who appeared frequently, led by Hankford, who appeared no less than twenty times, followed by his brethren Markham with seventeen and Gascoyen with fifteen.[31] Whereas the pleaders were by this time fully occupied professionally and well on their way to becoming a clearly defined and powerful group, the attorneys were still mainly acting on a part-time basis, using the law as a supplement to their normal avocation. Consequently in 1402 when the Commons petitioned in protest about the number of attorneys they expressed concern that there were men who were earning their living entirely from acting as attorneys as if that were an abuse and contrary to normal expectation.[32]

London was a special case because the conditions there were markedly different from those in the rest of the country and feudal relationships ceased to exist there long before they did elsewhere. 'The people of the City are traders and have need of speedy remedy for the grievances that are done unto them.'[33] From an early date the City had its own system of courts: the Lord Mayor's, the Sheriff's or Hustings, the Orphans', and Pye-Powder. Appearance by attorney was well established in the twelfth century and in 1218 was a matter specially enquired into by the judges. They asked how attorneys were admitted to the Sheriff's Court; a citizen could appoint one freely, but foreigners could not do so at all if they were plaintiffs unless the case involved their own houses and they had the King's writ authorising them to appoint. Appearance by attorney had become so common that it was thought necessary in 1259 to obtain confirmation from Henry III of the citizens' right to conduct their cases in person if they so thought fit. In a general re-grant of rights in 1268 Henry III confirmed that the citizens 'have liberty to appoint their attorneys as well in pleading as defending there as elsewhere in our courts'.[34] City ordinances from an early date regulated the numbers, duties, fees and appointment of attorneys. In 1290 the basic rules were made and thereafter they were several times re-enacted. Those who practised were to be admitted each

[30] The Legal Profession, p 113 (published anonymously in 1850).

[31] Ames Foundation edition of Year Books 12–13 Richard II, *passim*.

[32] 3 Rot Parl 504.

[33] Liber Albus, p 255.

[34] 1267 (52 Hen 3); see Bohun, Laws, Customs and Privileges of the City of London (1702), p 10.

year by the Mayor; they were not to prosecute false suits; they were to behave quietly in court. The distinction between counters and attorneys was established by prohibiting a counter being appointed an attorney. The numbers were also fixed: in the Mayor's Court there were originally six but that was reduced to four; in the Sheriff's there were eight; the two most senior clerks in the Sheriff's Court acted as the attorneys in Pye-Powder; and the most junior attorney of the Lord Mayor's Court acted as clerk to the Orphans' Court. As to their duties: 'The attorneys have not the custody of any records belonging to these courts; their business is only to take their fees due to them in every cause and to give their clients notice of declarations and trials and to advise them when and what to plead.'[35] They were, at any rate in the Sheriff's Court, not to sit among the clerks or meddle with the Rolls,[36] but here again the rules and practice must have varied, with each court the master of its own procedure. As to the fees, in 1356 the Lord Mayor and aldermen ruled that they were to be reasonable and not more than forty pence per case. They remained very much at this level. In the seventeenth century in the Sheriff's Court the attorney had the right to have three fees in every case—they totalled 8s 4d—and if a case was called on more than once he received twenty pence for each call after the first. The second attorney in the Mayor's Court was by that date also clerk of the enrolments and was paid 6s for each enrolment, which bears a close relationship to the twenty pence paid in the early fourteenth century to the Recorder, who also had an annual salary of £20. A defendant who wanted time to pay out a judgment had to speak to an attorney in the Mayor's Court (this was the case in whichever court the judgment had been given) and pay him 4s to mark the Lord Mayor's list and later another twenty pence for moving for time.[37] As to appointment, that was in the gift of the Lord Mayor and Court of Aldermen before whom the attorneys swore their oaths on admission. Discipline was a matter for the courts, and although it occurred in the seventeenth century the case of a Mr Hutton illustrates the way in which it was administered and the basis of it. Mr Hutton, an attorney in the Sheriff's Court, was summoned peremptorily to appear before one of the courts, but he refused to come on the ground that he knew not what authority the court had to send for him. The court held that the refusal was an offence which entitled it to dismiss him from his office of attorney as 'a subordinate officer of this City'.[38] The attorney in London developed earlier than in the provinces and he was by reason of his monopoly always more clearly an officer of the court than the professional attorney elsewhere. It was probably because of that status that the demarcation between attorney and pleader was firstly clearly established in the City.

[35] Bohun, op cit, pp 300–301.
[36] Liber Albus, p 492.
[37] Bohun, op cit, p 302.
[38] Ibid, pp 435–437.

Elsewhere the division of the legal profession into two branches had not become final but was deepening. The Ordinance of 1292 treated the apprentices and the attorneys together, and each did work which much later would have been regarded as the function of the other. Because the attorney could do whatever his principal could do there were obvious advantages in leaving matters entirely to him rather than incurring the expense of employing a pleader who did not have that authority. As the professional attorney gained more experience those advantages became greater, and it seemed in the early fourteenth century that separation into two branches would be unnecessary and would not occur. Certainly until 1340 attorneys are found pleading in court and for their part the pleaders did not consider it improper to consult with a client without the intervention of an attorney. The serjeants traditionally sat at St Paul's to await those who came to consult them regardless whether their clients came with an attorney or not. All in the profession were in the same business. Whether the formalities were below the consideration of the pleader or pleading above the capacity of the man who usually acted as an attorney was a matter for each of them and possibly their clients to decide in the light of the circumstances of each case. When after the fashion of the times in the mid-fourteenth century the lawyers organised themselves into corporations, in their case called the Inns of Court, a man was not excluded because he followed mainly the vocation of an attorney. Court officers such as prothonotaries and filacers were admitted. But separation there was. It was a long process and the first irrevocable steps were not taken until the latter part of the sixteenth century. There were some technical factors which made it easier to evolve. The pleader was a mere spokesman whose words could be repudiated if the client so wished; by contrast the attorney was the client's *alter ego.* The early writs appointing attorneys place them in the stead of their clients *'ad lucrandum vel perdendum'* and although the later writs simply stated *'N attornavit R'* the attorneys' position was not changed. The attorney was appointed under the authority of the King's writ or statute by each client; the serjeants were appointed by royal letters patent and their office was a hereditament. The attorney had to swear an oath to the court to do his office faithfully; the serjeant's oath was to serve the King and his people, and the ordinary brother of the coif swore simply to serve the King's people.[39] But the reality of the matter arose from the calibre and standing of the men performing the several functions. The serjeants were the advisers of the King and of the great men; it was from them that the judges were chosen. After 1275 no statute or ordinance was passed by Parliament or made in council affecting the discipline of the pleaders, for it was they who advised both on matters affecting the law. As legal proceedings became more complicated the art of pleading became more difficult and only those specially trained for it could master it. The serjeants and those following them left the mechanical work to others and

[39] Pulling, History of the Coif, pp 34–35.

drew away. Because they were little if any below the judges in status, to them was naturally committed the selection of their colleagues and the supervision of those intending to follow them. How this was effected is not known.[40] But the Inns of Court during the fourteenth and fifteenth centuries in fact acquired the exclusive privilege of calling men to the Bar and, by so doing, of giving them and them alone the right to plead in the King's courts. No doubt the process was gradual; it is unlikely that there was any formal act; the essential factor was that the judges were in control of the courts and they had all been in practice as serjeants.

The legal profession was taking shape. The right to appear by attorney had been conceded in almost all forms of action. The practice of appointing as an attorney a man who would require a fee and who had special knowledge was replacing that of appointing a friend or relative. The legal hierarchy was sufficiently clearly established for the members of it to be placed by the Treasury in categories. The attorney was in the poll tax assessments made in 1379 classed with the apprentices of least estate at 6s 8d; the 'other' apprentices were assessed at 20s; and the serjeants at law and the 'great apprentices' were assessed at 40s. In public esteem the attorney was beginning to suffer from the fact that he earned his living by the use of his wits, and one of the songs current about 1330 contained the lament or accusation that 'Attourneis in cuntre theih geten silver for noht'.[41]

In 1402 came the first major intrusion of Parliament. It had already in 1322 by the Statute of Carlisle[42] tried to stop some of the laxities which it thought had crept into the appointment of attorneys. Appointment by barons of the exchequer and judges other than the chief justices were to be made only at the places where they were sitting and in respect of cases with which they were dealing; specifically and significantly clerks of the court were prohibited from admitting attorneys. Already it had become difficult to say who was validly appointed an attorney. On any showing the change from the personal appearance system to one permitting a representative was proving difficult to digest. The Parliament Rolls at this time are full of petitions directed against the multiplicity and evil practices of attorneys. It is unlikely that there would have been any objection to the 'private' attorney. The objection was to the 'common attorney', that is, to the man who was making his living as an attorney, and the legislation seems only comprehensible on the footing that the courts were to refuse to appoint an attorney who was a professional unless he were approved by the court as a suitable man. The Act of 1402[43] provided that 'for sundry damages and mischiefs which had ensued before that time to divers persons of the realm by a great number of persons ignorant and not learned in

[40] The Inns of Court and Chancery (1912), p 44; and Prest, The Inns of Court under Elizabeth I and Early Stuarts (1972), pp 50–58.

[41] Political Songs, p 339.

[42] 1318 (12 Edw 2) c 1.

[43] 1402 (4 Hen 4) c 18.

the law, as they were wont to be before that time, ... all the attorneys should be examined by the justices and by their discretions, their names put on the roll; and they that were good and virtuous and of good fame should be received and sworn well and truly to serve in their offices, and especially that they make no suit in a foreign county; and the other attorneys should be put out at the discretion of the justices; and that their masters for whom they were attorneys be warned to take others in their places so that in the meantime no damage nor prejudice should come to their masters. And if any of the attorneys died or ceased, the justices for the time being by their discretion should make another in his place, which was a virtuous man, and learned, and sworn in the same manner as aforesaid; and if any such attorney should be thereafter notoriously found in any default of record or otherwise he should forswear the court and never after be received to make any suit in any court of the King.' A following Act[44] prohibited certain officials such as stewards, bailiffs and ministers of lords of manors of franchises from being attorneys. The Act of 1402 may be said to have constituted the attorney as a professional class; his association with the apprentices in the Ordinance of 1292 had disappeared; and for the first time enrolment was required. It was in theory at least still necessary for each warrant of appointment to be entered on the court rolls in each case, and repeated statutes endeavoured to enforce this requirement;[45] failure to do so was fatal until the statute of jeofails[46] cured it, and thereafter the practice fell wholly into disuse.

The Act of 1402 could not have been seriously expected to be immediately effective, but the Commons were not satisfied to wait and in 1411 they again petitioned the King, this time to impose some limitation on numbers. Again it must have been the professional attorney with whom they were concerned. The court rolls of the period record thousands of appointments of attorneys, and the Commons must have been aware of that fact and of the enormous increase in litigation in the late fourteenth and early fifteenth centuries. It would have been completely idle to suggest, as they did, that all the attorneys, whether at Common Pleas or King's Bench, should be examined by the justices and their numbers limited to six, eight or twelve for each county according to size, if they were thinking of all attorneys, professional or amateur. Lord Campbell estimated that at the time there were two thousand attorneys,[47] and if they were all professionals the Commons were proposing a draconian reform. Palpably they were not. What one is still seeing is a large number of men supplementing their incomes by part-time attorneying, probably with little knowledge and certainly likely to cause loss to those who were foolish enough to engage them. The Commons were impressed with the abuses which this

[44] 1402 (4 Hen 4) c 19
[45] 1439 (18 Hen 6); 1540 (32 Hen 8) c 30; 1575 (18 Eliz 1) c 18; 1704 (4 Ann 1) c 16.
[46] 1575 (18 Eliz 1) c 14.
[47] Quoted Christian, Solicitors—An Outline of their History, p 29.

part-time system caused,[48] and were manifestly trying to limit paid representation to a few reliable men. The petition might well have been granted, but the Commons had added to it a request that court officials, specifically filacers and prothonotaries, should not be allowed to act as attorneys. This arose from the obvious abuse that where officials in charge of the court records were also acting as attorneys for the parties the records could be and were altered. It was an abuse which was complained of again and again, but in 1411, as later, the vested interests of the officials caused them to react strongly. The King was prayed in the name of God and as an act of charity not to accept the Commons petition, which it was said was so grievous and insupportable that it could not be carried out. The result was that the whole matter was referred to the judges and nothing more was heard of it. The appointment of attorneys attracted a fee to the judge, and judges who were easy-going in the matter of appointment had more business and more fees. It was hardly likely that once the matter came to them they would act to the detriment of themselves and their own officials. After this flurry of activity the Commons in effect for another one hundred and fifty years abdicated in this respect in favour of the judges. Only in the counties of Norfolk and Suffolk and the city of Norwich was another attempt at limitation made. In 1455 the numbers in these cases were restricted to six each for the two counties and two for the city; the Act was ineffective and did not inhibit the growth of the profession in these places during the four hundred years it was on the statute book.[49]

At this crucial time in the development of the profession, its education, its discipline and its corporate interests were no man's business. In the City of London the restriction on numbers meant that no guild need be formed and the profession was denied the traditional nucleus of a professional organisation. Outside the City the attorneys might be subject to some control through the Inns of Court and Chancery being set up along the road to Westminster at this time, but there is no evidence of it. Generally the attorneys were left to such control as an uninterested judiciary might see fit to impose. In practice this meant that they were left to develop as need arose in the sphere of work which had become recognised as particularly theirs – the mechanical and highly technical procedures of the common law courts. In those courts the very technicalities gave them an effective enough monopoly, but that was not the case in the new courts which in the fifteenth and sixteenth centuries developed with the active encouragement of the Chancellors. These new Chancery and prerogative courts were intended to remedy the defects and limitations of the common law courts, which had become hide-bound in formality to the extent of creating injustice; the new courts introduced into English jurisprudence the doctrines of conscience and equity and their business rapidly expanded.

[48] Eg 'falsifications, deceits, and disinheritances'; and attorneys 'little or entirely unlearned in the law and some of tender age'.

[49] It was not repealed until 1843.

Between 1420 and 1450 it increased fourfold and in the Elizabethan court of Chancery at least five hundred cases were entered each year. In these courts, too, litigants required attorneys, but in this case only a court clerk could be so appointed. In Chancery the clerks were known as the Six Clerks, whose office persisted down to 1843, when it was extinguished with handsome compensation. The volume of business was too much for them to handle and accordingly each was authorised to have under-clerks, at first eight each, then nine, and finally ten. As late as 1674 these men were formally declared to be the only attorneys in Chancery. In the Court of Requests there were three clerks designated to act as attorneys; in the Court of Star Chamber at first there were two, but later four. But the work was too much for the officials, and if litigants wished their suits to make any progress they had to get expert help. The men they employed were called common solicitors—common because they held themselves out for engagement by any who would pay their fee; and solicitors because of the work they did. The title solicitor derived from the Norman-French *sollicitur*, which in turn derived from the Latin *solicitare*: to agitate, to urge, or solicit.

The title or name was of long standing. Solicitors had been employed from early times by the so-called men of great estate to facilitate their business, which included litigation about their property. Their status in the great houses in which they served was that of menial servants. Attorneys also employed men in much the same capacity and therefore called by the same name. The attorney's need was for a man who knew his way about the courts and was able to transact a good deal of the purely formal business which was within the attorney's province. He was defined as 'in our common law a man employed to follow suits depending in law for the better remembrance and more ease of attorneys who commonly are so full of business that they cannot so often attend the serjeants and counsel as the case may require'.[50] These men were, however, not common solicitors, for they served only one master. Partly because they performed for their clients the same sort of service that the private solicitor had performed for his master, and partly because they were recruited from men who had been private solicitors, the men who helped litigants in the new courts were called solicitors too. They had no formal status. As early as 1486 it was decided that a solicitor was not an officer of the court and was therefore not entitled to any privileges;[51] Lord Chancellor Egerton (1596–1617) refused to accord them any standing at all.[52] It was suggested that for that reason they were guilty of maintenance—that is, of assisting a party in litigation without lawful cause—and that they were not entitled to recover their fees or expenses by action.[53] This want of recognition

[50] Cowell's Interpreter (1607).
[51] *Corner's Case* (1656), Noy 112.
[52] Veall, Popular Movement for Law Reform in England, p 50.
[53] Hudson, Star Chamber (published in Hargraves, *Collecteanea Juridica*, 1791–1792,

meant that the common solicitor was subject to neither statutory nor judicial control except for contempt. The first statute in which solicitors are mentioned, the so-called Attorneys Act 1605 (3 Jac 1, c 7) required only that they should be of sufficient and honest disposition. The practice books of the seventeenth century, although they give in detail the procedure on the admission of attorneys, are silent about the admission of solicitors because there was no formality.

In these circumstances any man who wished to embark on this vocation might do so and many did. 'Every idle fellow whose prodigality or ill-husbandry hath forced him out of his trade or employment takes upon himself to be a solicitor'[54] and 'Every broken tradesman turns solicitor'.[55] If attorneys were vituperated they were less harshly done by than solicitors: 'In these last times there sprang up first under the wings of noblemen of great estate and for the help of the attorney in the judicial courts but as attorney in the prerogative ones, a creature called a solicitor; these men rob both lawyers and attorneys and all subjects';[56] and 'in our age there are stepped up a new sort of people called solicitors unknown to the records of the law who like the grasshoppers of Egypt devour the whole land';[57] and the solicitor was a 'pettyfogging sophister' who 'differed from a lawyer as a shrimp does from a lobster, a frog from an elephant, and a tom-tit from an eagle'.[58] But the force of circumstances was too great; the common solicitor performed a task which needed to be done and for which people were prepared to pay. His existence was first formally recognised in orders of 1557 and 1574 in the Inner and Middle Temples respectively, which excluded both attorneys and common solicitors from membership. The practice books of the seventeenth century are generally directed to both attorneys and solicitors[59] and by this time solicitors were performing in Chancery the same work as the attorneys were doing at common law.[60] They were still regarded as inferior to attorneys, and when in 1654 the judges made an order relating to the training of attorneys they provided that service as a solicitor for five years was to be one method of qualifying as an attorney. The distinction was, however, being eroded. There were in London in particular many men who were acting as both

but written before 1635), p 93: only a barrister, an attorney or their clerks could maintain a cause 'by profession': as late as 1716 it seemed 'questionable whether solicitors who are not attorneys can justify the laying out of their money in another's suit' (Hawkins, Pleas of the Crown, 1824 ed, Book 1, c 27, s 30).

[54] The Compleat Solicitor (1686), p 13.

[55] Gilbert, History of the High Court of Chancery, p 21.

[56] Hudson, op cit, pp 94–95.

[57] Cock, English Law (1651), p 44.

[58] Pamphlet *circa* 1680, quoted Christian, Solicitors—an Outline of their History, pp 102–103.

[59] Eg The Compleat Solicitor; The Compleat Attorney and Solicitor (otherwise The Practick Part of the Law).

[60] Sawyer, A History of Solicitors and Attorneys in Proc Annual Prov Meeting 1887, at p 94.

attorneys and solicitors and it was inevitable that sooner or later a full alignment of qualification and control should be made. In 1729 an Act 'for the better regulation of Attornies and Solicitors'[61] laid down the same regulations for admission to either part of the profession and it specifically provided that attorneys might be admitted as solicitors in Chancery; the reverse situation was, however, not dealt with until 1749, when solicitors were enabled to become attorneys automatically. From this point the distinction between attorney and solicitor was purely formal, although it persisted until 1875.

Although solicitors were much maligned, particularly by barrister textbook writers in the seventeenth century, the title 'solicitor' never became a term of contumely in common use, like 'attorney'. This was due in part to the work which they did. Chancery work was concerned mainly with property and originally with the device of 'uses'. Uses 'allowed a feudal tenant to enfeoff all his property before death thus avoiding the feudal incidents of relief and wardship for his heir and at the same time preserve the normal succession of the land by settling the use on his heir; and if he chose to bestow the use on somebody else he effectively achieved the devising of land by will which feudal law forbade'.[62] The scheme failed, however, if the person to whom the land had been enfeoffed chose to ignore the trust and act on the literal interpretation of the documents to claim the property as his own. Common law provided no redress, but the Chancellors by applying the principle of conscience compelled the trustee to act in accordance with the true intention of the donor. At the same period the tendency for money to be lent on the security of mortgages of land was increasing; the common law was unable to help the borrower whose time had run out, but the Chancellors could do so on the basis of an equity of redemption. This new jurisdiction was therefore fundamental to the new propertied society which was developing, and it was the solicitors rather than the attorneys who were concerned with it. In so far as the common solicitors were initially recruited from the men who had been employed as private solicitors by the great landowners this was work for which they were particularly suited. 'The earliest type of attorney to be called a solicitor was a kind of land agent who solicited or instigated pleas to defend or increase his master's estate.'[63] For the future the significance was that solicitors were involved with land, and because land was until the late nineteenth century the only really respectable form of wealth the solicitors through their connection with it somehow had a much higher degree of respectability than the attorneys, in spite of the much humbler nature of their origin.

[61] 2 Geo 2 c 23; the Act is normally referred to as the Attorneys and Solicitors Act 1729 and that practice is followed in subsequent references in this book at pp 20, 23, 52, 72, 73 and 108.

[62] Harding, Social History of English Law, p 101.

[63] Harding, op cit, p 176.

During the sixteenth and seventeenth centuries the two professions of attorney and solicitor were subject to another formative influence: the separation of the legal profession into two branches. The possibility had always existed and the trend had for many years been towards separation, but it was not until the mid-sixteenth century that the process of excluding the attorneys and solicitors from the Inns of Court started and with it a final commitment by the Bar to a divided profession. The initial steps seem to have been taken because the Benchers wished to preserve the standards which the Inns still had in education and training. In the mid-sixteenth century it was remarked that 'for lack of funds for allowances and exhibitions many a good witt is compelled to give over and forsake study before he have any perfect knowledge in the law and to fall to practising and become a typler in the law'.[64] The policy of the Benchers was to exclude those who had given up study and, perhaps from force of circumstance, begun to earn a living in the only business they knew, that of the law. Those already practising as attorneys therefore were not to be admitted; any man already admitted who dropped or neglected his studies to work as an attorney was to be expelled. The pattern of the numerous orders which were made in this sense was set by the first of them made in 1555 by the Middle Temple:[65] 'No common attorney should be admitted to the Company and in all admissions it should be implied that every gentleman when he refuseth study to practice attorneyship shall be dismissed from this Company and to have liberty to go and resort to the House of Chancery from whence he came.' The same theme appears in the orders made by Lincoln's Inn in 1556 and by the Inner Temple in 1557. It was repeated in a Privy Council order signed by Bacon, Burleigh and Walsingham in 1574 that 'if any hereafter admitted in Court practise as attorney or solicitor they be dismissed from their Houses thereupon unless they shall also use the exercise of learning and mooting in the House'. The demarcation line was being drawn. Either one became a barrister—the title itself dates from 1532 or thereabouts–and remained in the Inn or worked as an attorney and was expelled. If one worked as an attorney but still devoted enough time to attend the moots and lectures one might still remain and be called to the Bar. It is the familiar situation of men trying to find solutions for novel problems and being pulled one way and another by conflicting interests. In the early sixteenth century the nobility and gentry had sent their sons in large numbers to the Inns of Court and for social reasons these young men wanted to be rid of the attorneys. In 1617 some of them in the Middle Temple, with the remarkable and persistent ability of lawyers to adjust facts to the suit they are pleading, petitioned their Benchers that the Inns of Court had been originally established as nurseries for the gentry and 'which is more for the nobility of this land'

[64] Dugdale, Origines, c 61, p 193.

[65] Middle Temple Rec, vol i, p 104. On the subject of the exclusion of attorneys from the Inns of Court see Dr Bellot's article, *Law Quarterly Review*, 1910, pp 137–145.

but that the 'glorye of this society is faded by the swarms of attorneys which are nowe admitted ... whereby the gentlemen of the societye are outeaten in the hall and eaten owt of their chambers of the house'.[66] The Benchers may not have disagreed with this view. But on the other hand they had to think of their finances and the attorneys provided a useful source of income from entry fees and fines on taking chambers. Then there were chambers to be let, and that was increasingly important from the mid-seventeenth century onwards, when the gentry left the Inns, and chambers built with money provided by the Inns were not in such great demand. There was also the consideration that working as an attorney had been a convenient way for a poor student to earn his living until he had established a viable practice. Most important of all, exclusion from the Inns of men who had traditionally been members of it must have been a difficult step to take. Although it could be said of some of the attorneys that they were ignorant rascals, there were not a few who were of high standing, well known to and respected by the Benchers. In these cases the demarcation of functions was not so clear then as it afterwards became and it was not easy to exclude respectable and experienced men simply because of the type of work with which they were principally occupied. In the Middle Temple in 1635 there were some thirty-two members, some of them barristers, who were working as common attorneys[67] and they must have represented a fair proportion of the total membership. The result was that the Inns did not or could not enforce their orders strictly, and they were repeated in 1614, 1635 and 1656. The Privy Council supported the Inns and made orders in the same sense in 1630 and 1664. On the other hand the judges had to consider the problem of maintaining some degree of supervision over the attorneys and their own officials who acted as attorneys. Their interest was to have these men in places where they could be found, preferably in an Inn of Court or of Chancery. Consequently orders were made by the judges in 1654, 1677, and 1684 requiring attorneys to be members of one or other of the Inns of Court or Chancery or to give a convenient address for their places of business. The wretched attorneys were therefore being told by the Inns of Court and the Privy Council to leave the Inns of Court and on the other hand told to join them by the judges. By 1704, however, it is clear that the judges had recognised the policy of exclusion, and their order of that year to the attorneys was to join an Inn of Court 'if those Honourable Societies should be pleased to admitt them'. Exclusion was not really effective until the latter part of the eighteenth century when the Inns began to require a gap between cessation of practice as an attorney and call to the Bar; it became difficult, though not impossible, for an assiduous man to earn his living as an attorney while training for the Bar or at least keeping his terms.

[66] Middle Temple MS unclassified, quoted Prest, The Inns of Court under Elizabeth I and the Early Stuarts, p 42.

[67] Prest, op cit, p 43.

For suitable men exceptions could still be made. Mr Gregory, when President of The Law Society in 1875, recalled that he and his father before him kept terms in Lincoln's Inn whilst under articles,[68] and Thomas and William Gresham were still in Gray's Inn in 1872 defending their right to be members notwithstanding that they were attorneys. In their petition in support of their application for a mandamus to prevent their exclusion they stated that 'for upwards of a century attorneys at law have been admitted as members and students of the Inn', but the court refused their application and there is no evidence that they had help or support from their fellow attorneys.

These events had the most important consequences. The Bar had cut itself off from those members of the legal profession whom it stigmatised as ministerial persons of an inferior nature and had committed itself to the courts as the main sphere of its activity. From the seventeenth century utter and inner barristers ceased to act as attorneys. The day-to-day work and its necessary consequence, the day-to-day contact with the lay client, were left by the Bar to the attorneys and solicitors, and by so doing it gave these men the means to thrive. At the time Roger North noted with regret that barristers had very imprudently transferred to attorneys the work of personally examining witnesses. Two hundred years later the Bar, and particularly the junior Bar, contemplated also with regret what had been done and the work which had been lost. 'From all these functions the rule of the Inns of Court, enlarged and interpreted as it was by the social vanity of the Bar, excluded the members of the higher branch of the profession', and the Victorian barrister might well cry: *'Heu! quantum mutatus in illo.'* Another consequence, disadvantageous to the entire legal profession but particularly to the attorneys and solicitors, was that exclusion from the Inns of Court left those men with no form of professional organisation. They entered the eighteenth century despised, ridiculed and unprotected, without any means of professional education.

Another class of practitioner was developing in the ecclesiastical and admiralty courts, performing there the same functions as the attorneys and solicitors were performing in the common law and Chancery courts. These were the proctors, who can be identified as early as the fourteenth century. In the Court of Arches in London there were then ten proctors and at York there were eight, with lesser numbers at other consistorial courts. Like the attorneys at common law the proctors were *domini litis*, that is to say capable of acting in the suit in which they were instructed as fully as the client himself. But as was appropriate to a mainly ecclesiastical jurisdiction their oath specifically obliged them to give up any case which they found to be unjust. Perhaps because of this and because they worked in a much smaller community, the proctors never suffered anything like the same calumny as the attorneys and solicitors. In London they had the benefit of a close regulation by the Archbishop of Canterbury, under whose

[68] Annual Provincial Meeting, p 13.

jurisdiction they came. In 1696 their number was fixed at thirty-four; there were supernumerary proctors, but they could be promoted to proctor only when there was a vacancy among the thirty-four. The limitation appears to have been effective and in Browne's Law List published in 1775 there were only forty-four proctors listed. Articles could be given only by proctors of at least five years' standing; the period was seven years; the articled clerk must have been no younger than fourteen years old nor older than eighteen on entry and he must not have been employed as a writing clerk; he had to have a sufficient knowledge of Latin. The proctors were ultimately housed in Doctors Commons. There they seem to have flourished, but the reforms of the mid-nineteenth century were too much for them and they were with adequate compensation absorbed into the main stream. In 1857 the ecclesiastical jurisdiction was abolished and in 1859 the admiralty; in 1877 the ecclesiastical courts were opened to solicitors.

The other element in the formation of the profession also did not long survive the reforms of the courts in the mid-nineteenth century. The officer of the court had never given up his right to act as attorney for litigants in the court in which he was employed. At assizes it was common enough for the clerk of assize or his associate to act on behalf of one or other of the parties, certainly until well into the seventeenth century, and clerks of the peace did so at quarter sessions until the practice was stopped in 1749. When Parliament by the Attorneys and Solicitors Act 1729 was bringing some sort of order into the profession it specifically reserved the rights of officials in the common law courts to be admitted to practise 'in their respective courts and offices in like manner as they might have done before the making of this Act';[69] and the prothonotaries at Common Pleas and the secondary in the King's Bench were permitted each to have three clerks who, when they had served in their offices for five years, were entitled to be admitted as attorneys. In the 1740s the Six Clerks in Chancery pressed for similar rights and the Society of Gentlemen Practisers[70] objected. But when the 1729 Act came up for renewal in 1749 the request of the Six Clerks was granted, but so that not only they, but persons who had been articled to one of them for five years, could be admitted a solicitor and an attorney. For them it would appear to have been superfluous. They were nominally the attorneys of the Chancery litigants and until 1842 they were lavishly paid to do what others had in fact done. The most senior of them in the last three years of his sinecure received on an average £7,233 19s 1d a year and the compensation paid to them was so large that it remained a burden on the Chancery litigant and his solicitor for years. It was, however, a recognition of a practice four hundred years old of the court official acting as the litigant's attorney and being paid by him. In 1846 when the new county courts were being set up it was thought necessary to provide specifically that none of the officials should act as attorney

[69] Section 16.
[70] See p 73, *infra*.

for any party. It was not until 1888 that the old and original system finally ceased to operate. Even now it is still necessary for those who wish to be represented in court proceedings to seek out an officer of the court, now called a solicitor, who like his progenitors will be paid by fees and not by salary and like them will be subject to the control of the courts because he is one of their officers.

CHAPTER 2

Professional Organisation

If there had been any possibility of a professional organisation for attorneys and solicitors during their formative years it would have rested with the Inns of Chancery. These institutions, ten in number according to Fortescue but only eight according to Coke, were founded at about the same time as the Inns of Court and primarily for the same purpose: to provide accommodation for men who had business with the courts at Westminster. The best known were Clifford's, founded in 1345; Staple's in 1415; Lyon's in 1420; Barnard's in 1445; Clement's about 1478; New in 1483. How and when they came also to have the character of hostels for students cannot now be ascertained, but in course of time the practice was established of men belonging to these Inns prior to joining an Inn of Court. The Inns of Court from the first took an interest in the students. They usually allowed a student to reckon two years in commons at an Inn of Chancery towards his period of service of terms in their own Inns. They sent a barrister of ten years' standing as Reader at the Inns of Chancery and the men selected for that duty were usually regarded as on the way to becoming Benchers. In 1677 the judges decided that 'the government of the Inns of Chancery ought to be subordinate to the Benchers of every one of the Inns of Court to which they belonged'. But by that time the interest was rapidly declining and soon ceased altogether. As their own legal education arrangements fell into decay during the latter part of the seventeenth century the Inns of Court ceased to send Readers; and alongside the process of excluding attorneys from the Inns of Court ran the corresponding one of refusing to accept students from the Inns of Chancery. After the mid-seventeenth century hardly any were accepted, although fifty years earlier almost a quarter of the students in the Inns of Court had started there. By the end of the seventeenth century the attorneys were in complete control of the Inns of Chancery, but unfortunately those Inns never had any disciplinary powers or the right to admit men to practise or exclude them from it. Those powers in the case of the attorneys and later of the solicitors remained for another two hundred years firmly with the judges. The attorneys were in a kind of limbo—the Inns of Court which could have given them a professional cohesion did not want them and the Inns of Chancery to which they were sent could not do so. Being without duties or powers, the Inns of Chancery gradually declined until by the end of the eighteenth century they had become little more than dining clubs, and their importance and interest to the profession were mainly centred round the disposal of the proceeds of sale of their properties a hundred years later. They never had any significance in the organisation of the profession.

Not only were the attorneys and solicitors at the beginning of the eighteenth century without any organisation; there was also lacking the basic requisite of a reliable list of those properly entitled to practise. The result was that many men utterly unfitted to do so and certainly without any proper qualification acted as attorneys and solicitors and brought the whole profession into disrepute. There were two independent and spontaneous reactions to this state of affairs. In 1726 the West Riding of Yorkshire magistrates decided to petition the House of Commons for legislation to introduce some more effective control than then existed, with the result that the Act of 1729 'for the better regulation of Attornies and Solicitors' was passed, introducing for the first time a central Roll of Attorneys and Solicitors. Then in the early 1730s a number of London practitioners formed the Society of Gentlemen Practisers in the Courts of Law and Equity. They did so for the purpose of 'supporting the honour and independence of the profession, promoting fair and liberal practice, and preventing unnecessary expense and delay to suitors'. In the first minute of the Society which has survived, and which is dated 13th February 1739, 'the meeting unanimously declared its utmost abhorrence of all male and unfair practice and that it would do its utmost to detect and discountenance same';[1] and in June 1741 the committee of the Society was directed to 'take into consideration any matters relating to the benefit of suitors and the honour of the profession'.[2] The work of the Society in relation to conduct and discipline is dealt with later.[3] Looked at from the point of view of professional organisation, its importance was that there was for the first time a body of attorneys and solicitors formed for the purpose of improving the standards and representing the interests of the profession.

Unfortunately the Society never purported to be or tried to become an organisation of the profession as a whole. It began and remained a London society for a select few chosen on the club principle. Its membership never exceeded two hundred at a time when there were reckoned to be seven thousand attorneys and solicitors in practice. It never had any worthwhile financial resources and at the end of the century it possessed only £1,000 in consols and a little cash. It suffered from the outset from the fact that it had no premises of its own, so that its meetings were held in one place or another, generally taverns, in the vicinity of Fleet Street. From 1772 to 1806 the Society met and dined in Clifford's Inn or Furnival's Inn, but there seems to have been some problem about paying the waiters and it reverted to its former ways. The famous Freemasons' Tavern was then

[1] Freshfield, Records of the Society of Gentlemen Practisers, p 1.
[2] Ibid, p 5.
[3] See pp 73–75, *infra*.

the members' usual meeting place, though they also went to others. Their papers were carried by the secretary to whichever place they were using; he seems to have had no place to keep them, and once they were lost from some lodgings but happily were returned after a reward had been advertised for them. The general meetings held twice a year were generally well attended; the numbers present varied between forty and eighty. This may have been because the dinners were excellent and business was so arranged that it was finished in a reasonable time beforehand. At any rate the less convivial and more arduous committee meetings were a different matter. From time to time, and with increasing frequency as the century wore on, it was reported to the general meetings that much difficulty was being experienced by the committee in obtaining sufficient attendance for doing the business of the Society and 'much inconvenience caused to those inclined to attend and frequently did attend without being able to proceed to business'. Accordingly in 1800 a committee of twenty-four was appointed in the hope that out of that large number a quorum of six would always be present; this was reinforced by an obligation to find a substitute if a committee-member could not attend, with a penalty of five shillings in default. Even that scheme was unsuccessful. In 1807 no fewer than four attempts to hold a committee meeting failed for want of a quorum. The minute-books give the clear impression that the early enthusiasm declined as the inadequacy of the Society's organisation became more marked. Like many another law society it had become more an attorneys' dining club than a professional organisation. In 1872 Mr J M Clabon, looking back, referred to it as that 'Lowtonian Society with its grand meetings where Calapash and Calapse are in the ascendant'.[4] But in its day the Society had some considerable achievements for the benefit of the profession to its credit.

The theme that the Society was inadequate for the needs of the profession was the subject of determined propaganda by a London attorney named Joseph Day who at the end of the eighteenth century attempted to obtain legislation for the establishment of a corporation of attorneys and solicitors. His scheme was set out in An Address to the Attorneys at Law and to the Public published by him in 1796. Unfortunately a good deal of the book is devoted to self-vindication in the dispute between Mr Day and the Society of Gentlemen Practisers. But in its essentials the scheme had a great deal to commend it and at one time had much support. As Day said,[5] 'it is remarkable, however, that although there were societies in the metropolis honoured with royal sanction for the encouragement of philosophy, of the study of antiquities and of various branches of the liberal arts; and although the practice of medicine and surgery had been highly exalted and improved in consequence of the royal foundation of a college of physicians and by the incorporating the practitioners in sur-

[4] *Solicitor's Journal*, vol 16. He was President in 1880.

[5] Op cit, pp 17–18.

gery, no similar institution existed for improving and regulating the practice of the law and thereby raising its professors to the just place in consideration and regard which in this populous and commercial country they ought to hold; and it was most extraordinary that this had not taken place since societies for promoting the study of the law existed in the several inns of courts; and we perceived that in consequence of the knowledge and liberal conduct resulting from such associations, the gentlemen at the bar were most deservedly and universally deemed to be intitled to the respectable rank in life which doubtless they would ever hold'. His scheme was to establish an incorporated society under the control of the Lord Chancellor and the judges (on the basis that it was to them in any event that the control of the profession was committed). His society was to have the power to admit attorneys and solicitors to practise; all practitioners would have the right to join it; the Society of Gentlemen Practisers was to be consolidated with it; and most important of all it was to have a proper headquarters in London—'a good Hall near the Temple'. Day believed that the Gentlemen Practisers would co-operate in his scheme, but they took advantage of a misunderstanding about a meeting to withdraw from the discussions. They may well have disliked the emphasis which his scheme put on control by the judges. Day himself was very bitter, notwithstanding the fact that the Society paid him £100 for his trouble and £98 18s 2d for his expenses. His description of the Gentlemen Practisers was that 'it was hinted that a set of respectable gentlemen who call themselves the Law Society meet occasionally to regulate both the practice and conduct of the profession. It is much to be regretted that the good intentions and endeavours of these gentlemen have been attended with but little effect', and he thought that this would continue so long as the Society remained 'unknown to the Public and comprised only of such persons as are, by the mere favour of those before admitted to it, elected members'. Day has not generally been given much credit for his contribution to the organisation of the profession, but 'when the Law Society was founded in the nineteenth century its constitution bore a striking resemblance to that which he had advocated thirty years earlier'.[6]

For whatever reasons, the Gentlemen Practisers were either unwilling or unable to respond to ideas such as Mr Day's which were almost commonplace at the beginning of the nineteenth century.[7] It is hardly conceivable that they did not discuss the possibility of a scheme to realise these ideas, for some of them were at the time meeting at the Verulam Club, whose members were amongst the promoters of what was originally called 'The London Law Institute'. To these men 'it appeared singular that whilst various public bodies and commercial classes in the metropolis and indeed in many of the principal towns in the kingdom had long possessed places

[6] Robson, The Attorney in Eighteenth Century England, p 32.

[7] In 1804 a proposal was made for a Legi-Logical Institution for London—'with a complete and noble library'.

of general resort for the more convenient transaction of their business; and whilst numerous institutions for promoting literature and science among all ranks of Society had been long established and others were daily springing up, the attorneys and solicitors in London should still be without an establishment in London calculated to afford them similar advantages'.[8] This was the same consideration which had activated Mr Day; the words used were reminiscent of his. The leading promoter was Mr Bryan Holme and when his books were looked at after his death there was found an annotated copy of Mr Day's book. The promoters issued a prospectus in 1823[9] inviting support and subscriptions for a Law Institution—'London' had been dropped out of the original title because of the desirability of attracting country support. The central feature was to be a hall to be used as 'an exchange to be open to attorneys, solicitors, proctors and such principal officers at all hours of the day but some particular time to be fixed for the general time of assembling; to be furnished with desks or inclosed tables running on each side of the room for the whole length of it, affording similar accommodation to those in Lloyds Coffee-House'. There was to be a library, a club-room and offices. The reception of the idea justified the promoters in issuing a further prospectus;[10] a meeting at Serle's Coffee-house on 29th March 1825 appointed a committee to draw up a scheme for submission to a general meeting of subscribers. That meeting was held in Furnival's Inn Hall on 2nd June 1825. There was already an impressive list of subscribers and it was clear that the scheme had appealed to many as well suited to meet an urgent need.[11] The committee's proposals were unanimously adopted, and with them the committee's decision that the whole project 'ought to be established on the most liberal scale'. There was no reference to objects other than the severely practical ones of providing suitable premises and services. Perhaps larger designs would have appeared to compete, if not to conflict, with the Gentlemen Practisers. But after the manner of the times the moral value of the proposed Institution was not overlooked. The final prospectus stated the expectation of the promoters 'that individuals whose past conduct shall have excluded them from becoming members of the Institution in the first instance will begin to appreciate the advantages of a good character and be induced to alter their conduct in order to obtain admission at some future Time'.

The acceptance of the scheme was largely due to the work of two remarkable men. At the head and front of the promotion were Mr Bryan Holme, himself a Gentleman Practiser, and Mr Robert Maugham. Mr Holme

[8] *Legal Observer*, vol 1 (1831), p 37.

[9] A copy of the prospectus was published in the *Law Advertiser* on 23rd August 1823.

[10] A copy of this prospectus is included in the bound copy of the early Annual Reports in The Law Society's library.

[11] At this stage there were 292 subscribers for 1,335 shares, making a total subscribed of £33,375.

appears for only a short time in a leading role in the affairs of the profession. Having initiated the Law Institution, he was content to remain a committee member and never aspired to office or at any rate never achieved it. When he died the event was hardly remarked in the legal press. But Mr Maugham wrote in the *Legal Observer* a tribute worthy of one of the giants of the profession.[12] He was born in Lancashire in 1776 (he was christened on 29th December of that year) of parents whose home was Thurland Castle and who are said to have been small landed proprietors. After a local education he was articled when he was seventeen to John Baldwin in Lancaster and was admitted in 1800. He originally intended to practise in Lancaster but came to London and was made a partner in his firm by 1806. This perhaps encouraged him to marry in 1807; his wife was sickly and there is no record of any children. He practised for over fifty years, for he took out a practising certificate in 1856, the year of his death.[13] His main interest outside the law was the collection of old books and, as many likeable men do, he spent a great deal of his time in second-hand bookshops. His house in Brunswick Square and his office in New Inn were strewn with his purchases which he did not have time to arrange, and in The Law Society's library in Chancery Lane there are a good many old books which bear his signature. The library at the Law Institution was, because of him, inevitably the most important part of the whole project. After the fashion of his time he was a strict and perhaps a hard man: he confessed: 'My anger and resentment are strong and I am very unrelenting and unforgiving but I do not seek revenge. When a person offends me I avoid all communication with him afterwards and endeavour to wipe him entirely out of my recollection and to forget he exists.' Yet his last interest was to initiate and get much support for a benevolent institution for aged and indigent attorneys. When Mr Maugham in 1846 was telling the House of Commons Select Committee on Legal Education about the foundation of the Law Institution, which by then had become the Incorporated Law Society, Mr Bryan Holme's name was the only one he mentioned, and no man's knowledge of the matter was greater than his.[14] Mr Holme's full-length portrait hangs in the Society's Hall; he was the founder of the profession as we know it today.

Mr Maugham himself was regarded by some as the true author and begetter of the scheme for a Law Institution, and certainly none contributed so much to its establishment and development. He was born in 1788 and admitted an attorney in 1817; one of his grandsons became Lord Chancellor and another was Mr W Somerset Maugham, the author. He acted as secretary to the promoting committee from 1825 through the early stages up to the Royal Charter in 1831; he was then confirmed as secretary

[12] 1856 volume, pp 281–285. The memoir is anonymous, but nobody who has read Mr Maugham's books can mistake the style.

[13] On 15th July.

[14] Ans 2048.

in 1832 and he served until his death in 1862. He had already written in 1825 his Treatise on the Law of Attorneys and Solicitors and given to the profession a book of which they were in great need. As the *Law Magazine* commented: 'It is rather singular that in times so fruitful in bookmakers and with subjects so much in request attornies and solicitors should have been for more than a century one of the most wealthy and influential bodies in the state without having a special treatise devoted to them.'[15] He was a fluent author and followed this work by a number of others also of high quality. He was a tactful and able representative of the Society when need arose and gave his evidence carefully and with dignity. He was the proprietor and editor of the *Legal Observer*, which he founded in 1830, until it became the *Solicitors' Journal* in 1856. His outside interests sometimes got him into difficulties. The *Law Times* disliked him and perhaps for that reason criticised the Society almost up to the date of his death. At one time the *Law Times* was excluded from meetings of the Society and may well have drawn its own conclusions as to who had been responsible. His salary was £400 a year.

The formal basis of the Institution was a deed of settlement dated 16th February 1827. The date has some significance because Mr Maugham invariably gave it as the date upon which the Law Institution was formed. On a strict view he may well have been right since the Institution was not legally constituted until that date, but the date generally adopted is 2nd June 1825, when the scheme was approved by the subscribers. Others have been more ambitious and pushed the date much further back. Until the end of the nineteenth century nobody in the profession thought of anything earlier than 1823, but in 1890 some of the minute-books and other records of the Society of Gentlemen Practisers were found among the archives of The Law Society and their contents led to the claim that that Society was the parent of The Law Society and that they enabled the history of The Law Society to be traced back 'nearly a hundred years prior to the date assigned in the Calendar—or more exactly to the year 1739'.[16] This claim has been repeated consistently since. The Council in its Memorandum to the Monopolies Commission in September 1968 said: 'The Law Society was founded in 1826 [*sic*] as successor to the Society of Gentlemen Practisers in the Courts of Law and Equity which was an association of London solicitors founded in 1739.'[17] As both bodies existed side by side for a number of years the one cannot have been founded as successor to the other.[18] An amalgamation of two bodies with similar aims

[15] 1830, p 430.

[16] Mr Chamberlain's paper, 'The Parentage of the Law Society', Prov Meeting 1891, pp 161–172.

[17] Memorandum, p 5.

[18] The Gentlemen Practisers (then always called the Law Society) held an annual general meeting as late as 1830 and the resolutions passed were published in the *Legal Observer*, vol I, p 38; and as amalgamation was being discussed in 1832 the Gentlemen Practisers must have been in existence then.

was an obvious and sensible idea. Immediately after the Law Institution had obtained its Royal Charter in December 1831[19] a Mr Tooke proposed that an amalgamation should be considered and the management committee resolved that 'a deputation from this committee be authorised to confer with the committee of the Law Society for considering the means by which the objects of that Society may be conducted in concurrence with this Institution'. On 10th March 1832 the sub-committee reported and it was decided to ask for a list of the furniture which 'the Law Society proposed to be disposed to this Society'. The sub-committee was authorised to see 'the Law Society' members again but expressly directed 'not to pledge this Society as to admission of members or election to appointments'. Unfortunately the 'Report Book' in which the sub-committee's report was entered cannot now be found. There is no further reference to the matter beyond an authority given to the secretary to receive the papers of the Gentlemen Practisers into his custody 'for the time being' and to give some clerical assistance. Neither in the management committee minutes nor in the Annual Reports is there any reference to an amalgamation. The President in 1885 commented that it was a curious fact that in the printed records of the Incorporated Law Society there was not a single word to show that the older Society ever existed. The better view on the available evidence appears to be that the Gentlemen Practisers, already declining, were not able to continue in existence alongside the new Law Institution and passed into oblivion without any formal succession or amalgamation.[20] When their Society finally ceased to exist is not known, but it may be significant that on 30th June 1832 the Law Institution changed the name of its bank account to 'The Incorporated Law Society', which suggests that the name used by the Gentlemen Practisers had become available. By 1834 the Incorporated Law Society was undertaking proceedings against offending attorneys and the report of the first recorded case gives possibly the best account of what had happened:[21] 'One of the objects of this society is to promote fair and honourable practice and with this view where necessary to resort to the superior courts to punish the misconduct of practitioners. This was the principal design of the old Law Society established nearly a century ago and of the Metropolitan Law Society; and on dissolving these associations after the establishment of the present Incorporated Law Society it appears that the purposes of the former were grafted on the plan of the new Society.' This report had added authority since it appeared in the *Legal Observer*, of which Mr Maugham was editor. At no time when speaking or writing about the foundation

[19] See pp 32–33, *infra*.

[20] Cf Reader, Professional Men, p 28: 'not the ancestor of the present body'; Birks, Gentlemen at Law, pp 159–160: 'the two societies never amalgamated in the end, the old society was dissolved'; Christian, Solicitors: an Outline of their History', p 170: the Gentlemen Practisers 'suddenly ceased'.

[21] *Legal Observer*, vol 8 (1834), p 92; the name of the offending attorney was Robert Mark.

of the Incorporated Law Society did he say anything about its having succeeded or being amalgamated with the Society of Gentlemen Practisers, and no printed paper of the Incorporated Law Society in the first sixty years of its existence ever mentioned or claimed such succession or amalgamation. The only reasonably contemporary statement was made in 1844 by a Mr Lott, who had been active in professional affairs, that the Incorporated Law Society originated with the Metropolitan Law Society.[22]

The affairs of the Institution were in the hands of a management committee and its first task and responsibility was to ensure that it had a sound financial basis. It was estimated that £50,000 would be needed and it was decided to raise this by the then fashionable joint-stock method. There were to be 2,000 shares of £25 each, and to ensure a wide spread no individual was to be entitled to more than twenty-five shares. The issue got off to a good start, for by the inaugural meeting on 2nd June 1825 there were already 292 subscribers for £33,375. But it then tailed off: by 1st May 1826 there were 407 subscribers for 1,684 shares at £42,100; three years later on 20th June 1829 there were 575 subscribers for 1,958 shares at £48,950; and only on 1st July 1830 could it be reported that 673 subscribers had applied for the total issue. There was a fair sprinkling of country support and of the first list published twenty-one subscribers out of 160 worked or lived outside London. When the first call was made twenty-three of the subscribers refused point-blank and another 219 failed to respond. Eventually a Mr Harrison from the Old Kent Road was employed to press the laggards at a fee of 5s per name and 2½ per cent commission on the amount he collected. The original estimates proved to have been optimistic and when the Institution applied for a Royal Charter in 1831 it was decided to increase the authorised capital to £75,000. Perhaps to have something in reserve, only a further 800 shares were issued, bringing the issued capital up to £70,000. The joint-stock method, however, was found to be unsuitable for this type of organisation. The object had been to limit shareholders to members of the profession, but it was soon found that this would be difficult when shareholders died leaving their property to persons outside the profession. For those who were not attorneys or solicitors the shares were unattractive since there was no dividend and they were not entitled to use the amenities of the Institution. Accordingly in June 1842 it was decided that such shares as were held by persons not members of the profession should be bought in; and that where a member held more than one share one should be treated as an entrance fee and extinguished and the balance acquired for cash and extinguished. Most members had only one share, and because these steps were taken so early the new scheme was simple and inexpensive to put into operation. There was some delay because, as will be seen,[23] the proposals were made at the same time as

[22] *Law Times*, vol 3, p 445.

[23] See p 42, *infra*.

some constitutional changes which were opposed. However, the amendment was effected by the Charter of 1845.

The management committee's next task was the selection and purchase of a suitable site for the erection of the Hall which was the central feature of the scheme. It is typical of the energy and determination of the men of the period that within five years of the Deed of Settlement they had pieced together the half-dozen properties required to form the site, overcome a tangle of legal complications, particularly in relation to easements (and obtained an Act of Parliament to solve the most intractable of them), conducted a competition for the best design for the building, carried out the building work in face of many difficulties, equipped the Hall and opened it to the use of the members. In one period when activity was at its height—from October 1828 to March 1830—the management committee held twenty meetings and its members were involved in weekly meetings of sub-committees to which detailed aspects of the work had been delegated. The central site (since of course extended) was acquired by June 1828.[24] The total cost was about £17,000 and one of the properties bought was in Pope's Head Court which had been the Crown and Rolls Tavern and Coffee-house, one of the places where the Gentlemen Practisers had met in their early days. The site had a double frontage to Chancery Lane and Bell Yard. That done, the committee advertised a prize of 100 guineas for the best design submitted for the new building, with a second prize of fifty. They selected the design of Mr Lewis Vulliamy. At the time Grecian architecture was the fashion and Mr Vulliamy followed it. He 'had visited and made studies of all the principal monuments and remains of Grecian architecture in the various countries where it flourished and thrown into this front [ie the Chancery Lane façade] the true spirit of the originals'[25] without servilely copying any of them. His plans were circulated to all members of the committee so that they could make their comments and suggestions. Grecian architecture *à la* Vulliamy was perhaps not the most suitable for this purpose. It was found that 'huge Ionic columns surmounted by the classic pediment, and flanked by the correct, great plain windows, [made] it necessary that the erection should be of two storeys, and the rooms within of a loftiness which, useful enough in the case of the reading room and library, was very wasteful in the matter of space where offices and the smaller rooms were concerned'.[26] Somehow the Lloyd's Coffee-house concept had been dropped, though some fancy they see it in what is now the members' reading room. Within this classic exterior the accommodation was generous. The library occupied the height of two stories and was fifty-five feet long, nearly thirty-two feet wide and twenty-four feet high. It was divided into two unequal parts by a screen

[24] For a detailed account of the acquisition of the site, see Law Society's Handbook, 1932, pp 94–108.

[25] *Legal Observer*, vol I, p 292.

[26] *Solicitors' Journal*, 16th August 1902, p 713.

of columns and pilasters of scagliola and there was a gallery running round the whole room. The main hall was thirty feet high and nearly fifty-eight feet long; on each side it had wings or recesses behind columns of scagliola in imitation of Egyptian granite. The club-room on the ground floor was fifty feet long, twenty-seven feet wide and eighteen feet high. Around these main parts were the minor, more business-like rooms. There were a large committee-room and a meeting room; there were offices, and a flat for the secretary. For completeness there were rooms for dinner-parties and kitchens in the basement to serve them; there were rooms for what were called the 'resident officers'. Members could rent strong rooms or boxes in the basement—fifty-two were provided. For comfort there were in the basement 'two of Sylvester's largest sized stoves to give warmth and dryness to every part of the building' installed by the makers at a cost of £228.

The execution of these plans was delegated to a building sub-committee. Mr Vulliamy found them unrelenting in their zeal. In the first year they held no fewer than thirty-eight meetings and called for or received twenty-five reports from the architect. The work was to be done in stages and the first, which involved the erection of the carcase of the building, was put out to tender. Nine tenders were received and that of Lee & Sons for £9,214 was accepted. As was then the mode, the event was celebrated with a dinner. But the sub-committee was soon showing the inevitable anxiety of a building-owner at the slow progress being made. Anxiety in August 1830, however, had become keen disappointment by November. The contractor was urged to employ more men; he countered with explanations about the difficulty of getting supplies of materials. Rather than change horses the sub-committee gave to the same contractor the work of erecting the next section—the club-house. In December 1830 the contract for the internal fitting and decoration was given to Messrs Baker for £7,891. Every detail received the urgent and careful consideration of the sub-committee: the method of lighting, fire-proofing the library, securing the strong rooms, and a score of similar items were all on their agenda papers. In spite of all the anxieties the work progressed well enough for the fifth annual general meeting of the Institution to be held in its own Hall in July 1831. The formal opening took place on 14th April 1832 in the presence of the Lord Chief Justice, the Master of the Rolls, the Vice-Chancellor, the Chief Justice of Common Pleas and seven puisne judges. The building was opened to the use of members on 31st May 1832. The total cost of carrying out the scheme was £53,715 against the cost of £25,000 estimated in 1823 and the capital of £50,000. But the deficit had been foreseen and steps taken to raise the additional money.[27]

Although the building was inevitably the most important task at this stage, there had also been some constitutional changes because the vehicle of a trust had already been found to be inadequate to the Institution's purposes. It was decided to ask for incorporation by Royal Charter, and

[27] See p 30, *supra.*

this was granted on 22nd December 1831. Most of the provisions of the Deed of Settlement were incorporated in it, but it effected a change in the style of the Institution. The Attorney-General during the discussions leading to the grant suggested that 'some title should be taken which was more appropriate to the peculiar character of the Institution and as designating the members composing it'. It was therefore decided to adopt the cumbersome title of 'The Society of Attorneys, Solicitors, Proctors and others not being Barristers practising in the Courts of Law and Equity in the United Kingdom'. This remained the formal title until it was changed to 'The Law Society' in the Charter of 1903, but it was immediately found to be impracticable for ordinary use. In 1833 the management committee decided to use the title of 'The Incorporated Law Society of the United Kingdom' except when it was technically necessary to use the formal title, and that was the title which was invariably used even in statutes. Curiously enough the old name lived on, and until at any rate the end of the nineteenth century the Society's premises in Chancery Lane were still called the Law Institute.[28] The original prospectus had not referred directly to any object other than the creation of a Law Institution and specifically the building; but the Charter recited that the Institution had been founded by its members 'for facilitating the acquisition of legal knowledge and for better and more conveniently discharging their professional duties'. The Charter did not materially affect the constitution. The original management committee of twenty-four was still retained. At first there was no chairman or president as such, each member taking the chair in alphabetical rotation. On 11th May 1833 it was decided to appoint a chairman and vice-chairman each serving for six months, the vice-chairman automatically succeeding the chairman. Members of the committee retired according to the level of their attendance—the seven with the lowest attendance vacating office at the end of each year.

The master-stroke of the founders of The Law Society was the emphasis they gave to education and to the establishment of the profession as liberal. The library was in the forefront of the scheme. The Select Committee on Legal Education in 1846 asked Mr Maugham: 'What are the special objects of the society?' and he replied: 'The first and prime object is the formation of a library.'[29] The policy was set out in 1829: 'To contain a complete collection of books in the law and relating to those branches of literature which may be considered more particularly connected with the profession such as Votes, Reports, Acts, Journals and other proceedings of Parliament; County and local histories; topographical, genealogical and other matters of antiquarian research.' The first librarian was a Mr Henry Dobson at a salary of £150 and subject to fidelity bonds in the sum of £500. The library, with 6,000 volumes by 1846 and growing by means of purchases (£400 was then the annual expenditure) and

[28] Law Society's Calendar, 1895, p xlii.

[29] Ans 2082 and p 55, *infra*.

numerous gifts, became the most important law library in London. Its growth was faithfully recorded in each annual report. By the mid-1920s its stock was over 60,000 and in the mid-1970s it had reached 100,000. Its importance to the profession cannot be exaggerated. Throughout the crucial latter part of the nineteenth century it was a symbol of the 'liberality' of the profession.[30]

The remaining element in the original scheme as set out in the prospectus was the Law Club. A club in the early nineteenth century was an important element in the concept of masculine respectability and no doubt the prospect of belonging to a club with its innuendo of exclusiveness attracted many subscribers. The prospectus proposed the provision of 'a clubroom which may afford members an opportunity of procuring dinner and light refreshments on the plan of the University, United Services, Verulam and other similar clubs'. These names obviously set an attractive standard. The club was from the outset a separate entity from the Institution, and the management committee of the Institution resolved that the Institution was to be 'at no charge whatsoever other than providing the rooms and offices required for the club'. Membership of the club depended on election and payment of an entrance fee of five guineas and an annual subscription of the same amount with no reduction for country members. The reason for segregating the club finances and facilities was that 'as many members have no occasion for this accommodation it has been thought right to make it a separate subscription'. No serious problems arose until the 1870s, when some members of the Society alleged that the Society was providing the club with facilities at the general expense. The club had only some 300 members and the charge was made (and denied) that Society members who wished to join were black-balled if they happened not to suit the club members. The inference was that the club was limited to Council members and the wealthier London solicitors. The Council strongly resisted the pressure on it to close the club; it was helped by the violence of some of its opponents, and it had the justification that the club was an inherent part of the original scheme. In 1884 a Society member named Ford commenced Chancery proceedings to compel the Council to close the club, and within a fortnight the Council had done so. But it resurrected the club in another form which avoided the legal difficulties of which Mr Ford had taken advantage. The only difference in practice was that no election was necessary in the case of Society members, any of whom could become members on paying the entrance fee and subscription. The rules also permitted solicitors who were not members of the Society to become members of the club and Mr Ford's attempt to stop that by further proceedings in 1887 failed. Nevertheless the matter rankled. It was still seen as a means of segregating the members of the Society into first and second classes. In 1900 the opponents of the club declared that

[30] 'A short historical description' of the library by the present librarian, Mr F P Richardson, FLA, was published in *The Law Librarian* in August 1970.

there had been no greater scandal in the history of the Society than when, in response to the action of a private individual, the club had committed a happy dispatch but had resurrected itself in order to become a legal association. The meeting passed a resolution 'that the Council give the shortest possible notice to the Law Club to quit the premises and forthwith to make such arrangements for supplying refreshments to the general body of members as shall be the most convenient'. Naturally there were technical problems and the matter was referred to a strong committee to report. The committee reported with truth that 'the existence of the club has been the occasion for agitation and complaint from time to time for twenty-five years and that an adverse feeling towards it undoubtedly prevails however much it may be based on misconception'; and in effect it recommended the closing of the club. The Council itself was obdurate. The catering arrangements it made still preserved the club in all but name. Those who wanted refreshments had to pay a subscription of four guineas if they worked within a radius of half a mile of the Hall; two guineas if outside that radius but in London; and one guinea if a country member. Non-subscribers had to pay 8d table-money, which was a stiffish charge when a good lunch cost not more than eighteenpence. By 1905, however, the matter was pretty well settled. Table-money was reduced to 6d and the subscription was merely a commutation of that. It had all been badly managed. At a time when the Council and the Society needed to unite London and Country the dispute gave ammunition to those who said that the Council was a remote body of successful London solicitors who knew nothing of and wished to have nothing to do with the country solicitor.[31]

The constitutional history of The Law Society has been uneventful and has been primarily concerned with the gradual development of 'country' representation.[32] The 1831 Charter was surrendered and a new Charter was granted in 1845. This has remained the basic constitutional document and subsequent charters in 1872, 1903, 1909 and 1954 have been supplemental to it. Apart from the financial aspects which have already been dealt with the principal change effected by the 1845 Charter was the conversion of the former management committee into a Council consisting of not more than thirty and not less than twenty members, including the President and Vice-President who replaced the old chairman and vice-chairman. The first President, Mr Michael Clayton, and Vice-President, Mr Edward Rowland Pickering, were with the Council nominated in the Charter and the election of future Councils was provided for in the bye-laws made under the terms of the Charter. In 1872 when extraordinary members were first introduced the number of the Council was limited to fifty together with ten extraordinary members. The 1954 Charter abolished the extraordinary members and instead increased the maximum number

[31] The history of the later stages in this dispute is to be found in *Solicitors' Journal*, 1900, pp 104–105; and *Law Journal*, 1900, pp 668–669.

[32] See pp 36–41, *infra*.

to sixty-five; it has since 1969 been seventy. The 1954 Charter authorised the Council to appoint honorary members, but so far this power has not been exercised. Such members would be entitled to speak but not to vote at Council or general meetings. The practice for many years was for the Presidency to go to the Council member willing to accept the office who had served longest. In 1953 the Council indicated its intention of departing from this rule and nominating Mr Charles Norton (as he then was) for the Vice-Presidency with the normal succession to the Presidency in 1954. The senior Council member was Mr F H Jessop and he was nominated by members of the Society. The result was a victory for Mr Jessop. As a result in part at any rate of this the previous convention was changed. Nomination as the Council candidate for the Vice-Presidency ceased to depend on seniority. The Council was free to select whichever of its members it thought most suitable for the nomination subject only to the nominee having served ten years on the Council and not having reached such an age as would make him sixty-five when he entered office. The nomination has invariably by convention alternated between a London and a country member.

The Charter of 1845 with its supplements and the bye-laws governed the domestic affairs of the Society. From 1843 the Society undertook duties and functions in relation to the profession as a whole and not merely to its members. For these purposes legislation was necessary. The profession had, of course, been since its emergence a favourite subject of legislation and one of the first steps taken by The Law Society was to consolidate the seventy or so Acts which were in 1825 still on the statute book. In 1839 an outline of a consolidating Act was submitted to the Master of the Rolls and this resulted in the Solicitors Act 1843. That Act repealed sixty Acts and had the significance that it created the office of Registrar of Attorneys and Solicitors and appointed the Society to the post.[33] This was but the first of a series of Acts—1860, 1870, 1874, 1877, 1881, 1888, 1894, 1899, 1906, 1918, 1919, 1922, 1928, 1932, 1933, 1936, 1940, 1941, 1949, 1956, 1957, 1959, 1965, and two in 1974. The Acts of 1932 and 1957, and the Solicitors Act 1974, were consolidating Acts. A consideration of the law relating to solicitors involves a reference to nearly three hundred statutes, and no profession, trade or business can match that.[34]

The Society of Gentlemen Practisers was from beginning to end a purely metropolitan body with no country membership and little or no contact with the provinces. Yet the number of men practising outside London grew considerably during the eighteenth century, and they included many who were of the first importance. They were, however, without any form of professional organisation until local law societies were established. The first in point of time was that at Bristol in 1770, but by the time The Law Society had been formed there were only ten in the whole country. Not

[33] Section 21.

[34] See Cordery, Law relating to Solicitors (1968, 6th ed), table of statutes.

all of them formally adopted any specific objects, but they were all motivated by a desire for respectability and status, which they conceived would be best achieved by raising the standards of the profession. The objects adopted by the Gloucester and Wiltshire Law Society in 1817 best illustrate what they all had in mind: 'To sustain the character of a liberal profession by pursuing and encouraging an honourable course of practice and by discouraging whatsoever has a contrary intent or tendency and by marking with a becoming regard that is due to members of the profession at large any unmerited imputation against their character or conduct and also to afford relief to distressed members of the Society and such other distressed attornies and solicitors who are serving resident in the said County and City and their respective families.' The *Durham County Advertiser*, noting the foundation of the Sunderland Law Society in 1824, commented: 'The respectable and very numerous body of solicitors in Sunderland and neighbourhood lately formed a Law Society for the promotion of fair and liberal practice and for preventing abuses in the profession.' Unfortunately such societies had a tendency to become little more than attorneys' dining clubs and as professional organisations were in some cases of little significance.[35]

The founders of the Law Institution recognised the importance of the support of the country practitioner. As we have seen, the name originally selected was changed to avoid emphasis on London. The prospectus was sent out to country attorneys and met with a reasonable response. One hundred and twelve subscribed £4,625 for 187 shares out of the original capital, but there was little progress after that. The *Law Times* in 1843 analysed the reasons: 'We are aware that this was a portion of the original design of the Law Institution but there are many obvious reasons why it has not succeeded and cannot hope to accomplish it. There is necessarily too much exclusiveness in such a society, the cost of the share, the amount of the subscription, the purposes for which it is mainly applied necessarily throw it into the hands of the London attorneys ...';[36] and in 1848 it claimed that Mr Maugham had acknowledged in so many words that The Law Society was 'essentially a London institution alone'.[37] The animosity of the *Law Times* towards The Law Society necessitates some reserve in accepting its analysis, but the facts give it support. In 1848 the number of country members was only 288, in 1862 was 462 and in 1870 was 650, or less than one in ten. In 1857 there were not less than one thousand cities and towns where attorneys and solicitors practised where there was not one who was a member. The idea of belonging to a London-based society was naturally difficult for the country attorney to grasp, and there seemed more hope in the development of local law societies. The Law Society's Annual Report in 1836 expressed 'the hope that law societies will

[35] *Law Times*, vol II, p 412.
[36] Vol I, pp 444–445.
[37] Vol XI, p 282.

be established more generally throughout the country by means of which information might be collected and the benefits of the Society more widely extended'. Almost from the outset there was co-operation and local law societies sought the advice of The Law Society and reported to it cases of malpractice with which they were not able to deal locally. The difficulty was to co-ordinate the efforts of these societies. An attempt was made to do so in 1844 through a Provincial Law Societies Association, but it failed because it found that it needed a London office. Accordingly it merged in 1847 with the Metropolitan and Provincial Law Association then recently formed.

The Law Society itself was only too glad to find some activity among the country solicitors. In recording the foundation of the new Association it promised that 'so far as this Society can usefully and properly afford its co-operation they will always be ready to assist their brethren in carrying out their important objects'.[38] Those objects were 'promoting the interests of suitors and the better and more economical administration of the law; of obtaining the removal of the many and serious grievances to solicitors and through them to suitors; and maintaining the rights and increasing the usefulness of the profession'.[39] Slightly ungratefully, it stated in 1849 that the 'Incorporated Society must always be too expensive and too predominantly metropolitan in character and government fairly and satisfactorily to represent a body so scattered as the attorneys and solicitors of England and Wales'. It exhorted on the other hand every solicitor to become a member of one of the local law societies—'no class of the community has been so supine and inactive in the assertion of their own rights or permitted more passively aggression and encroachment'—and regretted the 'considerable hesitation felt by many of their professional brethren in taking advantage of this opportunity of uniting together'.[40] The Association deserved better support. Its proceedings show that in intelligence and knowledge its leading men were the equal at least of their counterparts in The Law Society. One of their most active members was Mr E W Field, who was the first solicitor to be commemorated by a public monument and a biography.[41] Every effort was made to arouse the interest and support of the provincial solicitor. Meetings were held in the provinces and the general committee, recruited mainly from the country, tried hard to get recruits. But out of some 6,000 country solicitors in 1849 only some 650 joined the Association; in 1868, in spite of an increase in the number of solicitors, the membership from the country actually dropped to 635.

The Association seemed to have lost its purpose. The *Law Times*, so

[38] Annual Report, 1846, p 9.

[39] Metropolitan and Provincial Law Association, Proceedings, vol I.

[40] Metropolitan and Provincial Law Association, Proceedings 1849, p 9.

[41] He was a typical 'self-help' Victorian; with no inherited wealth or influence he became by hard work highly successful; he was a leading figure in the agitation for new law courts and was appointed secretary of the board responsible for their erection in the Strand; typically he refused to accept for his own use the salary he was paid.

enthusiastic at first, was in 1858 already urging it to close down and its members to join The Law Society, which had 'been almost completely regenerated from the complaints of indolence and cliqueism which issued in the formation of another Society'.[42] It had no resources and it had often to refer matters to The Law Society for effective action. The relations between the two bodies had fortunately been friendly throughout; The Law Society provided the Association with rooms for meetings and other facilities; the Association regularly recorded its appreciation. An amalgamation was obviously sensible, but negotiations, which started in 1870, took a long time. The Law Society was in any event making a bid for better country participation. In the 1872 Charter power was taken to appoint not more than ten extraordinary members of the Council from among the members of the Society holding offices as president of a local law society. The extraordinary members were not eligible for election as President or Vice-President, but this was a start in the process of giving the country member direct representation on the Council. In the amalgamation negotiations The Law Society refused to enlarge country representation beyond the limits of the 1872 Charter, but it did agree to continue the practice of the Association in holding an annual provincial meeting. On the basis the matter was concluded and the Association went out of existence with the plea: 'Henceforth let the whole profession metropolitan and provincial give its undivided support to the Incorporated Law Society of the United Kingdom.' The first annual provincial meeting was held in Leeds in 1874. It was a success and the practice has continued ever since, though latterly as a 'national conference'.

A united effort was clearly needed. In 1873 The Law Society itself had only the sparsest representation even in the largest cities—thirteen in Manchester out of 295, sixteen in Liverpool out of 283, twenty-four in Birmingham out of 193, ten in Bristol out of 189 and five in leeds out of 104.[43] There were only thirty-five local law societies in the whole country, and sixteen counties and eighty-one major towns did not have one at all. Even with the accretion of the members of the Metropolitan there were only 1,336 country members out of a potential of about 8,000. The feeling that they required their own organisation died hard among the country solicitors. Just when the Law Society and the Metroplitan were amalgamating there was a meeting of the Birmingham, Manchester, Liverpool, Newcastle and Leeds Societies which resulted in the formation on 30th April 1874 of the Associated Provincial Law Societies. Membership of The Law Society itself was still inhibited by the feeling that it was interested only in London and in the big practices at that. The *Law Times*, now mellower since the early days, commented in 1887: 'The figures to say the least do not say much for the *esprit de corps* of a profession which at the lowest

[42] Vol 16, 1858, p 117.

[43] From a paper read by Mr T Marshall of Leeds to the Annual Provincial Meeting in 1873: see *Solicitors' Journal*, vol 18, pp 67–70.

computation cannot number far short of 15,000 persons, and we fear that the main cause is due to a general apathy on the part of the country solicitor ... Complaints are occasionally made against the Society ... but we have never found them to be justified.'[44] In 1891 the Vice-President agreed with this view: 'Many solicitors in the country had an impression that their interests are not cared for. That was a mistake.' It had been worse than that. The President in 1877 said that 'a feeling grew up especially among country solicitors that the constitution of the Council of The Law Society was such as to lead it to take a line of action antagonistic to the interests of the country attorneys'.[45] But gradually the country solicitor began to see the advantages of professional organisation and accordingly to support The Law Society and the formation of local law societies. By 1889 there were for the first time more country than London members; the figure given in 1891 was 3,330—still only a third of the total country strength but a substantial improvement. Between 1871 and 1900 a further thirty-six local law societies were formed. Their co-ordinating organisation, the Associated Provincial Law Societies, never set out to be, nor did it become, a competitor of The Law Society, and one of its main functions was and remained the selection of extraordinary members of the Council until that ceased with the constitutional changes made in 1954. It was kept in being in case of need, but it last met in 1966 and was wound up in 1975. Unfortunately its records were destroyed in an enemy attack in 1941.

The country representation on the Council had been further liberalised by the Charter of 1903, which enabled the Council to appoint as an extraordinary member any member, not necessarily a president, who was nominated by a local law society or a group of such societies. The restriction that an extraordinary member could not be elected President or Vice-President still applied, but that was not then of great significance. Until 1884 even ordinary Council members who were country solicitors refused the office of President when it came to their turn; Mr C T Saunders, who became President in that year, was 'the first country member of the Council who had sufficient energy to assume the office'.[46] The 1909 Charter removed the restriction to the extent of qualifying for the office extraordinary members who had served on the Council for four years, with the proviso that the offices of President and Vice-President should not be held in the same year by Council members holding country certificates, whether they were extraordinary members or not. The 1954 Charter completed the assimilation of 'country' members by abolishing the extraordinary member and placing all on the same footing. The method of election was made democratic by dividing the country into constituencies each electing a number of members approximately proportionate to the number of members practising in each. The rule against 'country' members holding

[44] Vol 83, p 218.
[45] Annual Prov Meeting Proc, p 6.
[46] Williamson, Recollections of Some Past Presidents of The Law Society, p 39.

the offices of President and Vice-President in the same year was formally abolished but has in practice been continued.

The local law society system upon which these changes were based was by 1954 substantially complete and by 1962 with the foundation of the Holborn Law Society entirely so. The original object of the founders of the Law Institution had been to have such a system so that there could be a ready means of interchange of information and views between it and its members, particularly those outside London, and that had been achieved. The Law Society was now in a position to find out what the profession wanted. Apart from the ordinary communication from 'Chancery Lane' to the local law societies, annual meetings were established for presidents and secretaries of local law societies to hear Council policy and to express their views on it and to make their own suggestions. The *Law Society's Gazette* was started in 1902 as a further means of communication; at first it was published monthly and it was said to be not much read though it deserved to be; from 1972 it has been published weekly and has been in that form a success. It provides those who wish to put their views to the profession with a ready means of doing so whilst the subject is still topical.

The slow rate of recruitment, mainly in the country but also in London, was a matter of great concern to The Law Society. The founders had made it exclusive in order to make membership something to be proud of and to strive for, but that became inconsistent with the role of representing the whole profession. It was not entirely a matter of apathy or suspicion which kept the run-of-the-mill attorney away; it was very much a matter of cost. The entrance fee at first was £15 and in those days that was a substantial sum. In the hard times of the 1840s membership actually declined because it could not be afforded, but when the entrance fee was reduced to £5 the rate picked up again. Nevertheless it was not until the Society had existed for eighty years that a majority of the profession were members. This meant that during the highly critical years between 1860 and 1905, when the Council was dealing with major problems such as legal education, solicitors' accounts and land registration, it could not take a strong line because it did not represent the main body. There was the further problem that many did not belong to any law society at all; in 1889 it was reckoned that 7,469 solicitors, or more than half the profession, fell into that category. The Council accordingly had to make as sure as possible that it was carrying the profession with it, but it had no means of putting its own proposals and reasons before the profession as a whole or getting the profession's reactions except through the legal press. The problem was particularly acute when the Council was proposing action which would impose a direct financial levy on all solicitors as in the case of compensation fund. There were therefore from time to time strong pressures inside the profession to make membership of the Society obligatory on all practising solicitors just as membership of an Inn of Court was obligatory on a barrister. The Solicitors Act 1957 made membership compulsory, but that provision was only to come into force upon an order of the Lord Chancellor made after a poll of all solicitors holding practising certificates had shown that two-thirds were in favour of compulsory membership. In fact no such poll was ever taken and the Solicitors Act 1974, which repealed the Solicitors Act 1957, did not contain a corresponding provision, so the power has now lapsed. The growth in membership has amply justified the policy of the Council to leave it on a purely voluntary basis:

Year	*Practising certificates*	*Members*
1841	10073	1205
1851	9957	1320
1861	10229	1802
1871	10576	2405
1881	12688	3567
1891	15175	6558
1901	16265	7712
1911	17000	9030
1921	14623	9120
1931	15608	10283
1951	17396	15590
1961	19438	17350
1971	25366	23542
1976	29406	27700

Inevitably there had been disagreements and much criticism. When the capital structure was being reorganised in 1842 and the 1831 Charter was to be surrendered in exchange for a new one, a group of dissidents entered a caveat and obtained an interim injunction to prevent the Council surrendering the existing Charter and thereby blocked any progress for more than two years. Their opposition was withdrawn only when the management committee with reluctance and reproach agreed to retain the existing provision which excluded from membership any person disqualified by a court order from practising and agreed to a clause which excluded from the Council set up under the new Charter any person not in actual practice as a solicitor or attorney.[47] In 1844 some of the younger members 'had long felt that their interests had not been adequately represented by The Law Society' and there was a move to form a Legal Protective Association to fill the gap;[48] and it may well have been that they agreed with the criticism implied in the reference in 1848 to the 'slumbers of the elderly gentlemen in Chancery Lane'. In 1845 The Law Society was described as 'the Legal Bazaar in Chancery Lane'.[49] In 1862 one highly regarded journal said that 'the constitution and purposes of the Society unfit it for the popu-

[47] This dispute is described from the point of view of the objectors in The Legal Profession, 1873, at p 224 et seq, and from that of the Committee in the Annual Reports 1842–1845.

[48] *Law Times*, vol 3, p 442.

[49] *Law Times*, vol 2, p 390.

lar and prompt action which is the necessity of a defensive organisation'[50] and in 1873 another referred to that 'most respectable but inefficient institution known as the Incorporated Law Society'.[51] In the seventies in fact the Society was under particularly heavy fire. The close relationship between the Council members and the Lord Chancellor and the judges and senior members of the Bar did not go unnoticed, particularly in the country, and for the first but not the last time the suggestion was made that Council members were too much part of the legal establishment to be able to represent actively the interests of the rank and file. One of the few solicitor-Members of Parliament of the period said to a meeting of solicitors in London in January 1873 that 'if he were to say that the Council of the Law Institution had become sluggish and apathetic he thought it would not be difficult to prove. If he were to say that for many years a seat in the Council of the Law Institution had been looked on rather as a place of retiring dignity than the place of active work he would be stating that which would carry along with him the feelings and judgment of those present.'[52] The Council was strongly criticised because it was said to oppose any active steps towards abolishing the annual certificate duty. This led to suggestions that a solicitors' committee should be formed to look after the interests of the profession, but these came to nothing. Throughout this period the general meetings of the Society were enlivened by a group of London members[53] who watched every action by the Council with the object of subsequent criticism embodied in numerous generally tendentious motions and questions. The profession was well served by a numerous and vigilant legal press[54] which devoted to Law Society affairs much more space than has subsequently been the case. The proceedings of the Society (including in particular the Annual Report of the Council in full), the attendance records of Council members,[55] every grievance at lack of activity or excess of zeal, correspondence from the profession on the Council's successes and failures, reports of local law societies and students' debating societies, all these received detailed attention and ample space. The amenities or lack of them did not escape attention: 'What resting place does he (ie the solicitor) find at The Law Society? He cannot even hang up his perhaps wet coat, much less obtain a frugal lunch.'[56] The age of Council members was studied and the conclusion

[50] *Law Magazine and Review*, vol 14, p 126.

[51] *Solicitors' Journal*, vol 17, p 484.

[52] Mr C E Lewis MP at the Freemasons' Tavern, reported *Law Times*, vol 54, p 204.

[53] The most active were Mr Charles Ford, whose particular interest was the club (see p 34, *supra*), and Mr Hastie, who concentrated on discipline and accounts.

[54] There were at least six weekly legal papers carrying general professional information and comment.

[55] The records were analysed and for instance in 1879 the *Law Times* concluded that of the sixty members of the Council 'the working members ... were under thirty' (vol 72, p 143).

[56] *Law Times*, vol 100 (1895), p 46.

drawn that they were too old. In 1895 it was said that half were over sixty and the youngest was well into his forties; in 1899 it was alleged that the average was sixty. But the problem was to find younger men who could spare the time to attend meetings. Efforts were made to disturb the ruling clique by contesting Council elections but without success. The Council members were not without their defenders: 'How can it be expected that they should do more than they now do when almost the only expression of opinion they receive from their constituents is that of contumely and insult?'[57] and it was true that too many preferred criticism to joining the Society. It was in the bitter struggle against compulsory registration of title that the criticisms and reactions were most severe. One of the great campaigners, Mr J S Rubinstein, commented: 'We cannot but be painfully alive to the fact that the Council have but small influence with the authorities. The sole responsibility for this unfortunate state of affairs must rest with the Council and must rest with them so long as they lack the courage of their convictions.'[58]

It was also the Society's policy in relation to conveyancing which was the chief motive force behind the creation in November 1964 of the British Legal Association and with it the appearance of the first national rival organisation in the profession for nearly a hundred years. But it was not the only cause. To some solicitors the Society's conveyancing policy was flaccid because of the dual role which the Society had gradually adopted, and to them this was only one aspect of a much wider problem, namely whether when it came to the crunch of an argument with the government the Society would act in the same ruthless way that for instance the trade unions were doing. To these solicitors the Society seemed to have become part of the establishment. At the Association's 1965 Conference, at which 133 solicitors were present, it was 'contended that the Society is too tightly built into the structure of government, too much part of the Establishment to represent adequately the views of the rank and file'.[59] Investigation of complaints about solicitors from members of the public had formerly been a matter for the courts, but now it was done by the Society, and inevitably it appeared that the Society was acting against its own members and was at best unable to help those against whom complaints were made; solicitors charged with professional misconduct were formerly dealt with by the courts but now came before the Disciplinary Committee, which nothing could convince the rank and file was other than a committee of the Society; examinations were formerly a matter for the judges but now for the Society; the Roll and admission procedures had formerly been a matter for the Petty Bag Office but now were functions of the Society. To these solicitors as to solicitors a hundred years earlier it seemed that the Council was too anxious to remain on good terms with the Lord Chancellor, the

[57] Ibid, vol 77 (1883), p 215.
[58] *Solicitors' Journal*, vol 56 (1912), p 68.
[59] Ibid, vol 109 (1965), p 326.

judges and the Bar; and that constant association and negotiation had made the Council and the Society staff unable or reluctant to take a tough line. That 'The Law Society is bureaucratic in its dealings with solicitors in exercise of its statutory functions but leans over backwards to appease others. Whom does it attempt to appease? First and foremost of course—Government' was and remained their opinion and they asked: 'Can The Law Society with its obvious conflicting loyalties—to the profession on the one hand and to the public on the other—be both the governing body of the profession and its professional association?'[60] To those solicitors who were the supporters of the British Legal Association the profession needed the trade union approach: solely and exclusively concerned with the immediate interests of their own members without any obligation to consider any other aspect. From the first therefore the Association modelled itself on trade union lines and was registered as a trade union on 23rd December 1970. It celebrated the event by inviting the Executive Council of the TUC to publish an advertisement meant to suggest to its members as good trade unionists that they should instruct in their legal business solicitors who were also trade unionists, that is to say members of the Association. The formal status was short-lived because of the definition of 'worker' in the Industrial Relations Act 1971, but the reality remained the same. The present rules adopted at the Annual Meeting on 20th March 1965 had made a passing reference to the public—'to improve and extend the profession's services to the public'—but in the objects adopted prior to registration as a trade union no word of the public interest appears.

By contrast the Council of The Law Society set its face resolutely against any change in the Society's traditional attitude. For it the public interest was a factor to be taken into account in all situations. It and its predecessors had always rejected the charge that the profession was concerned with its own interests when determining its policy in relation to law reform in any of its aspects. The philosophy was restated in 1964 by the then President: 'Before a calling can be called a profession it must be followed in the spirit of public service.'[61] Accordingly when employed solicitors raised the possibility of striking, the Council warned them that such action might render them liable to disciplinary proceedings on the grounds that a solicitor had a duty to his client or employer (who for the Council was in the same position as a client)[62] which overrode his own pecuniary interest and that it would be improper for a solicitor to exert pressure on a client or employer for his own benefit by withdrawing his services. In its statements relating to remuneration or the conveyancing monopoly

[60] *BLA Solicitor*, October 1975, pp 4 and 5.

[61] Mr R J F Burrows (as he then was), reported in *Law Society's Gazette*, vol 61, p 815.

[62] The employed solicitor is 'in every respect in the same position as those who practise on their own account'—*per* Denning MR in *Alfred Crompton Amusement Machines* v *Customs and Excise Commissioners* (*No 2*) [1972] 2 WLR 835, CA.

it reiterated the claim that it was recognising the public interest, which was best served by having this important business dealt with by trained men reasonably paid. If some members of the profession thought that as a result of this attitude the Society was any less efficient in securing the interests of the solicitor than a trade union would be, that view was not shared by outside observers. In 1867 it was said that 'probably the most perfect specimen of a trade union in what we may call the non-aggressive phase of development is to be found in the association of solicitors known as the Incorporated Law Society. Every attorney with any claim to respectability belongs to this body which exercises a sort of lax control over the conduct of its members. Its avowed object is to keep up the character of the legal community and any gross breach of recognised legal morality or etiquette is visited with expulsion from the Association.'[63] In 1967 it was said that 'by the 1870s The Law Society in co-operation with the provincial law societies had already established itself as an effective trade union as well as a powerful force for the social elevation of solicitors', and of the Society's achievements in the twentieth century in relation to conveyancing that 'The Law Society had proved itself a superb trade union'.[64] In 1971 the view was expressed that 'The Law Society is primarily a trade union bent on defending such restrictive practices as the solicitors' monopoly in conveyancing. But it also does something to coax its members into more up-to-date habits.'[65]

The Council would have no contact or discussions with the Association except on the most informal basis, though it agreed to notices of the Association's meetings being published in the *Gazette*. Whereas a hundred years before it had welcomed the formation of the Metroplitan and Provincial Law Association, with which it worked in harmony, now it resented the attempts of the new Association to displace the Council as the sole acknowledged representative of the profession and it considered that in the difficult times which the profession was facing division was bound to be harmful to its interests. The anxieties and doubts of the profession helped the Association in its early years. By 1966 it claimed to represent a tenth of all solicitors. Its much smaller and less formal organisation enabled it to react more quickly to topical situations than The Law Society could and therefore its views tended to be published. For a time it seemed as if it might obtain some recognition as speaking for the profession, and the possibility may well have made The Law Society more alert and forward-looking than it had tended to become. It was regarded as a thermometer for registering the feelings of the profession in relation to official (or Law Society) policy. But as The Law Society came to grips with the conveyancing and remuneration problems the influence of the Association seemed to wane. It was not consulted when important changes were made

[63] *St Paul's*, vol I (1867), p 49. This magazine was edited by Anthony Trollope.
[64] Abel-Smith and Stevens, Lawyers and the Courts, pp 187 and 197.
[65] Sampson, New Anatomy of Britain (1971), p 348.

in 1972 and all its Chairman could do was to protest in the legal press. In that year the attendance at its Annual Conference at Blackpool was 'minuscule' whereas the attendance at The Law Society's National Conference at Harrogate was 'massive'.[66] A minority of the profession might join the Association, but the vast majority preferred The Law Society with all its faults. The really important problems required its experience, resources and prestige. The outcome of the conveyancing battle of the 1960s and early 1970s, and particularly the outcome of the conveyancing remuneration battle, if they had not won the war, had fully vindicated the policy of the Council that in the face of what it regarded as unjustified attacks the profession should conduct itself with dignity and show itself capable of understanding wider issues than the immediate and pecuniary. In its essentials that was the policy that the founders of the Society had adopted as right at the very outset and maintained throughout. A membership of nearly 28,000, equal to more than ninety per cent of solicitors with practising certificates and on a purely voluntary basis, was the best possible vote of confidence in the Society as a professional organisation and of approval of the professional ethic for which it has stood.

[66] *Solicitors' Journal*, vol 116, p 840.

CHAPTER 3

Education

The profession suffered until the latter part of the nineteenth century in its business, social and public life from three grave defects in its educational system. First, there was no means of ensuring that men entering the profession had any semblance of a general education; secondly, there was no effective system of providing the articled clerk with a legal education during his articles; and thirdly, there was no effective examination to test his progress during his articles or his knowledge before admission.

That the general educational standard was low cannot be doubted. In 1630 members of the profession were described as the 'unlearned and unconscionable crew';[1] in 1688 the author of The Compleat Solicitor asked: 'Do not all men know that there are many solicitors who have much practice and great dealings that have never been bred to such things? Simple fellows who have not the wit or honesty to learn a mean trade and in truth cannot write their own names and yet are accounted brave fellows in the business.'[2] A hundred years later the same things were being said. In 1796 Mr Joseph Day considered that 'a dreadful proportion of the lower class of them proved to be men totally devoid of education'.[3] Looking back to the beginning of the century, a speaker told the Provincial Meeting in 1899 that 'it is probable that with comparatively few exceptions the mind of the average London practitioner was uninstructed and narrow'.[4] In 1846 Sir George Stephen, speaking of his contemporaries, said that 'looking at the profession generally it consisted certainly of inferior men both in point of station and education'.[5] There was no sort of test of a would-be attorney's general education before he entered into articles, and many did so who had been taught little more than to read and write.

A liberal education had a particular significance for the profession. Attorneys and solicitors were throughout the nineteenth century concerned about their status and particularly their social status.[6] They were anxious that their profession should be recognised as conferring on its

[1] Attornies Academy, p A3.
[2] The Compleat Solicitor, p 17.
[3] An Address to the Attorneys at Law and to the Public, p 15.
[4] Mr Devonshire's Paper.
[5] Select Committee on Education, 1846: ans 1963.
[6] As to this generally see Chapter 11, *infra*.

members the status of 'gentleman' and it was axiomatic that a gentleman must have a liberal education. It followed that so far as possible entry to the profession must be limited to men with such an education as would entitle an articled clerk on admission 'to be, as he will be called, a gentleman, and to assume the social status of a gentleman. When it is known that no person can become a solicitor without having proved himself to be what is called "the educated man" the very fact of being a solicitor will become a passport to society and the profession will be raised in esteem and therefore in status.'[7] When Parliament was considering in 1821 the desirability of shortening the period of service under articles for graduates the Society of Gentlemen Practisers welcomed the proposal because, as their secretary Mr Flexney told the Select Committee, it would be 'highly beneficial to the Profession by raising its respectability',[8] and Mr Thomas Allen an eminent London attorney, told them that such a measure by rendering the profession accessible to men of education would give it 'increased respectability'.[9] Sir George Stephen said in 1846 that a liberal education would make his brethren 'a more gentlemanly set of men and as such stand in a greater degree of confidence in each other and their clients'.[10] The *Law Times* in 1843 in its first year analysed the problems facing the profession particularly in relation to its status and discipline; it stated the solution in capital letters: EDUCATION.[11] Ten years later it drew attention to another aspect. The business which the profession was transacting was 'of a better class, requiring more intelligence to conduct and demanding that the attorney shall be a man of quite another grade, mentally, morally and socially from that which he was when he was but a ministerial officer of the Law Courts—a man of technicality and form, of quibble and quirk. To conduct well such business as the wants of society impose on him, the attorney must now be a scholar and a gentleman; he must take rank socially with those whose fortunes are intrusted to his honour and intelligence.... But this will not be accomplished by a stamp duty; and it is for the interest of the public that some better test should be applied and that test is—education.'[12] The desire of the attorneys and solicitors to improve their status was not peculiar to them; it was shared by many in mid-Victorian Britain. In the great class competition the trump card was education.[13]

There was an even more substantial problem in relation to professional education. In the thirteenth and fourteenth centuries attorneys learned their business in the offices of the courts in which they worked as officials or practised as common attorneys. When the Inns of Court and of Chancery

[7] *Law Times*, vol 35, p 333.
[8] Parl Proc 1821, vol 4, p 325.
[9] Ibid, p 326.
[10] Select Committee on Education, 1846, ans 2004.
[11] Vol 1, p 215.
[12] Vol 22 (1853–1854), p 90.
[13] Best, Mid-Victorian Britain, p 170.

were founded from the latter part of the fourteenth century onwards the attorneys who were members had an opportunity of attending the moots and lectures which gave the Inns the character at that time of a legal university. But it is not likely that many took advantage of it, because their daily work was both too exacting and alien to the subject-matter. Those who had no time to study were gradually excluded, and that in the end included all the attorneys. The facility was therefore short-lived, perhaps a century at the most. It had ceased to have any significance for attorneys or solicitors by the time the profession was well established in the sixteenth century. Such training as the would-be attorney or solicitor received he obtained in his master's office. That this training was and is by itself insufficient was and is accepted. Yet until the mid-nineteenth century it was the best that was available and Lord Brougham once publicly declared in Chancery that if he had to recommence his legal studies he would begin as a clerk in an attorney's office. The fact was indeed generally recognised and many who intended to follow a career at the Bar spent their first years of training with an attorney. Lord Tenterden, Lord Wynford, Sir William Grant, Lord Chancellor Thurlow, Lord Mansfield, Lord Kenyon, Sir Samuel Romilly, Lord Campbell and many others followed this course. In addition to Thurlow five Lord Chancellors—Somers, Macclesfield, King, Hardwicke and Truro—started their careers in an attorney's office, as did Ashburton, who was expected to reach the Woolsack but failed. But these men were exceptional and for the general run of articled clerks the conditions under which they worked and the training they received were no sort of preparation for their intended profession. Indeed, given the fact that until the 1830s there was no entrance examination worth the name, there was no compelling reason why the articled clerk should be given any training at all beyond what might be useful to his master. In 1833 the *Westminster Review* asserted that 'the pretence of examination which the judges used to require is now abandoned and many men enter the profession ignorant of the commonest principles and practices of the Law'.[14] This had long been the case. The articled clerk of the eighteenth century was often little more than a servant in the domestic establishment of his master—he was housed, fed and taught like the apprentices of petty tradesmen[15] and, as to teaching, 'He is taught by form or precedent rather than by principle. His knowledge is in the end as limited as the means by which he is instructed.'[16] In the nineteenth century he might no longer live in his master's house, but it was a general complaint that very little attention was paid by his master to the direction of his studies. In fact it could hardly be expected from a busy practitioner whose time was so much taken up with his clients' affairs that he should devote any time to looking after the articled clerk's training. It very much

[14] Page 69.

[15] Jeafferson, A Book about Lawyers, vol 2, p 283.

[16] Preston, Conveyancing, Preface, p ix.

depended on the clerk himself; he was left almost entirely to his own devices and unless he qualified himself nothing was put in his hands beyond what any person could do, namely copying.[17] Accordingly such training as he got came mainly from the managing clerks, who were jealous of him and only employed him when pressure of work in the office required every available hand to be used. Looking back on the early years of the century, the *Law Journal* said: 'The solicitor or rather the attorney of the period ... was fed on the husks of practice. He had five years of office education without even the tincture of scholarship and liberal arts which most barristers his contemporaries brought from the universities and which so many solicitors now enjoy. Small wonder if such training—shorn of all that ennobles the profession of the law—tended to produce the Dodson and Fogg type of practitioner, proficient in the arts of pettyfogging and chicanery.'[18] Yet the cost of this training including stamp duties was estimated by the *Westminster Gazette* at not less than £1,000.[19] Premiums for articles were high. They could be as much as 500 guineas and an average would be 200.

If the training which the articled clerk got from his master was defective, there was until 1833 no other means by which he could acquire a knowledge of the laws which he was subsequently to assist in administering than the study of the manuals which from the beginning of the century poured from the press.[20] It has been suggested that the Gentlemen Practisers initiated some form of education for articled clerks. But their records show only that in 1751 they welcomed the initiative of a Mr Felton who had at his own expense distributed 'many thousands' of copies of his 'Friendly Hints to Young Gentlemen who are or intend to be bound by Articles to Attornies or Solicitors' and made a contribution of fifteen guineas towards his expenses; and that in 1807 they considered the formation of a Society for Articled Clerks but took no further action on it. Mr Maugham lamented in 1825: 'We possess neither college nor hall, library nor society yet the necessity of every possible assistance in legal studies is surely equal to that of any other science and none can be more important.'[21] It had in any event not been thought that attorneys and solicitors needed to know much law. In the eighteenth century 'lawyer' meant barrister; Roger North in his Autobiography written about 1730 wrote that formerly 'conveyancing

[17] Select Committee, p xiv.

[18] *Law Journal*, vol 35 (1900), p 354.

[19] 1833, p 69.

[20] As examples: 1804—Bridgeman, Reflections on the Law; 1815—Wright, Advice on the Study and Practice of the Law (this had three editions by 1828); 1829—Thompson, Practical Suggestions and Instructions to Young Attornies and Articled Clerks; 1830—Dawson, A Practical Treatise ... with an Appendix containing suggestions as to the course of study to be adopted; 1831—*Law Magazine*: Course of Study for Articled Clerks; 1835—Warren, A Popular and Practical Introduction to Law Studies; 1845—*Law Times*: Education and Training of Articled Clerks; 1854—Wheston. A Manual for Articled Clerks.

[21] Treatise on the Law of Attorneys and Solicitors (1825), Preface.

was done by the lawyers, now the attorneys have the largest share'. A scheme in 1800 for a professional law school contemplated that those intending to be attorneys should leave at sixteen but those going to the Bar should continue. In 1853 the *Law Times* looked at the past and into the future: 'The attorney of the future requires to be a very different personage from the attorney of the past because he has very different duties to perform. The attorney of the past was little more than a ministerial officer of the court, a man of parchment and paper who scarcely ventured to be a legal adviser; that office being assigned to counsel who were the "lawyers" properly so called.'[22] Legal knowledge in family solicitors was 'the least part of their value'.[23] As late as 1873 it could be said that not a single text-book in common use 'even for the usual practice of an attorney's office had been written by one of themselves'.[24]

There was an equally melancholy situation in the arrangements for examination after entering articles and before admission. Before 1729 the ordinances, rules and statutes relating to the admission of attorneys had referred to the judges admitting only those who were apt for the profession and the elimination of those who were not. But in practice there was no test of any sort as to the applicant's legal knowledge. At its highest the standard was that described to the committee hearing the evidence in support of the petition which led to the Attorneys and Solicitors Act 1729. Sir George Cooke, who was in charge of the Book of Attorneys for Common Pleas, said that 'to his knowledge he never entered any clerks in his office but such as had served their time, or were well recommended by practisers that he knew or the master with whom they served their clerkship'.[25] That was all. The Attorneys and Solicitors Act 1729 provided that the judges were to enquire and examine 'by such ways and means as they shall think proper touching his [ie the applicant's] fitness and capacity to act as an attorney' and the same provision applied to solicitors.[26] But the only fee allowed to the judges for this duty was one shilling for administering the statutory oath, and the examination was perfunctory or altogether non-existent. It remained as it had been described by Sir George Cooke. Mr Joseph Day described the procedure at the end of the eighteenth century: 'The verbal certification by the clerk to the judge before whom the affidavit of due service is sworn, that he knows the party to have been in the habit of transacting professional business during a considerable time, was together with the affidavit usually deemed sufficient; or if the clerk had served in the country a like certification by his master's agent that he thought the clerk duly qualified, usually occasioned any examination to be dispensed with and under these circumstances, in

[22] Vol 21, pp 185–186.
[23] Johnston, England As It Is (1851), p 171.
[24] *Law Magazine and Review* (1873), p 52.
[25] House of Commons Journals, 1728, p 267.
[26] Sections 3 and 4.

either case a fiat was granted as of course.'[27] When the Society of Gentlemen Practisers considered objections to an admission it was practically without exception on the ground of some defect in service and never as to knowledge. Mr William Hickey in his Memoirs describes his own admission, which was conducted by the judge, a friend of his father, at the judge's own house over the judge's breakfast of French rolls and muffins; the admission was so far as examination was concerned limited to an enquiry as to how he liked the law and how long he had been out of his clerkship.[28]

Palpably this was not good enough, and in 1836 a rule of court was made entrusting the examination to the masters and twelve examiners annually selected from the Council of The Law Society. This arrangement was given legislative sanction in the Solicitors Act 1843, under which orders were made in 1846. In practice there were five examiners at each examination; one of the masters presided and he was assisted by four solicitors selected by the judges from the Council. There was no oral examination. One unsuccessful candidate who wanted one tested the point before the judges but was refused. The whole business was done in one day. The subjects were common law and equity (which were compulsory) and one other chosen by the candidate from conveyancing, bankruptcy or criminal law.[29] The examiners at the end merely certified whether the candidates were 'fit and capable of acting as attorneys; the degree of fitness or capacity the examiners [did] not consider themselves warranted to determine'.[30] In 1836 all 207 candidates passed and, from that date until 1846, out of 3,994 candidates only 200 were, as it was euphemistically termed, 'postponed'.[30] The questions were palpably not difficult: 'What is the difference between a verdict and a judgment?' Mr Samuel Warren said that the examination would not have been passed by one in ten of the attorneys then practising;[31] if he was right in his estimate then the legal knowledge of those already admitted before 1836 must indeed have been abysmally low.

There was mounting unease inside and outside the profession at this state of affairs. In 1845 the *Law Review* put it: 'In England where the importance to the public interest of having educated lawyers is the greatest, the provision for legal education is the smallest.'[32] On 8th April 1846 a Select Committee of the House of Commons was appointed to consider the state

[27] Day, An Address to the Attorneys at Law and to the Public, p 15.

[28] Memoirs, i, pp 331–332. Until The Law Society introduced admission ceremonies in 1947 admission seems always to have been a disappointment to the candidate. In 1883 'one of many' described how the oath was administered to him and others in a corner of the court by an official whilst the ordinary business of the court went on and said that he signed the roll in one of the recesses in a corridor. 'Now here was an imposing ceremony and one calculated to impress a young man with the importance of the step he had taken and the position he was called upon to occupy' (*Law Times*, vol 85, p 234).

[29] Select Committee on Education, anss 2133, 2134.

[30] Ibid, p xvi.

[31] Quoted Christian, Solicitors—An Outline of their History, p 181.

[32] Vol 1, p 146.

of legal education in Ireland as if there was no need to consider the position in England. The absurdity of that was so manifest that on 5th May 1846 the Select Committee was authorised to extend its consideration to England too. The Select Committee acted with commendable and extraordinary speed and reported on 25th August 1846. Speed did not involve any lack of thoroughness. As to the general situation it came to the following resolution: 'That the present state of Legal Education in England and Ireland in reference to the classes professional and unprofessional concerned, to the extent and nature of the studies pursued, the time employed, and the facility with which instruction may be obtained, is extremely unsatisfactory and incomplete and exhibits a striking contrast and inferiority to such education, provided as it is with ample means and a judicious system for their application, at present in operation in all the more civilised states of Europe and America.'[33] This indictment was all the more remarkable when one considers the firm view of most Englishmen of the day that British institutions, and particularly the British legal system, were superior to all others. The resolution was founded on the most compelling evidence. That of Lord Brougham summarised the rest: legal education was 'at as low an ebb as it is possible for education to be in any country'.[34] It was not only the attorneys and solicitors who were ill provided. The Bar with its ampler resources and longer traditions was if possible in even worse case and had shown less intention than the attorneys and solicitors to improve matters. The two Universities provided nothing that was worth while. In all the committee found 'as a general fact to which there are very few exceptions that the student professional and unprofessional is left almost solely to his own individual exertions, industry and opportunities and that no Legal Education worthy of the name of a public nature is to be had in either country'.[35] It was a conclusion which nobody disputed.

The Select Committee made clear recommendations as to the way in which this situation should be remedied, and the history of legal education for the profession since 1846 has been mainly a matter of achieving by persistent effort the standards which the Select Committee set and the means it recommended. The committee, which at no time wasted words on idle or insincere flattery, recognised the work which The Law Society had already done: 'The profession generally have so felt these defects that with a very laudable zeal, seconded by much discretion and intelligence, they have endeavoured under different forms to provide by individual exertion a more efficient course of instruction for the young pupil; with this view ... in 1827 [*sic*] the Incorporated Law Society was founded by Mr Bryanholme [*sic*] and many leading solicitors of the time.'[36] Its recommendations for the attorneys and solicitors were:

[33] Report, p lvi.
[34] Select Committee Minutes, ans 3774.
[35] Select Committee Report, p lvi.
[36] Report, p xv.

(1) There should be a preliminary examination before entry into articles to show that the would-be entrant had a sound general education; the examination should 'embrace in addition to the ordinary acquirements of a so-called commercial education, a competent knowledge of at least Latin, Geography, History, the elements of Mathematics and Ethics, and of at least one more modern language'.[37]

(2) There should be opportunity for the articled clerk to attend lectures provided by The Law Society and others.[38]

(3) The final examination should be conducted more in reference to general principles than technicalities.[39] The present examination had received short shrift from the committee, who asked whether it was not merely a guarantee against absolute incompetency.[40]

(4) There should be a College of Law—albeit at that stage only in relation to the Inns of Court. The committee envisaged, however, the articled clerk having access to facilities provided by the Inns.[41]

As the committee had handsomely recognised, The Law Society had already made a start. Indeed the committee probably rightly—and they were speaking of comparatively recent events—considered that it was education which was one of the motives for the foundation of the Society. At any rate Mr Maugham told the Committee that the Society's 'first and principal object is the foundation of a library'.[42] The library had opened in 1831 as soon as the building was ready for it; by 1846 it contained 6,000 books, of which many had been presented. At this time the Society was spending £400 a year on books besides providing proper staff. The librarian was second to the secretary in the staff hierarchy. The Society's action was the more significant because at the time there was no other institution in London providing a law library. As to lectures, the Society as soon as it had the necessary premises set to work. A sub-committee was formed by resolution passed on 23rd February 1833, a date which may be taken as the starting point of legal education in the profession. By 9th March notices had been put up announcing the forthcoming lectures and inviting suggestions as to lecturers; by 17th March Mr Wilde of counsel was invited to give the first lectures, which significantly enough were to be on conveyancing. Other lecturers were not so easily come by, but by Michaelmas Term 1833 all was set and the first series of lectures for articled clerks started. Originally the lecturers were paid one-half of the fees paid by the students, but by 1846 each received 100 guineas for each course of twelve lectures. They then covered common law, conveyancing, equity, bankruptcy and criminal law. The attendance was originally

[37] Recommendation 25.
[38] Recommendation 26.
[39] Recommendation 28.
[40] Select Committee Minutes, qu 2139.
[41] Recommendation 15.
[42] Minutes, ans 2082.

300 or so but dropped by 1846 to about 200. Articled clerks of members paid £2 a year, others paid £3. In order to help students they were permitted on paying an extra £1 a year to use the 'outer' library. This was not particularly generous because a London member paid only £2 a year for all facilities including the lectures and the library. Some articled clerks complained that The Law Society was overcharging, and others whose principals were not members of the Society complained that they could not use the library at all. But at any rate in 1859 fifteen articled clerks sufficiently appreciated the kindness and attention which they received of Mr Lapworth, then the librarian, to present him with an inkstand. A room was placed at the students' disposal for meetings and debates. The lectures were of course much more useful to the London than to the provincial man, and this may have been the reason why the number attending was less than half the number sitting the final examination. In Manchester the local law society started lectures in 1844 in commercial law, evidence, conveyancing 'in every department', criminal law, and landlord and tenant. The Manchester Law Society told the Select Committee that for the future it intended to arrange for lectures to be given on 'such subjects as of more general or immediate interest'.[43] The lectures were free and the attendance was good. The Select Committee was plainly impressed. It dismissed the other thirty or so provincial law societies then in existence in a sentence: 'The other societies spread over various parts but especially in the north of the kingdom do not materially differ in constitution or object from this of Manchester though inferior in the efficiency with which their arrangements are carried out.'[43]

Such was the situation which The Law Society and the profession generally had to face in the mid-nineteenth century. The first problem to be tackled was that of a preliminary examination. Mr Maugham when before the Select Committee had given a qualified approval to that concept, particularly for those articled as young as fourteen or fifteen,[44] and in 1854 The Law Society took the first steps towards requiring would-be articled clerks to pass an examination in science, literature and the classics. There was some opposition on the ground of the hardship which this would cause, particularly to the writing clerks who had been given their articles. Eventually, however, the Solicitors Act 1860 authorised a preliminary examination in such branches of general knowledge as the Master of the Rolls, the Chief Justice and the Chief Baron might approve. The Act authorised these judges to grant exemptions from the examination in special circumstances.[45] The exemptions were freely given. In 1867 a deputation from The Law Society saw the judges and 'it was then intimated that after the Act had been in operation for about ten years orders for exemption

[43] Report, p xvi.
[44] Minutes, ans 2158.
[45] Section 8.

would only be given in exceptional circumstances'.[46] This, however, was not to be. Chief Baron Kelly, who had started life as an office-boy in an attorneys office, was exceptionally kind and in two years exempted 141 men; thus in 1878 eighty out of the 100 who applied were granted exemption. The death of the Chief Baron in 1880, and the Solicitors Act 1877 which emphasised the fact that exemption was to be given only in special cases, enabled the matter to be brought under control. Thereafter the applications were referred to The Law Society and its recommendations were normally accepted.

The general improvement in education in the country (Foster's Act introduced compulsory education for all children in 1870) and the much higher standard of education of those entering the profession robbed the preliminary examination of much of its significance and purpose by the time it was fully operative. As early as 1835 Mr Samuel Warren observed that the articled clerk of that time 'is or ought to be a very different person from the attorney's clerk of 1735 ... The youth who now enter that walk of the profession are for the most part of great respectability and have received a liberal education.'[47] The new entrants were now coming from the grammar and public schools, so that many of them had in any event attained that standard of the fifth form boy set by Sir George Stephens to the 1846 Committee. In 1878 it was said that 'for years past men of education from the universities and all the great schools of learning and men of high social position are in our ranks';[48] in 1881 that 'our profession is now largely recruited from the public schools';[49] and in 1882 that 'the solicitor of to-day is a well-educated gentleman with a social position second to none'.[50] Unfortunately the position was not quite as good as that. In the presence of each other at general meetings or after dinner solicitors were apt to exaggerate. But as the *Law Times* put it in 1883, 'as a body they say they have the respect of all classes of their fellow-subjects ... Yet by men of culture who generally deny attorneys a place in the learned professions at all they cannot be considered even an outermost twig', not to mention 'a lower branch'; and the writer went on to say that 'Attorneydom with a large class is a current expression for the lowest form of Brummagem intellect, a beauteous compound of cunning vulgarity and the self-confidence of ignorance'.[51] As to the university graduate, although there were concessions as to the term of articles to be served in the Acts of 1843 and 1860, and the 1877 Act exempted graduates from the preliminary, the profession did not attract university men in any numbers until nearly the end of the century. In 1874 only two applicants for admission

[46] Law Society's Handbook: Origins and Progress of the Profession of Attorney and Solicitor.

[47] Warren, A Popular and Practical Introduction to Law Studies, 1835, p 80.

[48] Annual Provincial Meeting, p 54.

[49] Ibid, p 139.

[50] Ibid, p 129.

[51] *Law Times*, vol 40, p 621.

had a degree;[52] and during that decade it was reckoned that the percentage was not higher than five.[53] At the 1881 Provincial Meeting it was claimed that sixteen per cent of all new entrants had a degree; in 1882 out of 808 new entrants eighty-seven were graduates; in 1886 out of 882 there were 106; and between 1892 and 1897 out of 4,189 there were 680. It was still being argued whether a university training was the right thing to undertake before articles. In 1876 it was said on the one hand that it was 'still a long way from the time when it will be generally deemed to be in the interests of a youth who is to be articled to a solicitor that he should have had a university training'; and on the other hand (in the *Saturday Review*) that 'of all the investments that a young man intending to be a solicitor can make the best is to obtain a university education'.[54]

Nevertheless there were those who thought that the preliminary examination should be toughened. In the early 1880s a Mr Hastie successfully proposed at a Law Society general meeting that this should be done, though every Council member present voted against him. The Council was reluctant to raise the standard not only because of its traditional tenderness to the 'ten-year man' but because there were a number of exempting examinations such as the entrance examinations of the universities which had a low standard and the Council feared that if they raised their own sights the only result would be that would-be students would choose the alternative examinations.[55] In 1899 when Mr Hastie returned to the charge in the legal press a correspondent who disagreed with him on other points conceded that the preliminary examination was 'childish when compared with that required by almost every other profession' and 'did not offer a guarantee that men with a deficient general education shall be shut out'.[56] The standard of general education in the profession undoubtedly improved immeasurably during the century, but that was not due to the preliminary examination or to any action by the profession or The Law Society.

Professional education was also widening its scope. The text-books of the eighteenth century written for the attorney tended to be of the handbook variety purporting to give in one volume all that the attorney might require over a wide field. Typical was The Attorney's Pocket Companion, published in 1733, which dealt primarily with the King's Bench procedure but only with legal principles so far as was needed to make the procedure intelligible; or in 1725 The Attorney's and Solicitor's Companion or the Compleat Affidavit Man; or Bird's Pocket Conveyancer or Attorney's Pocketbook in 1796. They were the successors of The Compleat Solicitor of the previous century and emphasised their completeness in one volume.

[52] *Solicitors' Journal*, vol 19, p 29.
[53] Univ Oxford Minutes of Evidence, Parl Proc 1881, qu 1151.
[54] Quoted *Solicitors' Journal*, vol 21, p 8.
[55] These were eliminated by the Solicitors Act 1922.
[56] *Law Journal*, 9th December 1899, pp 678–679.

In the nineteenth century there was an enormous increase in the number of text-books of a much more special nature. In 1844 the *Law Times* reviewed sixty text-books; by the end of the century the number was 160 a year. In 1830 the *Law Magazine* reviewed in one issue three works on the law of attorneys and commented that it was 'rather singular that in times so fruitful to bookmakers and with subjects so much in request, attorneys and solicitors should have been for more than a century one of the most wealthy and influential bodies in the state without having a separate treatise devoted to them'[57] and now suddenly there were three. The profession was equally well supplied with periodicals and law reports. Between 1822 and 1885 there were no fewer than fourteen weekly or monthly papers, of which three published reports and statutes.[58] The subscribers were mainly attorneys and solicitors, judging from the list published by the *Law Times* when it started publication.[59] The *Legal Observer*, founded in 1830, was owned and edited by Mr Robert Maugham, the secretary of The Law Society. It was said at the time to have been started mainly to mount an opposition to the Bar and a metropolitan deeds registry, and certainly it was always orientated towards the solicitors' profession. It was generally at loggerheads with the *Law Times* and when it was being re-organised in 1856 there was a most acrimonious exchange. The *Law Times* accused the leading members of The Law Society of misrepresentation if not worse in trying to persuade its subscribers to favour the new weekly, and they certainly did suggest that the *Law Times* was pro-Bar and anti-solicitor. In fact the *Law Times* was anti-Law Society because of what it regarded as the Society's London bias and was pro-country attorney because that was the source of its strongest support. In one way or another therefore the profession was well informed, and these

[57] Page 43.

[58] The following is a not necessarily complete list:

1790 *Lawyers and Magistrates Magazine*
1822 *Law Journal*—a new series started in 1866
1823 *Law Advertiser*
1825 *Legal Advertiser*
1826 *Property Lawyer*
1828 *Law Magazine*
1830 *Legal Observer* (which became the *Solicitors' Journal* in 1856)
1831 *The Lawyer's Magazine*
1837 *The Jurist* and *The Justice of the Peace*
1838 *Monthly Law Magazine*
1843 *Law Times* (amalgamated with *Law Journal* in 1965 as *New Law Journal*)
1844 *Law Review* (amalgamated with *Law Magazine* as *Law Magazine and Review* 1856)
1846 *Legal Practitioner*
1885 *Law Quarterly Review*

[59] There were 1,313 country and 191 town attorneys and solicitors and forty-three barristers. The paper was founded, owned and edited by a barrister named Edward William Cox who eventually became a serjeant at law. He and Mr Maugham were therefore in exactly the same position as founders, owners and editors of their papers and they neglected no opportunity to attack each other.

papers show that the profession had not only widened its horizons but took a lively interest in all that concerned it, and was eager for instruction. As most of these ventures had a long life it is reasonable to suppose that they were well supported.

But this was primarily for admitted men. Articled clerks had, for years to come, to make do with what they were taught in their offices and with such lectures as The Law Society and some provincial law societies provided. Some of them in 1846 wrote to the Lord Chancellor and the Master of the Rolls complaining that there was no organisation or society to help articled clerks, but they got no more than expressions of sympathy.[60] There was some degree of self-help with the encouragement of The Law Society and a Students' Debating Society was founded in London. In the provinces similar societies were established; there were at least eight in 1848 and in the 1870s the proceedings of fifteen or so were being regularly reported in the legal press. In 1872 the movement was sufficiently well established to justify a National Congress being held in London. But between the time when the 1846 committee reported and the end of the century the education provided for articled clerks outside their offices had hardly improved at all. The example of the Manchester Law Society in providing lectures was followed by Liverpool in 1871; and the Yorkshire Board of Legal Studies was established with some financial help from The Law Society in 1898. Otherwise the provincial articled clerk was left largely to his own devices. The Law Society itself had only small resources and in any event until after the end of the century represented less than half the profession. It could therefore 'only try to improve its own library facilities and expand its own system of law lectures'.[61] To encourage articled clerks to attend the lectures the Society eventually gave effect to the 1846 committee's recommendation by agreeing that articled clerks should have three months' leave of absence from their office work to prepare for the intermediate examination which had been set up under the 1860 Act and six months' leave to prepare for the final. But this operated only to the advantage of the law coaches, who had by this time started giving tuition to supplement that supplied by The Law Society. Advertisements for coaching began to appear in the early 1860s. Then the Reverend M A Molash offered to provide board and tuition for the preliminary examination at five guineas a month. More serious names soon appeared. In 1876 the most famous of all the coaching businesses was established by Messrs Gibson and Weldon, a firm of solicitors practising in Chancery Lane. The competition from them and the other coaches was such that by 1883 'seven-eighths of the candidates did not attend any Law Society lectures at all and less than three per cent attended the whole'.[62] The Law Society lec-

[60] *Law Review*, vol 4, pp 365–367.

[61] Report of the Select Committee on Legal Education (1967) (the Ormrod Report: see p 63, *infra*), p 9.

[62] Kersley, Gibsons, p 2.

turers were of good quality: a rising young barrister named H H Asquith was one of them in the 1880s. But perhaps they were not practical enough and in 1893 the numbers attending had fallen to such a point that The Law Society stopped the lectures and started classes conducted by solicitors and continuing right through the year. Clearly The Law Society was trying to copy Gibsons, but the change does not seem to have succeeded and Mr Justice Cozens-Hardy in a lecture to solicitors announced that The Law Society had ceased to educate and now only examined its articled clerks. In 1903 the Society at last established its own law school.[63] Although attendance was at first voluntary, it increased slowly and steadily,[64] in spite of a fall in the number of articled clerks. By 1906 it was claimed that 73·7 per cent of all London articled clerks were attending the school.

The establishment of a school or college of law had been recommended in 1846 by the Select Committee. It was even then not a novel proposal. Cardinal Wolsey projected an institution to be founded in London for the systematic study of all branches of the law; and Sir Nicholas Bacon presented a similar scheme to Henry VIII in 1537. At the beginning of the nineteenth century there had been a scheme for a college of law which was to have power to examine the legal attainments, the character, and the professional prospects of all candidates for admission, and was to deal with both London and provincial men. Nothing came of that or of the Select Committee's recommendation, although the deficiencies of the existing system were constantly exposed in the legal press and at meetings of the profession. In 1870, however, a small committee of provincial solicitors which had been concerning itself with the problem converted itself into the Legal Education Association with the principal object of setting up a 'General School of Law' based on the Inns of Court but intended to provide legal education for articled clerks as well as for Bar students. The Council of The Law Society was opposed to the scheme, but there was a strong body of opinion inside the profession in favour. The scheme required legislative sanction and when it was debated in the House of Commons Mr Jessell alleged that 'the more eminent and experienced members of that Society were opposed to the change ... but a large majority of younger members had called a meeting and outvoted the Council'.[65] It was true that a special meeting had been called to consider whether the profession should support the scheme; the attendance was heavy; the debate lasted three days and the supporters of the scheme resisted every attempt to put them off. In the end resolutions to support the scheme were passed by overwhelming majorities. Whether the majorities were made up as Mr Jessell said is not known, but those who favoured the scheme included men like Mr Freshfield and Mr Clabon (after whom the Clabon

[63] *Law Magazine and Review* (5th Series), vol 28 (1902–1903), p 391.
[64] 1903–1904: 212; 1904–1905: 214; 1905–1906: 235; and 1906–1907: 278.
[65] *Law Times*, vol 51, p 235.

Prize was later named), and nobody could be more eminent and experienced than they were. The Metropolitan and Provincial Law Association was also in favour and so were the great northern law societies. Behind the opposition was the fear in both professions that the idea of a common education for both branches would lead to fusion. The Law Society Council's spokesman in the House of Commons, Mr Gregory, asserted that fusion was the real object of 'the young and ambitious spirits' who favoured it. The proposal was narrowly defeated in the House of Commons by 116 votes to 103. The chief sponsor was Sir Roundell Palmer, who shortly afterwards became Lord Chancellor as Lord Selborne. In 1874 and 1875 when he was in opposition he tried again to get acceptance: in 1875 the scheme was actually approved by the House of Lords but was lost in the Commons. He claimed that the Bill had the support of eighty per cent of all practising solicitors, but it was of no avail and he gave up the struggle. He attributed his failure to 'the jealousy of the University of London ... to the innate conservatism of the Inns and to the fear that a common education would lead to fusion of the two branches of the profession'.[66] The result was the same mixture as before: a library and some lectures. In 1873 'the legal education of this great country could be supplied ... by something less than the average teaching staff of the law faculty of a third-rate German University'.[67]

There were a number of chances before the century was out. In 1884 there was a suggestion in connection with the then pending re-organisation of the University of London to merge the Society's training facilities and needs with those of the University and King's College and the Inns. On this occasion the Society refused to co-operate, but in 1891 changed its mind when it was proposed to establish what was intended to be called the Gresham University for London. The law faculty for the new University would have been too small without the students from the Inns and The Law Society. On this occasion the Inns refused to agree and the scheme came to nothing. A third chance arose when Clifford's Inn and New Inn were to be sold. It was held in *Smith* v *Kerr*[68] that the proceeds of sale of Clifford's Inn were subject to educational trusts and the same principle was applied to New Inn. The net proceeds were £150,000 and the proposal was to use the money to establish a general school of law. The scheme was strongly supported by The Law Society, but the Bar Council and the Inner Temple were equally strongly opposed to it. The result was that the proceeds of sale had to be invested and half the income paid to The Law Society for educational purposes. In 1974 that share of income was £2,836, which was a poor enough result but at least the fate of the proceeds of sale of Clement's Inn, Barnard's Inn and Staple Inn had been avoided. They went to the principals and commoners of the

[66] Ormrod Report, p 10.
[67] *Solicitors' Journal*, vol 18 (1873), p 78.
[68] [1900] 2 Ch 511.

respective Inns, except for the fund which constitutes the Clement's Inn Prize.

It had in this way taken almost sixty years to establish a School of Law which bore some resemblance to the ideal put before the whole legal profession in 1846 by the Select Committee. The School was assured of pupils because The Law Society in 1922 introduced a compulsory 'academic year' for all articled clerks other than those with a law degree or ten-year men.[69] This meant that before taking the intermediate examination articled clerks had to attend lectures at the Society's School of Law or at a centre arranged by a recognised institution, which normally meant a university. The Society paid subsidies to the universities who provided the courses. Legal education was put in the charge of a Legal Education Committee consisting not only of members of the Council but of up to six persons representing local law societies and law students' societies. Nevertheless the fact remained that most students continued to find it prudent also to attend courses provided by one or other of the law coaches, of whom Messrs Gibson and Weldon continued to be the most popular and successful.

The final stage was reached in 1961. After the War Messrs Gibson and Weldon found it increasingly difficult to maintain a proper staff; on the other hand something was needed to make the Law Society's School of Law really effective. The matter was all the more urgent because of the increase in the number of would-be solicitors. The Law Society decided to acquire Messrs Gibson and Weldon's business in 1961 and to set up with the partners in that business a College of Law. It withdrew its subsidies to universities who were providing courses and it made its own courses compulsory for the Part I examination which by that time had replaced the old intermediate examination. In addition to the existing premises at Lancaster Gate in London the Society had acquired Braboeuf Manor in Guildford and by 1970 had some 2,500 students taking courses in London or at Guildford, and another 3,500 taking correspondence courses. Courses were also available at Birmingham and other provincial centres. Advocates' training courses have also been established.

This system was of course based on the traditional service under articles. Criticism of the system had never ceased and in the post-1945 period was even stronger because of the difficulty of finding solicitors willing to accept an articled clerk, or at any rate sufficient for the large numbers seeking entry into the profession. The whole problem of legal education was referred to a Select Committee under the chairmanship of Mr Justice Ormrod in December 1967. The committee recommended[70] that the training of a solicitor should be in three stages: (1) the academic stage, which meant that he should have a law degree; (2) the professional stage, which meant that he should attend what was called a vocational course for one year; and (3) a period of three years in a solicitor's office. These recommenda-

[69] Solicitors Act 1922, s 2.
[70] Cmnd 4595.

tions were in accordance with The Law Society's memoranda to the committee, but their implementation immediately ran into difficulties.

The trend towards having a university degree before starting articles, already noticed, appeared at one time to be continuing steadily towards becoming normal procedure. By 1937, of the 188 candidates who obtained honours ninety-nine had a degree; and it was estimated that by 1960 sixty per cent of all entrants were university men.[71] But then the numbers tended to decline or at any rate to remain static. In 1964 the percentage was 44·8; in 1969 it was 46·8. The would-be solicitor found that it was difficult to get a place in a university law school; on the other hand he found that, with or without a degree, newly qualified solicitors readily obtained well-paid posts. To go to a university involved delay and therefore loss of money, so that there were good reasons for going straight into articles after leaving school. In addition the profession itself was not convinced. Many if not the majority of solicitors had no degree and they could find no fault with that. But the vocational year was the most difficult problem, primarily because of money. When the Ormrod Report was published the Young Solicitors Group of The Law Society said that 'a solicitor after seven or eight years of practice can reasonably be expected to meet a levy of up to £1 per week if this is necessary', but not all the potential contributors thought as they did. To bring the matter to a head The Law Society in 1974 circularised local law societies with the question: 'Is the proposal acceptable that there should be an increase in the practising certificate fee to subsidise the pilot course which had been planned for 1975 and subsequent pilot courses?' The profession overwhelmingly rejected the proposal, which would have added £40 a year to the practising certificate fee. This reaction meant that the Ormrod scheme could not be implemented at all, and the profession continued as before with the much-criticised articles system.

In the meantime the profession had been raising its entry standards. In 1922 some of the examinations giving exemption from the preliminary examination were excluded and for general purposes the standard was the qualifying examination for entry to a university.[72] After 1967 the entry qualification has been either a university degree or at least two 'A' levels[73]—in other words the new entrant has to be university material. Mere attendance at the College of Law is not sufficient. The student has to satisfy the College that he has been diligent; failure to pass such tests as he may be set can result in his losing the benefit of his period of attendance for qualifying purposes. The preliminary examination has been retained only for the ten-year man and can be taken only by those over

[71] *The Times*, 14th November 1961.

[72] Solicitors Act 1922, s 1.

[73] Training Regulations 1967, reg 6 (2) (*d*). The qualification has been made even more stringent by the Training Regulations 1972.

twenty-eight years of age. For these men it represents a palpable obstacle and the failure rate runs as high as thirty per cent.

The third of the educational and training problems which the profession had to tackle was that of examinations during articles and before admission. The 1860 Act introduced not only the preliminary examination but also the so-called intermediate, which was intended to be taken about half-way through articles and to deal with the general principles of law. The subjects were real property, contract and tort, public law—the constitution and the courts—and trust accounts and book-keeping. There were no set books but some were recommended, and generations of English solicitors were brought up on Stephen's Commentaries. The final examination had been criticised in 1846 as providing no real test of knowledge, and thirty years later it was clearly not a very difficult obstacle. In the year 1876–1877 eighty-two per cent of all candidates passed. Entry to the profession was thought to be too easy, and there was a practical aspect of that in the concern at that time at the size of the profession. The standard was sharply raised in 1887, with the result that the failure rate for the first time became significant. In 1890 it was as high as fifty per cent. The candidates then seemed to adjust themselves to the new conditions and the failure rate dropped to about twenty per cent just before the 1914 War. In the 1930s, however, it had crept up again towards forty per cent and that proportion continued after 1945. In 1957, for instance, only 711 passed out of 1,216; in 1960 only 792 out of 1,658; and in 1974 there were 6,155 out of 8,847 but that includes partial passes. The 1846 committee had also commented adversely on the fact that no indication was given of a candidate's performance other than that of pass or failure. In 1856, however, The Law Society started a prize system; the Clement's Inn and Clifford's Inn prizes were instituted in 1858; and thereafter the interest of the profession in education was shown by the foundation of other prizes, national and local. By 1936 there were no fewer than twenty-eight. In 1859 an honours system was introduced based on performance in the final examination; in 1880 that was changed by having a special honours examination; in 1964 that in its turn was changed and honours were thereafter awarded on the final examination.[74]

The 1846 committee had in a matter of three months arrived at certain recommendations for providing solicitors with a satisfactory educational system. There was to be a high standard of general education before entry into articles, a college of law to provide a sound professional education, and a proper test of professional knowledge before admission to practice. It needed not much less than one hundred years to give effect to those recommendations. That was a long haul. The profession had never seemed able to make up its mind about legal education. It wanted to establish itself as a liberal profession and it accepted the need of a sound and liberal general education. With more hesitation it accepted the idea of severe

[74] Students Regulations 1962.

qualifying examinations. Professional education was a different matter. In spite of all that was said and written about it, the provision for legal education by the profession through The Law Society for the profession was in 1933 no different from what it was in 1833. The difficulties had been considerable. This was an issue which the profession generally shirked when it came to the crunch. It was sharply divided in the 1870s and 1880s about a college of law and an opportunity was lost then which was not realised for another eighty years; it has come to the brink of becoming a wholly graduate profession but it has pulled back; it refused to bear the cost of trying out practical training outside the articles system which for generations it has generally condemned. The Law Society and the profession were breaking new ground and at each stage it was necessary to convince a conservative body of men that changes in a familiar system were necessary and that the ones proposed were the right ones. There was the awkward fact that until the twentieth century The Law Society did not represent a majority of the whole profession or more than a quarter of those in the provinces. The Society could not compel; it could only hope to convince professional opinion that it was right. Its resources were limited, and it was certain that any changes which involved a financial contribution from the profession would be rejected by the profession or defeated in Parliament. The problem was bedevilled by anxieties about the effect which any solution might have on the relationship between the Bar and solicitors; if both branches were to be recruited from the same sources and given the same professional education, why have two branches? Yet the ideal was never lost sight of and there were always men who kept legal education an active issue. When The Law Society celebrated its centenary in 1925 the President could with justice say that 'we have been and are to-day pioneers in professional legal education in this country'.[75] In 1934 an independent observer, Professor Harold Laski, summed the matter up: 'The Law Society ... has made an effort comparable in quality to that of the great medical schools to send out students into practice whose training indicates a general level of competence with which the public may feel satisfied.'[76] Since 1945 the effort has been much greater. Not only was the College of Law adequately established and organised but there was a large measure of post-admission education which the profession welcomed. The total expenditure of The Law Society itself on legal education has not been stated, but in 1974 the net expenditure after allowing for all income from examination fees, grants and the like was £154,000.

[75] *Solicitors' Journal*, Centenary Supplement, p 12.
[76] Cmd 4663, p 16.

CHAPTER 4

Conduct and Discipline

Until the Solicitors Act 1888 authorised the establishment of a Disciplinary Committee consisting entirely of solicitors, the responsibility for the discipline of the profession had rested with the courts. Originally the attorney was in precisely the same position as the litigant whom he was representing and the courts exercised control over his conduct in the same way and on the same basis as they would have done over that of his client had the client been in court. Because in theory the client was always present personally, so was the attorney, and therefore the court assumed the power to treat as contempt, and accordingly punishable, acts which the attorney committed outside the court.[1] When the attorney was a court official he was also subject to the court's discipline on that account. As the professional attorneys gradually excluded the court officials from the work of representing litigants but still did the work which the officials had done, the attorneys came to be regarded as subject to the same discipline as the officials had been. 'Our jurisdiction depends on the authority of the court over its officers.'[2] It was inherent in the relationship between the court and those it had licensed to represent litigants. In these circumstances there was little statutory provision. The Statute of Westminster 1275 fixed a penalty of imprisonment for a year and a day and exclusion from pleading for those who deceived the court and, although this specifically referred to serjeants and pleaders, it was interpreted as applying also to attorneys. The Ordinance of 1292 imposed a duty of selecting proper persons to be attorneys,[3] but there is little evidence that the judges ever discharged it. On the other hand there is ample evidence that the judges dealt strictly if not harshly with the attorneys who were engaged in cases which they were trying. It might be a matter of want of authority: the Attorney Hugh of Grantchester was admonished that 'at the time when you waged law for your master it was commanded that he should come in person to make his law and thus your power was extinguished. You deserve punishment. Therefore keep your day on Monday to hear judgment … as to your punishment.' But Hugh took advice and did not appear and there is no

[1] *Law Quarterly Review*, vol 25, p 245.
[2] *Ex parte Fisher* (1819), 1 Chitty 694.
[3] Chapter 1, pp 6 and 7, *supra.*

record that he was punished.[4] It might be a matter of the court record: Attorney Soke excused his non-attendance because he had been set on when on his way to the court and imprisoned. This was an excuse not infrequently given and generally accepted in the conditions of the times. But in this case it was proved by production of the court roll that Soke had been in court that day on another case; Soke pleaded an error in the roll, but the court rejected the plea on the ground that if it were accepted that would be an end of any sort of judicial order; it decided that 'All England cannot save this default'.[5] It might be a case of neglect of a client's interest: an attorney failed to comply with the formalities and caused a woman to be delayed in her dower; he was told: 'You will go to gaol until you are well chastised.'[6] Or it might be one of plain chicanery, as in the case of an attorney who on redeeming a bond showed the lender the money and thereby obtained possession of the bond but then absconded with both money and bond.[7] Or the court might relieve a client of the consequences of the mistake of a witness and stupid attorney. Such was the pattern which was in its essentials followed for the next five hundred years. The courts dealt with such cases of malpractice as might come to their notice, but it was a haphazard business.

At the end of the fourteenth century Parliament again took a hand. The employment of court officials as the professional attorneys of litigants had obvious risks because of their opportunities to tamper with the court records to the advantage of their clients. This was a chronic problem which was tinkered with from time to time without success. Two attempts were made in 1384 and 1410. The 1384 Act imposed a penalty of a fine or ransom at the King's will on any person who entered false pleas, erased the rolls, or changed verdicts;[8] the 1410 Act followed complaints of 'favourable' writing by the clerks 'a grant meschef, damage, et desheriteson de lieges', and provided that pleas should not be amended or impaired by new entering of clerks.[9] The overall problem of the professional attorney was dealt with in an Act of 1403 which confirmed the jurisdiction of the judges over attorneys and imposed on them specific disciplinary functions. The Act provided that 'all the attorneys should be examined by the justices and by their discretion their name put on the roll; and they that were good and virtuous and of good fame should be received and sworn well and truly to serve in their offices, and especially that they made no suit in a foreign county; and the other attorneys should be put out by the direction

[4] Year Book (1 Ed 2) Selden Society, vol I, p 99.

[5] Year Book (4 Ed 2) Selden Society, vol 6, pp 20 et seq.

[6] Year Book (3 & 4 Ed 2) Selden Society, vol 4, pp 194–195: *Broke* v *Tayland*.

[7] Selden Society, vol 10 (1386), Case 2. At the time it seems to have been common for a judge to address an attorney as 'my fair friend'—as in 'My fair friend, do you warrant' (YB 3 Ed II, Selden Society, vol 3, p 80: *Gaunt* v *Gaunt*)—when preparing to criticise. Both Beresford CJ and Staunton CJ used the expression in this sort of context.

[8] 1384 (8 Ric 2) c 4.

[9] 3 Rot Parl iii, 306, No 28 and 1410 (12 Hen 4) c 3.

of the justices; and that their masters for whom they were attorneys be warned to take others in their place so that in the meantime no damage nor prejudice should come to their masters. And if any of the attorneys died or ceased, the justices for the time being by their discretion should make another in his place which was a virtuous man and learned, and sworn in the same manner as aforesaid; and if any such attorneys should thereafter be found in any default of record or otherwise, he should forswear the court and never after be received to make any suit in any court of the King.'[10]

There is no evidence that the judges performed their duties under the 1403 Act any more effectively than their predecessors had performed those imposed by the Ordinance of 1292.[11] It would have been remarkable if they had done so, for these were troublesome times in which the discipline of attorneys was completely unimportant. Men had ceased to look to the courts for protection or justice. The courts, if one were powerful enough, were simply a means of gaining one's own ends. 'From the beginning of the fourteenth century and all over the country men were becoming more and more in the habit of forming illegal associations to defeat the ends of justice particularly by corrupting and coercing juries.'[12] The judges were corruptible. In 1340–1341, in 1350 and in 1365 the judges of the King's Bench were summarily dismissed and put on trial for misconduct; Chief Justice Fortescue (1394–1406) for all his smugness was said to be not above taking bribes. Major offenders either were not brought to justice or were pardoned. In the fifteen years from 1381 to 1396 out of 485 persons indicted in Lincolnshire only eighty-one were tried and of these all but five were acquitted or pardoned; in 1446 there were 3,319 pardons and in 1485 2,424 for crimes as serious as murder and rape. 'Maintaining' suits was a commonplace reinforced by bodies of armed retainers to threaten or maim or kill counsel, jury or adversary. The Court of Common Pleas might still sit at Westminster and the judges go their circuits at the appointed term, but litigants were exasperated at the delays and the ineffectiveness of the common law courts and they resorted either to violence or to arbitration through the Chancery.[13] In these circumstances the moralists might complain about the attorneys, but judges were too much concerned with greater problems to trouble themselves about this one. Although the Tudors introduced some degree of law and order there was little improvement in their time in the standard of administration of justice. In fact, the men who had previously been able to get their way by force and intimidation now had to use the courts. Juries were notoriously corruptible and at assizes opponents of important local men found it difficult to get a fair trial and often hard even to get legal representation. 'Less influential litigants

[10] 1402 (4 Hen 4) c 18.
[11] See pp 6 and 7, *supra*.
[12] Selden Society: Select Cases King's Bench Ed III, p xxvii.
[13] See Lander. Conflict and Stability in 15th Century England. p 172 and *passim*.

might resort to detaining witnesses, rigging the trial jury, stealing the record of preliminary proceedings, or irregularly procuring the *postea*.[14] In these, as in other insidious devices for ensuring a favourable outcome, litigants could always rely, for a consideration, on the unprincipled assistance of a local attorney.'[15] The judges themselves continued to do as they had done in the previous two or three hundred years, occasionally punishing some attorney by pillory or prison or fine for having overlooked some formality or otherwise given offence, but not taking any effective action towards establishing a standard of conduct or a means of enforcing it. They 'proved as regards attorneys an inefficient substitute for the corporations which regulated trades'.[16]

In the seventeenth century the picture became a little clearer. There was a procedure for admission of attorneys, though as yet none for solicitors. The oath which was set out in Powell's Attourney's Academy in 1623 was said by the author to have fallen by then into disuse, so that it seems reasonable to suppose that by that date the formalities of which the oath was a principal part were of quite long standing. Although the oath in its full form may have fallen into disuse, it was still printed in The Practick Part of the Law in 1676 as part of the admission procedure, so that it is possible that the practice varied from court to court. Its significance is that it sets out the rules which the attorney was to observe as from time to time established by statute or practice: 'You shall do no falsehood nor deceit nor consent to any being done in this Court and if you know of any to be done you shall give knowledge thereof to my Lord Chief Justice or other his brethren justices of this Court that it may be reformed.[17] You shall delay no man for lucre or malice, you shall increase no fees but be contented with the old accustommed fees.[18] You shall plead no foreign pleas nor sue any foreign suits unlawfully to hurt any man but such as shall stand within the order of the law and your conscience.[19] You shall seal all process as you shall sue out of this Court with the seal thereof and see the King's Majesty and the Lord Chief Justice discharged from the same. You shall not wittingly or willingly sue nor procure to be sued any false suit nor give aid or consent to the same on pain of being expulsed from the Court for ever.[20] And further that you shall use and demean yourself in the office of an attorney within this Court according to your learning and discretion.' Apart from the oath, whether in this form or merely swearing allegiance as Powell stated, the admission was a mere formality without

[14] The '*postea*' was the enrolment of the verdict with the judgment of the court and took its name from the first word of the record.

[15] Cockburn, History of English Assizes 1588 to 1714 (1972), pp 144–145.

[16] Christian, Solicitors—an Outline of Their History, pp 60–61.

[17] This paraphrases the Statute of Westminster 1275 (*supra*, p 6).

[18] This was apparently an established practice and was repeated in the 1654 Order (p 7, *supra*).

[19] The prohibition of foreign suits repeats 1402 (4 Hen 4) c 18.

[20] This is supported by 1384 (8 Ric 2) c iv.

any enquiry by the judges as to the applicant's training or knowledge or suitability. Having sworn before the chief prothonotary the oath required of him, the applicant paid 20s into the judge's box, 12d to the chief prothonotary's secondary, 12d to the clerk who entered his certificate, and something to the other hangers-on, and then proceeded to the clerk of warrants, who entered his name on the roll and received 4s 4d for doing so. That done, the new attorney paid a 4d term fee. He sought admission in the court where he intended to sue out his writs, and the more attorneys chose a particular court the more were the fees which the officials of that court received both on admissions and for later business. It is not likely that chief prothonotaries were discouraging to applicants by being over-nice about their qualifications.

In 1605 Parliament made another attempt to control admissions and conduct. The Act was primarily concerned with the fact that 'the practice of the just and honest serjeants and counsellors-at-law' was greatly slandered by the abuses of sundry attorneys and solicitors who did not pay the fees due to the serjeants and counsellors. As the whole Bar structure was based on the convention that it was not entitled in law to fees, it seems inconsistent that its members who were so numerous in the Commons should have sought parliamentary help to recover them. For the purpose of discipline the Act provided that none should be admitted as attorneys in any court of record but such as had been brought up in the same courts and found by their dealings to be skilful and honest; as to solicitors, only men of sufficient and honest disposition were to be admitted; attorneys were not to allow others to use their names for acting as attorneys, and those who did were liable to be fined £20 and excluded from practice. In 1610 the Privy Council ordered the judges to take whatever steps were necessary to limit unnecessary fees, which at the time were said to be the ruin of many. In 1633 the judges on assize were instructed to compile a detailed list of attorneys in the counties they visited and of their addresses as another attempt to limit the size of the profession, stigmatised in the order, as was customary, as 'sowers and fomenters of suits'. The judges were themselves now making some effort. They made a series of orders in relation to Westminster in the same sense as the 1633 order, that is to say with the object of ensuring that attorneys had an address where they could readily be found. That would if observed have been one means of ascertaining who was and who was not entitled to practise.[21] The ideal was to have the attorneys entered into one of the Inns of Court or Chancery to give them the corporate spirit and self-discipline of the guilds and other trade corporations, but that could not be achieved. Another attempt at the same objective of making the profession primarily responsible for its own discipline was made in the judges' order of 1654. Every three years the courts were to empanel a jury and able and credible officers, clerks and attorneys to enquire into and reform abuses. The jury was to present

[21] Chapter 9, *infra*.

to the court for removal all attorneys and clerks who were notoriously unfit. Every Michaelmas term the courts were also to appoint twelve or more able and credible practitioners to act for the ensuing year in the examination of applicants for admission before they were presented to the court to be sworn. The scheme was sensible, but although the panels continued to be appointed there is no record of their having achieved anything practical, and at the beginning of the eighteenth century Parliament was again invited to intervene.

However much one may discount all the criticisms of the profession, there is the most ample evidence that by and large the fact of being an attorney disqualified a man from decent society in the seventeenth and much of the eighteenth century. The problem which had first to be resolved if this situation was to be cured was that of controlling admissions. The system, whatever it was, had broken down. Almost anybody could be admitted; but it did not greatly matter, for many acted as attorneys and solicitors without troubling to be admitted. The West Riding magistrates in 1728 petitioned the House of Commons for legislation to put an end to the scandal and the evidence put to the Select Committee led to the Attorneys and Solicitors Act 1729.[22] This Act provided the foundation upon which all subsequent legislation relating to the discipline of the profession has been based—the establishment and maintenance of a roll or rolls and the exclusion from practice of those not enrolled. The Act laid down the requirements for admission and applied the same to both attorneys and solicitors.[23] The applicant must have been articled to an attorney or solicitor for five years before admission;[24] the judges were to examine him and satisfy themselves 'by such means as they shall think fit and proper touching his fitness to act as attorney';[25] and he had to take a simplified oath that 'I will truly and honestly demean myself in the practice of an attorney (or solicitor) according to the best of my knowledge and ability' and the oath of allegiance.[26] The applicant had to enrol himself in all the courts in which he intended to practise. No attorney or solicitor was to have more than two articled clerks at the same time.[27] The Act had only a very limited success. The judges were to an extent to blame for the failure of the Act to secure a reasonable standard of knowledge and moral character as a condition of entry, because from the outset they did not examine the candidates. This may well have been partly due to the fact that no

[22] Chapter 2, p 23, *supra*.

[23] The Act made the curious distinction between the two parts of the profession that attorneys could become solicitors automatically but the converse did not apply until 1783 by virtue of 23 Geo 2 c 26, s 15.

[24] Sections 5 and 7.

[25] Sections 2 and 4, and ss 6 and 8: ss 2 and 4 applied to persons practising at 18th December 1730; ss 6 and 8 to subsequent entrants.

[26] The oath of allegiance was abolished in 1888.

[27] Section 15: this provision was probably intended to restrict the entry (see Chapter 6, *infra*, p 107).

fee was payable for performing this duty, but also it may be attributed to their lack of interest in attorneys and solicitors. But it would be unfair to blame them for the almost total absence of any post-admission discipline. They could deal only with cases which arose in their own courts and of which they had personal knowledge or with those which somebody chose to bring to their notice. It was highly unlikely that there would be many dissatisfied clients who would incur further expense and trouble to bring their former attorney to book[28] and the panels set up under the 1654 order had become obsolete.

The same concern was beginning to be felt inside the profession. In 1739 the Society of Gentlemen Practisers was already established. Its object[29] in general terms was the suppression of malpractices in the profession. Its achievements in this as in other fields have been exaggerated, but bringing the Society into perspective does not mean that one should disparage what it did and what it meant. It represented the first spontaneous gesture from within the profession to discipline itself and in the long run to get rid of the rogues and rascals who disgraced it. The example it set was followed in the provinces, and if it and the other law societies founded in the eighteenth century eventually became little more than attorneys' dining clubs they were evidence of a better element in the profession prepared to take a lead. The Gentlemen Practisers' principal weapon was the Attorneys and Solicitors Act 1729. The Act was in the first instance to be in operation until 1739; it was then renewed until 1749; and then made perpetual on its next renewal in 1757. The Society took the opportunity of the renewal in 1749 to strengthen control on admissions and over training under articles. It had been found that articles were being back-dated so as to enable a candidate to be admitted without serving his five-year term; the 1749 Act required that an affidavit of due execution should be made and enrolled within three months of the entry into articles.[30] To secure as far as possible that articled clerks got some sort of training, only attorneys and solicitors in actual practice were to have articled clerks;[31] and the clerk must throughout his articles be actually employed in the business of an attorney or solicitor carried on by his principal and at the conclusion of his articles swear and file an affidavit that he had been so employed.[32] The control on admission was reinforced by orders of the judges in Common Pleas and King's Bench in 1791 and 1795[33] that the names of all candidates for admission and of the persons to whom they had been articled had to be entered in a book kept available for inspection in the

[28] For instance Attorney Brounsall was brought before the court after his conviction for felony not by the original complainant but by the magistrates 'to prevent the neighbourhood receiving any injury' (Cowp Rep 829).

[29] Chapter 2, *supra*, p 23 et seq.

[30] Section 3.

[31] Section 7.

[32] Section 8.

[33] Trin Geo III 1791; and Trin Geo III 1795.

office of the court in which the application for admission was to be made. The Society concerned itself primarily with checking whether or not the applicants had complied with the statutory formalities, especially in relation to their service under articles. Particularly after the orders of 1791 and 1795, it was able to check who was applying and with whom articles were claimed to have been served; and if they were not satisfactory it entered a caveat against admission. If then not satisfied, the Society pursued its objection to the court itself.

Supervision of admissions was a constant operation; malpractices by attorneys and solicitors came to the Society's attention or activated it only rarely and spasmodically. In 1741 the general meeting resolved that the committee should meet as often as it thought fit to take into consideration any matters relating to the benefit of suitors and the honour of the profession;[34] in 1750 it directed the committee to take cognisance of and prosecute at the Society's expense any attorney guilty of illegal practices, and every member of the Society was desired to give notice to the deputy secretary of all such practices that came to their knowledge.[35] They do not seem to have had much business and the proceedings of the Society do not disclose more than a dozen cases where it took any action against an attorney for malpractice. The most notorious case was that of a Mr Wreathcock, a suborner of witnesses and a provider of men of straw at Westminster Hall.[36] He had been fined £50 in December 1725 for contempt of court on the ground that he and his partner had filed a writ claiming damages and an account in respect of a contract between two highwaymen as to the division of their spoils; the fine was backed by committal to the Fleet until payment was made. This conduct was not then of sufficient gravity to justify striking off, and Mr Wreathcock reappears in 1735, when he was convicted of robbing a Dr Lancaster of £35. For this offence he was sentenced to death, but the penalty was commuted to transportation. He was still on the roll in 1756, when he was committed to prison for various misdemeanours and contempt; there was another complaint against him of malpractices in Common Pleas. The Society was able to get an order for him to be struck off. In 1753 the Society took action against one Sparrow for acting as attorney for one Jones while he himself was a prisoner in the Fleet, and it considered whether or not it should seek an amendment of what was by then the 1749 Act to prevent attorneys and solicitors from practising whilst in gaol, because there were several

[34] Minutes, 18th June 1741.

[35] Minutes, 21st February 1750.

[36] Jeafferson, A Book about Lawyers (1867 ed), pp 360–361; Wreathcock was commemmorated in the following lines:

> 'The criers their attorneys call;
> One of the gown, discreet and wise,
> By proper means his witness tried;
> From Wreathcock's gang—not right or laws,
> He assures his trembling client's cause.'

'unfortunate attorneys and solicitors confined in prison' who took it upon themselves to bring and defend suits in law and equity.[37] There were also a couple of cases involving attorneys who had been put in the pillory.[38] In a period of over seventy years, at a time when by all accounts malpractice was rife, this was little more than a start, but at least a precedent had been established which the Incorporated Law Society was readily able to follow.

Had the 1729 Act and its additions and amendments been efficiently enforced, it would have provided for its times a reasonably satisfactory code for securing at any rate the essential basis for a liberal and respectable profession, in that new entrants were given an adequate preliminary training and were before admission able to satisfy the judges that they were suitable and knowledgeable. Unfortunately that did not happen. Not only did the judges neglect their duties but the Act was circumvented to defeat its provisions as to training. According to Mr Day articles were executed one day and the clerk presented for admission the next: 'The occasional Acts of Parliament which gave further time to such persons as omitted [to file the affidavit of due execution of the articles of clerkship] afforded in this most important instance an opportunity to inrol the articles at the last moment of the supposed time; and those who were bad enough to engage in such a transaction were not likely to be at a loss for the means of obtaining an affidavit that the articles were executed on the day they bore date and the clerk then swearing that he had served the whole term of five years according to the intent and meaning of the articles the admission followed as of course.'[39] The restriction on the number of articled clerks which an attorney or solicitor might have at any one time was evaded in the same way. The principal did not have to swear an affidavit that the clerk had duly served his articles; that was left to the clerk himself. Mr Day may be thought to have been a harsh and prejudiced critic, but three petitions presented by attorneys and solicitors to the House of Commons in 1786 and supported by the Gentlemen Practisers complained that the Act was 'greatly defective, daily experience confirming that many improper persons gain admission to the Roll'.[40]

If the Act was not effective the action of the courts was not much more so. The eighteenth century no doubt saw a considerable improvement in the respectability of the profession, but there were still a good many rogues

[37] Minutes, 9th August 1753.

[38] Mr Landen Jones, who had been put in the pillory in 1745 and struck off the roll of attorneys, continued as a solicitor and the Society had him struck off that roll, too; Mr Daniel Alexander was pilloried in 1752 and the Society had him struck off, too.

[39] An Address to the Attorneys at Law and to the Public, pp 13–15. Ironically the 'occasional Acts' to which Mr Day referred were in some instances initiated by the Gentlemen Practisers, eg 33 Geo 2 c 16 and Minute Book 20th January 1752, p 48.

[40] British Parliamentary Papers, House of Commons Journals, vol 41, 7th March 1786. The petition, which related to other complaints of the profession, was simply ordered to lie on the table.

in it. Nevertheless 'from a cursory inspection of the rolls of the court at Westminster it would appear that more solicitors are struck off the roll to-day in one year than were struck off during the whole of the eighteenth century'.[41] Two important principles were established. Lord Mansfield had a high opinion of the better elements in the profession: 'That part of the profession which is carried on by attorneys is liberal and respectable as well as useful to the public when they conduct themselves with honour and dignity'.[42] He it was who laid down the principle on which professional discipline was to be based: 'Having committed a felony we think that the defendant is not a fit person to be an attorney.'[43] It was also in this period that the courts decided that an injured client might sue his attorney or solicitor for damages for negligence as distinct from fraud.[44] In relation to professional conduct there was little guidance available to the profession. There were by the end of the century some five hundred relevant decisions scattered through the reports, but until Mr Maugham published his Treatise in 1825 nobody had presented to the profession a coherent statement of their effect or of the statutory provisions and rules of court which were also germane.[45] Of course, there was no professional body to whom the practitioner could turn for information or help.

Until the end of the nineteenth century the discipline of the profession remained entirely a matter for the courts. They could of their own initiative take such punitive action as appeared fit 'where the subject-matter of the complaint arose in proceedings in an action or suit or in a matter so connected with the professional character of a solicitor as to afford a presumption that his character formed the ground of his employment'.[46] In relation to matters outside this area the courts acted on the application of some person aggrieved by the attorney's conduct or of some interested body such as The Law Society or a bench of magistrates. The Law Society took up the task of applying in these cases as early as 1834,[47] in fact as soon as the Society of Gentlemen Practisers had ceased to exist, and the annual reports invariably refer to the number of cases taken before the courts. The normal procedure was that the court ordered the complaint to be investigated by one of the masters; the investigation often took many

[41] Birks, Gentlemen at Law, p 109.

[42] *Pitt* v *Yalden* (1767), 4 Bur 2061.

[43] *Ex parte Brounsall* (1778), 2 Cowp 829. Because of the importance of the point to the profession Lord Mansfield consulted all the judges before giving his decision and in the course of it he said they were unanimous.

[44] *Russell* v *Palmer* (1767), 2 Wils 325; and see Winfield, Select Legal Essays (1952), p 38.

[45] Considering the importance of the matter the profession was for long ill-served with text-books. The standard work on the law relating to solicitors, 'Cordery', has never dealt with professional conduct or etiquette in any detail. In 1960 The Law Society published in book form lectures (edited for publication) given by Sir Thomas Lund in 1950 and 1951; and in 1974 a Guide was also published by the Society which gave the first comprehensive survey since Maugham's 1825 Treatise.

[46] *Re Gray* [1892] 2 QB 440.

[47] Chapter 2, p 29, *supra*.

months to complete, but when it was complete the master's report came before the court, where the relevant facts were again sifted. The attorney was under a grave disadvantage. Normally the original application was widely publicised, but no further reference would be made in public if the master found that the original complaint was unjustified. The public naturally tended to remember only the original complaint. There was the further problem that the standard to be applied was uncertain. It had been assumed since Lord Mansfield's dictum[48] that a criminal was not fit to be an attorney so that a criminal conviction would be automatically followed by striking off. The rule seemed to be confirmed in these terms in 1867 by Mr Justice Blackburn: 'It was necessary for the protection of the public that no one should be allowed to exercise the office of attorney who was not a person of character and honour.'[49] But in 1889 Baron Pollock decided that the rule was not absolute and refused to strike off an assistant solicitor who had embezzled a large amount of money.[50] In 1893 the Court of Appeal decided that there was no absolute rule but that conviction of a serious criminal offence put the onus on the solicitor to show why he should not be struck off or otherwise made subject to some professional penalty, but 'the mere fact of a man being convicted of a criminal offence punishable with imprisonment and hard labour is not in itself sufficient to justify his being struck off or even being suspended from practice'.[51]

Discipline through the courts was manifestly unsatisfactory from every point of view, and self-help was in the spirit of the time felt to be a better method of raising the standard of conduct. Those who thought about the matter had no doubt of what that standard was: it was that of a gentleman. The promoters of the Law Institution in their prospectuses sounded a note which was often repeated: they hoped that men whose previous conduct had caused them to be excluded would mend their ways in the hopes of election. Local law societies were particularly important because it was 'difficult for the most impudent to exhibit the character of a knave in the presence of gentlemen'.[52] A Metropolitan and Provincial Legal Association[53] was formed in 1844 for the purpose of purging the profession of improper practitioners and to call in the 'interposition of the court in all cases where we can prove improper practice', but it failed from want of resources and support. There were suggestions of boycotting men who were guilty of malpractices and even of marking their names in a privately printed Law List. The latter suggestion was repeated from time to time,

[48] In *Ex parte Brounsall*, p 76, *supra*.

[49] *Law Journal*, vol 32, p 242.

[50] *Re a Solicitor*, decided QB 7th May 1889, reported *Solicitors' Journal*, vol 33, p 441.

[51] *Re Weare a Solicitor* (1893) 2 QB 439, confirming Divisional Court, reported *Solicitors' Journal*, vol 37, p 527.

[52] *Law Times*, vol I, p 164.

[53] It must be distinguished from the Metropolitan and Provincial Law Association formed in 1847 (p 38, *supra*).

but it was pointed out that this would be a useful means for clients with unsavoury business to transact to find the sort of practitioner who would do it. The first substantial advance towards the profession having its own disciplinary system was made in the 1843 Act by which The Law Society was made the registrar of the roll then instituted. The official roll was still kept in the Petty Bag Office. To abolish that would have been a reform too difficult to effect at the time, and the dual system meant that men being admitted had the inconvenience of having to register both with the Society and at the Petty Bag Office. The death of the holder of the Petty Bag Office, a Mr Murray, in 1888 enabled the dual system to be ended[54] and the Society was then in control of admissions and re-admissions subject only to appeal to the court. The complaints of improper admissions which had formerly been so frequent ceased after 1843. The problem of dealing with cases of misconduct was more difficult. Until 1874 the Society had no status to enable it to appear on applications to strike off or otherwise punish a solicitor unless it was itself the applicant. It was in exactly the same position as any other person or body. The Solicitors Act 1874 provided that notice had to be given to the Society of any application for the removal of a name from the roll and that the Society should have the right to be heard on such applications.[55] The significance was that for the first time there was an opportunity for the profession's own attitude to a particular case to be expressed. The burden on the Society was, however, heavy. All applications had to be investigated by the Society to determine the course it should take, even though many of them turned out in the event to be frivolous. Moreover, the system was over-complicated. Formerly there had been two investigations: one by the master and the second by the court on his report. Now there were three with the addition of the Society's own enquiry. Accordingly in 1887 the Society prepared a Bill to give itself the power and duty to investigate and determine complaints subject to the solicitor's right of appeal to the court. Because of the opposition which was threatened in the House of Commons the Bill was watered down to an application for power to appoint a committee to make preliminary enquiries on complaints and then to report to the court, that is to say, to amalgamate the work being done by the masters and the Society. This also was refused, but the Solicitors Act 1888 provided that the initial enquiry should be carried out by a committee nominated by the Master of the Rolls from the members of the Council of the Society and that the application to strike off should come before the court on the report of that committee. The importance to the profession was that it avoided an application in open court until the facts had been investigated and it had been established that there was a case of substance for the solicitor to answer. The publicity about the legislation and the fact that a complaint

[54] By the Supreme Court of Judicature (Officers) Act 1879 the Petty Bag Office was to close on the next vacancy in the office of its clerk.

[55] Sections 7–10.

could now be made without the need to employ solicitor and counsel led to an increase in the number to be investigated. Moreover, there was no opportunity for the committee to pass any opinion as to the gravity of the offence or as to the penalty which it might think appropriate. Of immediate practical importance was the large additional expense to which the Society was put. The closing of the Petty Bag Office in 1888 must have resulted in a substantial saving in servicing the profession, but it was not until 1897 that the Treasury agreed to make a modest contribution to the expense of disciplinary enquiries.[56] The wider problems remained. Before the First World War attempts were made to obtain power to set up a Disciplinary Committee with full powers to deal with matters of professional conduct, as was by that time the case in other professions. On each occasion, although the proposal had the support of Lord Loreburn, then Lord Chancellor, the Bill, having passed the Lords, was not reached in the House of Commons. A third attempt after the War seemed likely to meet the same fate, but Sir Gordon Hewart (as he then was) as Attorney-General persuaded the Cabinet to adopt the Bill as a government measure and it became law as the Solicitors Act 1919. The effect of the Act was that the Society retained its investigating role;[57] and the determination of complaints was a matter for a Disciplinary Committee appointed by the Lord Chancellor from members of the Council or former members practising as solicitors,[58] subject to appeal to the court.

The increasingly active part played by the Society in disciplinary matters and particularly the establishment of the Disciplinary Committee had disadvantages. It was immediately pointed out that the new system set up in 1888 meant that the Society investigated complaints, then prosecuted, and finally through a committee composed entirely of Council members adjudicated. The Law Society was said to have 'become a more prosecuting Society than ever'[59] and there were proposals for a defence fund. It was questioned whether the Society could reconcile its duties to member of the profession and its public functions; and solicitors against whom complaints were made considered that their professional body was hostile just at the moment when they needed its help. The paradox was more apparent than real; the Society's interest was the welfare of the profession as a whole and that was best served by demonstrating the profession's determination to investigate and if necessary deal with complaints against individual members. That was particularly so at the time when the Disciplinary Com-

[56] The original subvention amounted to £2,500.

[57] Exercised through the Professional Purposes Committee; the cost of that committee (whose work covers much besides investigation) was in 1974 £275,000, or about one-quarter of the total income.

[58] The number was originally not less than three nor more than seven; the maximum was increased to twelve by the Solicitors Act 1957 (s 46). The Solicitors Act 1919 enabled the Master of the Rolls to nominate from former members in addition to existing members of the Council, to which he had been limited by the 1888 Act.

[59] *Solicitors' Journal*, vol 33 (1889), p 627.

mittee was established because there were then and for the next decade a number of scandals which severely shook public confidence. Accordingly there were a good many solicitors who thought that the Disciplinary Committee was being unduly kind to solicitors with the innuendo that as some of the defaulters had been men of eminence the kindness was due to the Committee's acquaintance with them. At the general meeting in 1900 the President had an awkward passage: *Question:* Does it frequently occur that a solicitor in default has time given him to pay up the money? *Answer:* That may happen in certain cases. I can conceive that it will happen. *Q:* It does happen? *A:* I have no doubt. *Q:* In many cases? *A:* Yes. In fact since its improved powers had been available through the 1874 Act the Society had been vigilant. Whereas the number of disciplinary cases had previously run at the rate of six a year or one in two thousand of the profession, the President was able to tell the 1889 general meeting that the number had doubled, though he stressed that it was still only one in a thousand. It was difficult to strike a happy medium. In 1911 Judge Rentoul said: 'I do not think the Society investigates nearly as many cases for their own honour and the honour of the profession as they might do.'[60] The consciousness that it was their own Society which would receive, investigate, and prosecute if need be, complaints by their clients undoubtedly affected the attitude of many solicitors to the Society. The idea of a defence fund or other similar organisation was brought up from time to time and it was this which was one of the factors behind the formation in 1964 of the British Legal Association.[61] In 1968 that Association set up its defence fund, which as the BDA Defence Fund Ltd is a separate entity from the Association itself.[62] Its purpose is to provide assistance, advice and representation to members of the Association who find themselves the subject of investigation or disciplinary proceedings.

If the dual role of The Law Society caused some concern to some of its members it also did not please some sections of the public, who were assisted by some legal journalists to formulate their objections. Although it was repeatedly emphasised that the Disciplinary Committee was independent of The Law Society, none of the critics accepted that it was so, and judges not infrequently used words which showed that even they thought that it was simply another committee through which The Law Society carried out its duties. The facts that the committee was appointed from present or former members of the Council, that its staff were Society officials, and that it sat in Society premises did not help to support the independence of the committee in the public view, although in fact it was true. The critics further alleged that it was quite impossible for a complainant to obtain justice from a committee consisting entirely of the professional brethren of the accused solicitor and argued that, although solici-

[60] *Solicitors' Journal*, vol 55, p 831.
[61] See p 44, *supra*.
[62] It is now known as the Solicitors' Defence Agency.

tors were eloquent in their support of the ideal of justice manifestly being seen to be done, they did not apply it to their own case. The Society resisted any change and their justification was that only members of the profession with long experience could properly judge cases where professional misconduct was the issue. The mood of the times, however, was against that standpoint, and other disciplinary bodies, particularly that of the police force, were also under criticism, if not attack. When the Council in 1972 introduced a new Solicitors Bill with provisions for additional financial powers the opportunity was taken by Members of Parliament who supported the idea of reform of the disciplinary system to block the Bill until the Council agreed to introduce an element of what was called lay representation. The investigation which The Law Society carried out into complaints in order to decide whether there is a prima facie case to take before the Disciplinary Committee was to be subject to examination by a 'lay observer' appointed by the Lord Chancellor and given the powers necessary to obtain any information he might think desirable.[63] The title 'Disciplinary Committee' had led to the impression inside and outside the profession that the committee was one of the committees of The Law Society; the title was accordingly changed to 'The Solicitors Disciplinary Tribunal'. The Tribunal was in future to consist of solicitors of not less than ten years' standing and of lay members not being either solicitors or barristers. The previous requirement that solicitor members should be either present or former members of the Council was dropped, no doubt further to emphasise the separation of the Tribunal from the Council. The hearings are now held by a panel of three members of whom one must always be a lay member, on which there must always be a majority of solicitor members; in other words the Tribunal in session consists of two solicitors and one lay member.[64] The salaries and expenses of the lay observers and the lay members are met by the Treasury as a further confirmation of their independence of the profession and the Society.

The rules governing the conduct of the profession were until 1933 to be found in innumerable decisions of the court and to a lesser extent of the Council of The Law Society, but the Council had no formal authority to make rules. The Solicitors Act 1933[65] directed the Council to make rules relating to solicitors' accounts[66] and authorised it to make rules 'for regulating in respect of any other matter the professional practice, conduct and discipline of solicitors'. The first rule made under this discretionary power (which has to be exercised with the approval of the Master of the Rolls) was made in 1933 to deal with the problem of touting and 'ambulance-chasing'. The present sets of Practice Rules are six in number and deal with such matters as touting, acting for both parties in conveyancing

[63] Solicitors (Amendment) Act 1974, s 7.
[64] Section 11.
[65] Section 1.
[66] Chapter 5, *infra*, p 103.

transactions, sharing of fees with non-solicitors, firm names, and the supervision of branch offices.[67]

The history of the development of the disciplinary system and of a code of professional conduct has been one of consistent progress since the foundation of The Law Society in 1825. The profession has devoted a great deal of time and money to a solution of the problems which then existed or have since arisen. Through The Law Society it has adopted a very high standard, and the findings of the Disciplinary Committee have but rarely been disapproved by the court. The recent changes are irrelevant because both the Society and the committee have placed the public interest in the forefront of their considerations. That has been recognised in the public attitude. No member of the profession can read the literature at all levels in the nineteenth century without feeling somewhat abashed. 'The vulgar laughs, the caricatures of the stage, the misrepresentations of the novelists, the abuse of the democratic newspapers'.[68] were bad enough, but still worse were the measured comments of respectable men and the constant reports of prosecutions. All that has changed, and one of the main causes has been recognition of the fact that the profession is determined to exclude those who fall below its high standard. The number who do is small. It is remarkable that of a profession with an annual intake of between three and four thousand men and women from all walks of life and a total strength of nearly 30,000 not more than fifty on average come before the Disciplinary Committee in a year and of these about half are found guilty of offences of sufficient gravity to require their removal from the roll.

[67] These are (except the rule relating to branch offices made in 1974) set out in the Guide to the Professional Conduct of Solicitors at pp 185–189.

[68] *Law Times* (1865–1866), vol 41, p 611.

CHAPTER 5

Finance

Money is a constant theme running through the history of the profession. Hardly had attorneys started being paid for their services than there were complaints about their avarice, and it would be idle to believe that solicitors in the twentieth century are entirely acquitted by the public of giving a high priority to the amount of their fees. Money has always been one of the most important criteria of a solicitor's success and was for long the means by which he escaped from the toils of the profession and climbed the social ladder; money has in any event always been the subject-matter of most of the profession's business. How successful the profession was financially has tended to be something of a mystery. In 1885 it could 'safely be said that there were no surmises so uncertain as those which contain statements as to the position of the legal profession as a money-making business';[1] in 1967 the position was said to be that 'both the British Legal Association and The Law Society find it very difficult to give any clear indication of what solicitors earn';[2] in 1976 the Attorney-General told the House of Commons: 'No reliable information is available as to ... average annual earnings of ... solicitors.' Solicitors have regarded their earnings as something which was no concern of others and when the subject has been unavoidable they have preferred to restrict themselves to generalisations.

Although the complaints of lawyers waxing fat at their clients' expense started early, there is little likelihood and no evidence that they did so. The number of attorneys seeking business, the ease with which the profession could be entered, the size of the disputes—these were all factors which must have tended to depress the earnings of individuals. It may well have been, therefore, that being an attorney until well into the fifteenth century was for many a supplementary occupation but not enough of itself to provide a living. Yet the amount of business, certainly in litigation, was growing rapidly. By the end of the fourteenth century there were 40,000 cases a year entered in the Common Pleas alone, so that even if the vast majority of litigants acted in person or through unpaid friends or relations there

[1] *Law Quarterly Review*, vol I, p 314; Roscoe, The Position and Prospects of the Legal Profession.

[2] *Solicitors' Journal*, vol 111 (1967), p 780.

must have been a tolerable amount of work for the professionals.[3] It is, however, quite unprofitable to speculate on earnings or income at this date if only because the difference in the value of money and the general level of earnings then and now is so great as to make any figures meaningless. The picture becomes a good deal clearer during the later Tudor period and the early seventeenth century. There is a mass of evidence that then the legal profession, including the attorneys and solicitors, had a rich harvest. The nobility had in the fifteenth century and earlier been accustomed to assert by physical force what they regarded as their rights; the stronger central government of the Tudors prevented them doing so in the sixteenth century, and they turned instead to litigation to get by right what they could not get by might; and they relied heavily on their attorneys to ensure that the court decided that they had right on their side. The nobility ruined itself as much by litigation as it did by building and pleasure. The legal costs of the Earl of Northumberland (1562–1632) were regarded as modest enough but they were of the order of £300 a year.[4] Anne Countess of Warwick complained that 'suits and troubles by law have emptied my purse and pulled down my estate'. One suit was reckoned enough to break the back of any man of reasonable wealth,[5] yet the Earl of Devonshire had thirty actions current in 1630 and Lord Berkeley had fifty in his lifetime, of which one ran for thirty-eight years. Whereas costs had formerly been small,[6] they rose rapidly. The cost of obtaining a writ of habeas corpus increased by five times between 1558 and 1576; an attorney would be paid as much as £8 on a claim resulting in 15s damages and another £7 on a £20 claim. It was not only in litigation that the attorneys and solicitors were busy. The dissolution of the monasteries, the final breakdown of the feudal system, and the development of trade and a wealthy merchant class, all meant that land had become a freely transferable form of wealth at a time when those who owned it were prepared or forced to sell it and those who wanted it had the money to pay for it. The attraction of London for the nobility began in this period to be so strong that more and more landowners found the need to employ professional agents, generally attorneys, to look after their properties in their absence. There was money to be borrowed and there was money ready to be lent. There was for more people than ever before wealth to be disposed of by will.[7] All these were matters which brought business to the attorney. It is no wonder that the Commonwealth squibs and tracts represent the attorneys of the time as living with no less luxury and even

[3] This figure is taken from Ames Foundation: Year Book of Richard II, p xvi.

[4] *Economic History Review*, vol 9, p 449. This would convert to about £10,000 at 1975 values.

[5] Ibid, vol 18, pp 1–41, on this subject generally.

[6] In the Star Chamber in 1532 officials acting as attorneys were paid 3s 4d per term in each case they handled, and although this was not necessarily all that a professional attorney was paid it must have borne some relationship.

[7] In the sixteenth century proving a will could cost £200 to £300 in legal fees.

pomp than the country squires and amassing large fortunes which enabled them to educate their sons, and their sons in their turn to purchase the lands of the clients their fathers had impoverished. It is probable that the authors confused the attorneys with the Bar, which certainly reaped the benefit of the quarrelsome habits of the wealthy. The manor-houses which at the time began to decorate and dominate the English countryside can often be traced to a successful barrister but rarely to a successful attorney. Nevertheless it is at this period that the first attorney of really great wealth appeared. Captain John Somers, the father of Lord Chancellor Somers, is an instance of 'the affluence, gentility and power which were possessed by country attorneys of the highest grades in the time of the Commonwealth'.[8] At a lower level but nevertheless clearly comfortably off was John Skynner, junior (1596–1669), practising like his father before him in Hitchin and doing well enough to be able to found some almshouses. His partners and their families could afford such luxuries as tea and chocolate served by an African page-boy,[9] and at Cuckfield in Sussex Mr Barrell, farming a small estate with a staff of six alongside his attorney's business, recorded in his diary many payments for professional work in kind—haunches of venison, twenty-four china oranges, eighteen woodcock and so on.[10] Books for the profession began to appear in some numbers and they were bought well enough to justify further editions for most of them. The boom began to tail off during the latter part of the seventeenth and the early part of the eighteenth century. On the Home Circuit there were only 122 cases in 1713 compared with 411 in 1672. But taking the legal scene as a whole an economist reckoned that in 1688 the average income of lawyers in England was £140 a year, which would be tolerable considering that the Provost of Eton was at the same period paid £50 a year.[11]

For the run-of-the-mill attorney income seems to have remained pretty well at this level throughout the eighteenth century. The figure of £100 a year is quoted too often by contemporary observers for it to have been very wide of the mark. In 1732 the *London Magazine* said that, taking one with another, each attorney made 'yearly of his business £100';[12] the economist Massie calculated the same figure in 1759–1760;[13] and in 1785 the average income was guessed at £130.[14] The cost of living remained almost stationary during the period, so that these men were on the same level as their fellows of the previous century, and they compared not unfavourably with the clergy and the naval and military officers. The profession remained sensitive to allegations that its members made large

[8] Jeafferson, A Book about Lawyers, vol 2, p 323, and see p 190, *infra*.
[9] Hine, Relics of an Uncommon Attorney, p 48.
[10] Burnett, A History of the Cost of Living (1969), p 115.
[11] *Economic History Review*, vol 10, p 42.
[12] Page 240.
[13] *Economic History Review*, vol 10, p 42.
[14] A Free Enquiry into the Enormous Increase of Attorneys—quoted Christian, Solicitors—An Outline of their History, p 157n.

incomes, and believed then, as before and afterwards, that it was advisable to claim that most earned only enough to keep alive. One attorney declared: 'Upon my honour, I do not believe there are thirty in London who get one thousand a year; and the greater part can scarce keep their heads above water.'[15] Yet there is ample evidence that in the eighteenth century many attorneys were doing very well financially and some were doing handsomely. They had long since ceased to be concerned with purely legal business and many were closely involved in the commercial and industrial developments then taking place. It is literally impossible to find a major enterprise or type of business in England at this time in which attorneys were not taking a prominent part. 'The country attorney touched eighteenth century economic life at many points and was undoubtedly a key man.'[16] As early as 1692 an Ormskirk attorney was specialising in placing investments in Lancashire cotton.[17] The navigation and canal companies relied heavily on attorneys for finding capital and for managing the enterprises. Charles Barnard and Charles Buck of Leeds provided £3,000 and £3,500 respectively for the Aire and Calder Canal, and that represented a substantial part of the whole capital; George Huxley, a London attorney, in 1711 took over the Itchen river project from a bankrupt client and with family money carried it to fruition; Samuel Worral, a Bristol attorney and banker, provided money for the Kennet and Avon Canal.[18] In Bristol and elsewhere attorneys at the end of the century were advertising money for loans at 4½ per cent p a interest and carrying on businesses as brokers and dealers in shares in joint stock enterprises, particularly canal shares. In banking inevitably the attorney played a prominent part because his clientele formed a useful source of capital for his banking partners.[19] Unfortunately for some like Samuel Worral this way led to financial ruin. In the North Country Jasper Gibson of Hexham was providing the capital and managing the operation of a number of turnpike trusts[20] and a neighbour named Clayton was founding a fortune which when his attorney grandson died a century later was worth £728,746. Peniston Lamb in Nottingham was getting together the fortune which amounted to £100,000 when he died. It was not only in commerce that the attorney was in demand. With the proliferation of local administration there were innumerable offices created which only the local attorney could adequately fill. At the peak

[15] A Word to the Wise etc by an 'Untaxed Attorney', quoted Robson, The Attorney in Eighteenth Century England, p 16.

[16] Pressnell, Country Banking in the Industrial Revolution (1956), p 39.

[17] For instance, he found an investment in Manchester cotton business for £260 for a Preston woman: as to the part played by attorneys in the cotton trade see Wadsworth and Mann, The Cotton Trade and Industrial Lancashire (1931).

[18] As to attorneys in the canal movement see Ward, Finance of Canal Building in Eighteenth Century England.

[19] Pressnell, op cit, p 44, gives 'three dozen' as the minimum number of attorneys engaged in banking at the end of the century.

[20] Pressnell, op cit, p 41.

in this respect was Job Brough of Nottingham, who in 1791 was Town Clerk of Newark, Clerk of the Peace for Nottingham, Clerk to the River Trent Navigation Company, Clerk to the Commissioners of Sewers, Steward of the Duke of Newcastle, Steward of the Copyhold Courts of the Manor of Newark, and clerk and treasurer of a handful of turnpike trusts.[21] In Cumberland and Westmorland the Sandersons were equally dominant. With their substantial incomes subject to no tax worth speaking of, this section of the profession was amassing considerable capital wealth. Their prosperity gave substance and permanence to their businesses and the period saw the foundation of firms which endured. It was noted in 1897 that there were in Birmingham seven firms which had been founded more than a century earlier, one of them as early as 1760; in London firms were being established which still exist—Messrs Janson, Cobb and Pearson in 1728, Messrs Freshfields in 1743 and Messrs Collyer Bristow in 1750.

Behind these leading figures was a much more numerous body of men not earning anything like such large incomes but nevertheless very comfortably off.[22] It was a commonplace that in the country towns the best houses were generally occupied by attorneys and the attorneys were as like as not the leading men in local government and business. Accordingly parents were prepared to pay large sums to article their sons to substantial firms. Five hundred guineas was not out of the way as a premium and a fair average would be of the order of two hundred. In London there were more than a hundred and fifty attorneys of sufficient status and prosperity to belong to the Society of Gentlemen Practisers and in the country there were others setting up local law societies. The profession was like a pyramid with a very wide base of men earning just a decent living and not much beyond and tapering upwards to a very high peak. In the middle were the attorneys who, having started in practice in the eighteenth century, were by the start of the nineteenth well enough off to contemplate with confidence the establishment of their own Law Institution on the most liberal scale and of whom something over one in ten working in London subscribed in a year the present-day equivalent of nearly a million pounds.

The development of legal journalism and a much freer interchange of information might have been expected to throw some light on the profession's finances in the nineteenth century. The numerous comments made on the matter were, however, generally directed to proving that contrary to public belief the profession was hard pressed to make ends meet. In 1831 the *Legal Observer* complained that the 'costs now allowed are totally inadequate to the time and trouble occupied in the prosecution of actions'.[23] The *Law Times* attributed the falling off in the number of new

[21] Pressnell, op cit, pp 39–40.

[22] A typical man was Mr Christopher Wallis, who, practising in the West Country between 1799 and 1805, saved nearly £14,000, and whose earnings, albeit partly from 'non-legal' business, averaged about £2,000 a year—see Robson, op cit, p 162.

[23] Page 259.

admissions in the years 1845–1852 to the drop in profits and claimed that it was not exaggerating when it estimated the fall at one-half since 1825. Mr Maugham expressed the same opinion in 1846.[24] When in 1851 *The Times* published what was called a vituperative attack on the profits obtained by the profession through its control of access to counsel[25] a correspondent to the *Law Times* replied that 'those who know how to trace many firms who have been eminent in their days would be able to show that the individuals comprising them have often died possessed of very little property at all'.[26] In 1880 the President of The Law Society said that 'he never knew a solicitor who kept his carriage out of the money he received in his profession';[27] in 1896 Mr Christian wrote: 'The rewards are few. The most a solicitor can hope to achieve is a competence and not all solicitors do that';[28] and in 1906 the President warned articled clerks that it was no use 'to think that because they passed the final examination ... they would be sure to make a living'.[29] The outside observers were not able to reconcile these statements with the available evidence, and were probably more accurate in their conclusions: in 1832 it was said that 'in the incomes of attorneys there are great diversities. Some few in London make £10–11,000 a year, a great many more about £3–4,000 and some obscure practitioners do not clear more than £100 a year.'[30]

There were certainly a sizeable number who were earning large incomes, in some cases almost princely ones. The railway boom of the 1830s and 1840s and the joint stock company boom in the 1860s and 1870s, coupled with a generally high level of prosperity and negligible taxation, all contributed to the wealth of the successful solicitor. In 1850 the prospects were described in optimistic terms: 'With the increased and increasing wealth of the country and the extending practice of life assurance there are more wills and settlements to be made and managed. The Succession Duties Act alone will bring an immense accession to the business of the Attorneys.... Still more has been the influx of business to the Solicitor arising from the mercantile growth of the country.... The multiplied joint-stock companies and the complicated law connected with them, in their formation, their management and their winding-up have been and will continue to be a source of revenue to the Attorneys the total amount of which would astonish themselves. It is true that these sources of emolument are not widely scattered but they are prizes open to all.'[31] This state of affairs persisted. In 1885 'the great increase in population, the increased facilities

[24] Select Committee on Legal Education, qu 2118: p 109, *infra*.
[25] 5th November.
[26] Vol 19 (1852), p 41.
[27] *Law Times*, vol 69, p 405.
[28] Op cit, pp 230–231.
[29] *Solicitors' Journal*, vol 50, p 208.
[30] The Extraordinary Black Book, p 298.
[31] *Law Times*, vol 22 (1853–1854), pp 89–90.

for obtaining legal assistance, and the steady growth of joint stock enterprises' were given as reasons for the incomes of firms dealing with commercial matters being 'more considerable than they used to be'.[32] What incomes were is necessarily a matter of conjecture. In 1821 the five partners of one of the leading London firms were sharing unequally £15,000 a year according to their articled clerk Mr Benjamin Disraeli, whose information was probably more reliable than that of most articled clerks since he was contemplating marrying the daughter of one of the partners. In the same period Mr Hanson, Lord Byron's attorney, presented his client with a bill for £12,000 when he visited him in Italy shortly before his voyage to Greece. In 1849 the *Law Times* mentioned that a solicitor's bill in respect of a railway flotation had been taxed at £240,000; the bill ran to 10,000 folios and the taxation had taken twelve months to complete. The work done by proctors in Doctors Commons was not so very different from that done by the better class of solicitors, and the assessment of compensation on the closure of Doctors Commons in the 1870s gives some evidence of earnings. The compensation was to be based on the last three years' profits. One had earned £9,000 a year; another had earned £31,432 in five years; and a third had earned between £2,000 and £3,000 a year. One of the embarrassments was the publication from time to time of the details of the very large estates of deceased solicitors. In 1895 the *Daily Telegraph* commented that 'notwithstanding the frequent complaints of solicitors that their branch of the profession is sadly overcrowded some of them manage to acquire and leave very substantial fortunes' and proceeded to list forty-four cases arising in the previous five or six years where the average amount was £117,000. These would have been men who had been in practice from 1840 onwards. It was conceded that in some cases much of the money had been inherited or had been the result of speculation or investment rather than from professional earnings, but the general public drew a different inference. Only one very wealthy solicitor threw any light on the matter. Sir John Hollams was in practice from the 1820s to the end of the century, so that he covered the whole of the period now being considered. In his Jottings of an Old Solicitor he said: 'I had a very moderate partrimony, sufficient to keep me from borrowing' and 'I devoted the whole of my time to my profession—never speculated nor sought to make money in any other way'.[33] When he died in 1910 his estate was valued at £601,587, which was no mean achievement for the son of a Kent curate. The legal wags at the time reckoned it represented 6s 8d for every quarter of an hour of his long life. Others have suggested that perhaps he was fortunate in taking a hand in Rhodesian finance.

These men were exceptional. For the men relying mainly or entirely on professional earnings the most reliable information is that disclosed by the Inland Revenue to the Anderson Committee on the Pay and Condi-

[32] *Law Quarterly Review*, vol I, p 315.
[33] The book was published in 1906: pp 239–240.

tions of Service of State Servants in 1923 as to the incomes returned for tax purposes in the year 1913–1914. If anything the value of money increased during the nineteenth century. Taking 1900 as 100 the cost of living was 172 in 1820 and 113 in 1914, so that in taking the 1913–1914 figures as a yardstick one is not overstating the position for earlier years. The Inland Revenue figures showed that ten per cent of the profession, that is between 1,000 and 1,500 depending on the period, earned £1,410 a year of more.[34] This was close to the figure of £1,500 which in 1883 was said to be the income of a solicitor in good practice and 'the reason for the salaries of chief clerks and taxing masters who must have been ten years in practice being fixed at £1,500—there are some who make more but they are speculators and capitalists as well as solicitors'.[35] The highest paid appointment held by a solicitor was that of Solicitor to the City of London, who was paid £2,200 a year. Income tax was until the end of the century a negligible factor and at the minimum earning level in this group would not amount to more than £70 a year. It began to bite a little after that. Lloyd George's People's Budget put the rate up to 1s 2d in the pound, though his super-tax did not affect those with less than £5,000 a year. The partners in Letts Brothers met to consider whether with tax at this rate it was worth continuing in business at all.[36] Even so the income after tax of the lowest earners in this section would by 1975 standards represent about £12,500 a year and a gross income of about £30,000. This income and the number of those in receipt of it exposed as ridiculous the statements so frequently made of solicitors not earning enough to keep a carriage. More sensible and accurate were the statements in the *Law Journal* in 1866[37] that 'it is well known that in this branch there is open to merit and ability a sure pathway leading if not to honour and fame at all events to the more substantial rewards of retired ease and wealth' and to the Provincial Meeting in 1902 that 'solicitors except in rare instances cannot by a proper exercise of their profession attain wealth but many do by care and diligence make a moderate competency on which they could retire at a reasonable age and leave the field to younger men'. One man gave his own experience on that score: 'I have been fourteen years in practice as an attorney and have made what will keep me in competence.'[38] For professional earnings the top limit except for a few was estimated by an adviser on the choice of a profession in 1857 at £2,000 a year.[39]

The same Inland Revenue statistics showed a 'middle class' in the profession about 3,000 strong with professional incomes of between £800 and £1,400 a year. These figures are corroborated by the salaries offered for

[34] Routh, Occupation and Pay in Great Britain 1902–1960 (1965), p 62 et seq.
[35] *Solicitors' Journal*, vol 28, p 44.
[36] Letts, The Old House (1942), p 51.
[37] Vol 1 (1866), p 48.
[38] Ibid, vol 7 (1872), p 9.
[39] Thomson, Choice of a Profession (1857), p 134.

the middle to upper type of public appointment. The town clerkship of Salford in 1874 carried £1,000 a year, that of Newcastle-upon-Tyne at about the same time £1,200; in 1896 the London County Council paid its clerk and solicitor £1,200 a year, though it increased that to £1,350 in 1902 because the holder of the appointment then had completed twenty-one years' service and would 'in future have control of the whole of the business including conveyancing';[40] at the end of the century the Inland Revenue paid its own solicitor £1,000 a year. These incomes were considered at the time to represent a substantial degree of worldly success. It is difficult even at this short distance of time to relate the financial situation of these men who formed the core of the profession, but there are enough Victorian household budgets published to show that they had the means to enjoy a great measure of solid comfort. Below them were the young and rising men or those who had tried and not been so successful. These, about 2,000 in number, were earning between £400 and £800 a year. The extent to which this represented a standard of living above genteel poverty depended on location and other personal circumstances. A young professional man and his wife could live in a flat in London in tolerable comfort and have two maids on about £500; in Bristol on £700 a year it was possible to run a family house with the inevitable two maids, have two months' holiday abroad and still save £200 a year.[41] There was a prevalent view that £500 a year was about the right income for a solicitor. A future Lord Chancellor said in 1840 that no solicitor ought to have a professional income of more than that.[42]

The most significant statistic of all was that one-half of the profession had an income of £390 a year or less and that a quarter had less than £185. Again these incomes can be corroborated from the salaries asked and offered in the legal press from 1840 down to 1914. One man—a 'solicitor and commissioner'—in 1884 sought a post in Liverpool at £1 a week and many young men were prepared to accept nominal salaries to get a start and some practical experience. There were many well-qualified men prepared to accept as little as £100 a year, and when The Law Society started a register of posts wanted and available in 1902 there were generally about fifty men advertising for jobs and not more than two or three employers advertising for staff. The employers who did advertise knew they were in a buyer's market. In 1895 one of them specified his requirements: 'I am wanting an admitted solicitor not a manager. Must be a good advocate and well up in all branches of conveyancing and trust matters; hard-work essential and willing to do anything put before him; office hours long—9 to 6.30—and about three nights a week later at times very late; the highest references as to abilities and culture required also photo; salary not less than £100 or more than £130 according to abili-

[40] *Law Times*, vol 113, p 218.
[41] Burnett, op cit, pp 233–242.
[42] Annual Provincial Meeting, 1881, p 137.

ties.'[43] One in five of all solicitors was a managing clerk getting the same salary as or less salary than an experienced but unadmitted man. 'The advertisements of admitted men seeking engagements which appeared in The Law Society's Register and the salaries which they ask and upon which they cannot live provoke a mingled sense of shame and despair.'[44] In human terms these figures meant that there were some 8,000 solicitors earning less than was necessary for a married man with a family to live decently and about 4,000 who were a great deal worse off than that. These large numbers made it possible to say that the average income of solicitors was about £300 a year, but that was just as inaccurate in respect of the lowest paid as it was in respect of the better-off.

The Inland Revenue figures for 1922–1923 showed that the higher earners had fared less well than the lower ones. Their incomes had risen by seventy per cent, but the cost of living was three times as high as in 1914 and income tax had increased from 1s 2d to 5s. On the other hand the men in the lowest income bracket had incomes which had increased pretty well in line with the cost of living and they were less affected by tax. The median—that is the income level at which one-half of the profession numerically is above and the other half below—had gone up from £390 to £811. The advertisements in the legal press confirmed that this was so. Solicitors advertising for posts in and about 1925 generally quoted salaries of between £250 and £300, whereas in 1902 they had asked for £150 or less. Unfortunately the position did not improve for the man who was making a start. In the *Law Society's Gazette* in 1936 about half the solicitors seeking posts quoted £200–£250 and under ten per cent ventured to ask for over £400. One solicitor with over seven years' experience, first-class honours in the final examination, and three Law Society prizes asked for between £450 and £500. For the others there are at present no detailed figures available to show how they were faring in the immediate pre-1939 period, and one is limited to averages which have manifest drawbacks, not the least being possible variations in methods of calculation. For the years 1935–1937 the average has been calculated at £1,238[45] and in 1950 the Lord Chancellor gave to The Law Society the figure of £1,180 for 1938–1939, based on information supplied to him by the Inland Revenue. The figures for 1913–1914 and 1922–1923 calculated on the same basis as the average for 1935–1937 were £568 and £1,096 respectively. The average was, after allowing for variations in the cost of living, better than it had ever been, but this was achieved by an increase in the earnings of those who had previously been so badly paid and not by relative increases in earnings at the higher levels. The Law Society in 1939 gave evidence on the Committee Stage of the Solicitors Bill 1939 that the average income of solicitors

[43] *Law Times*, vol 99, p 25.
[44] Ibid, vol 121 (1906), p 228.
[45] Routh, op cit, p 64.

then was of the order of £400.[46] But that can only have been a well-intentioned guess.

In the immediate post-1945 period there was no significant change. It might have been expected that the sharp fall in the size of the profession due to the war would have resulted in a corresponding rise in earnings, but that did not happen. The official Careers Booklet No 23 published in 1945 said that the newly qualified solicitor generally obtained employment as a managing clerk and that the commencing salary was generally about £200 a year. Business began to pick up and earnings increased. The Lord Chancellor told The Law Society that the average income in 1949–1950 had gone up to £2,432, which was about double the average he had given for 1938–1939. The cost of living had also doubled, so that this was no improvement in real terms and was a decline if one took taxation into account. At the time The Law Society was starting its campaign for better remuneration and, although it appreciated the effect of inflation and taxation, it found these figures difficult to answer, primarily because it had no figures of its own at the time. One result of this lack of positive evidence from the profession itself was that in the 1950s there was considerable speculation as to what solicitors earned. In 1951 the estimate was that 'not many solicitors can look forward with confidence to taking £2,000 a year out of their practices and incomes of £5,000 a year or more are very few';[47] in 1955 Professor Break of the University of California sent out his own questionnaire and came to the conclusion that thirty-nine per cent earned less than £2,000; twenty-three per cent between £2,000 and £3,000; and sixteen per cent over £4,000, and that of this last group a sixth, ie two and a half per cent of the whole, earned £10,000 or more; in 1958 the *Financial Times* guessed that not more than a third earned more than £2,000 a year and said that the prospects for a newly qualified man were £600–£700, with little chance of rising to more than £1,500 a year as an assistant in a private office. Very large firms with correspondingly large incomes for the partners were said to be exceptional.[48] But although these figures were not large the question was already being asked: 'Is life too lush for the lawyers?'[49] The Law Society decided that it should have some reliable information and sent out a questionnaire to 450 firms chosen at random in 1956, but the results were not published. They were soon overtaken by events, because in 1960 the Inland Revenue gave to the Royal Commission on Doctors' and Dentists' Remuneration the figures based on income tax returns for the year 1955–1956.[50] Treating these figures on the same basis as those quoted earlier for 1913–1914 and 1922–1923, they showed that the top ten per cent started at just under

[46] Ans 196.
[47] Lewis and Maude, Professional People, p 247.
[48] 11th October 1958.
[49] *Sunday Express*, 18th December 1955.
[50] The Report is published as Cmnd 939 (1960).

£4,000 and the top twenty-five per cent below that group at £2,630. The most significant figure was that of the lowest paid group which had increased, from £185 in 1913 and £434 in 1922, to £1,041. The top group had increased by two and a half times on the 1913 figure and the bottom by nearly six times. As a result the average had gone up to £2,038, but again that had been achieved by an increase in the lower ranges and not by an overall increase. The average was misconstrued. It led to statements such as 'It was rather surprising to find the Secretary of The Law Society alleging in 1963 that the solicitor's net income was "less in purchasing power than in 1939"'.[51] In fact the Secretary was right even if one ignores taxation.[52] In 1956 the median figure was £1,688 as compared with £811 prewar and that was not enough to balance the fall in the value of money. Dr Routh in his study of the relationship of salaries in the professions concluded that 'the solicitors have done badly'.[53] That was also true in a comparative sense, for whereas until 1939 solicitors' incomes had been better than those earned by the three most comparable professions—the Bar, medicine, and dentistry—they were in the middle 1950s only marginally better than the Bar and markedly worse than the other two. At this stage 'a fair view promised no more than a reasonable livelihood' for the large majority of the profession.[54] A man of thirty-two earning £2,000 a year as a solicitor in 1958 had sufficient news value for the *Solicitors' Journal* to ask 'How many men can claim a comparable record?' and to point out that when the *Sunday Times* ran a careers article with advertisements there was not one for a solicitor.[55]

In the 1960s business generally was good and particularly so in property development, which gave solicitors the best profit. The demand for staff meant that young solicitors were able to command much higher salaries than ever before and there were many more opportunities in commerce and industry and central and local government. A starting salary of £2,000 a year became not unusual and the demand for capital as a requirement for a partnership became less and less frequent. The profession became subject to more and more criticism for the fees which it charged, particularly in conveyancing transactions, and yet felt itself in some areas to be badly underpaid. Solicitors were convinced that in relation to people with comparable or less skills they were being left behind in the earnings battle. They were particularly bitter therefore when they were one of the first professions to be made the subject of an investigation by the Prices and Incomes Board in 1966. The Board's investigation was the first into the financial affairs of solicitors and its three reports provide a mass of information. The Law Society was never able to contradict any

[51] Abel-Smith and Stevens, Lawyers and the Courts, p 400.
[52] His article was published in the *Sunday Times*, 15th December 1963.
[53] Routh, op cit, p 65.
[54] *Solicitors' Journal*, vol 101 (1957), p 846, in a review of the previous hundred years.
[55] *Solicitors' Journal*, vol 102 (1958), p 866.

of the Board's statistics, either because it had no statistics of its own or, if it had, then because those statistics corroborated those of the Board. It contented itself with general comments intended to cast doubt on the validity of the Board's conclusions. The British Legal Association made a submission based on information supplied by 1,762 solicitors. This gave a median line of £3,176 in the North of England, £4,300 in the East, and £3,500 in London; one-sixth of solicitor-principals in London had returned incomes of less than £2,000 and the average hourly net earnings of all London solicitors who supplied information was 30s. But it may be doubted whether a sample of not more than twelve per cent of the profession was large enough to be valid. The Board's first Report stated that in 1966 there were about 6,720 practices with a total annual gross income

	Income	*Income after tax*	*Income after tax adjusted to 1968 value of £*
Upper Quartile:			
1913–1914	800	750	4,500
1922–1923	1,450	1,220	6,100
1955–1956	2,650	1,850	2,727
1968	7,000	4,500	4,500
Lower Quartile:			
1913–1914	185	180	1,100
1922–1923	435	400	2,000
1955–1956	1,040	900	1,350
1968	3,000	2,300	2,300
Average:			
1913–1914	455	425	2,550
1922–1923	900	800	4,000
1955–1956	1,786	1,400	2,100
1968	5,373	3,773	3,773

Note: tax is calculated in round figures on basis of a married man with one child.

of about £170,000,000; and its second Report stated that in 1968 there were about 6,580 practices with a total gross annual income of £200,000,000. The 'upper quartile' started in 1966 at £6,135 and in 1968 at £6,968; the figures for the 'lower quartile' were £2,640 and £3,000. It was in this section that the variation from 1955–1956 had been most marked, with an increase of 200 per cent. The great disparity in professional earnings was disappearing; in the nineteenth century the top figure for the lower quartile had been only an eighth of the starting figure for the upper quartile, but now it was nearly a half. The result was that the average had trebled between the two dates—from £1,786 to £5,373. The increase was more apparent than real: in the same period the purchasing power of the pound had fallen to sixty per cent of what it had been in 1955. Of course, the joker in the pack was the effect of tax which was charged on the assumption that an income of £2,500 or over warranted a charge to surtax. In spendable income the upper quartile was back at the pre-1914 level but substantially worse than it had been between the wars; the lower quartile was better off than it had ever been, though not a great deal better than between the wars; the average was fifty per cent better than pre-1914 and nearly twice as good as in 1955–1956, but was no improvement on the position between the wars. The table on p 95 illustrates.

The rise in solicitors' incomes which had already become marked in the mid-sixties accelerated in the seventies. The combined effect of the Remuneration Orders of 1953 and 1972 enabled solicitors in all non-litigious or non-criminal business to fix their own charges subject only to the right of the client to ask The Law Society to certify what was a reasonable charge or to apply to the courts for taxation. Although the right to refer to The Law Society was exercised in a substantial number of cases, the proportion of clients who did so was minimal. Inflation was at that time getting into its stride and people were losing their capacity or will to trouble about what services or things should cost. The general level of remuneration escalated rapidly and against a background of constant and large wage claims the charges made by solicitors seemed to be lost. Until the end of 1973 there was an unprecedented boom in land prices, and that meant for most solicitors a golden harvest. Legal aid was another major contributor. The increase in crime and the greater sophistication of the people accused meant that there was a greater demand than ever before for solicitors' services and legal aid meant that by and large those services were reasonably paid. In fact at all levels and in all situations there was an upsurge in legal business. It was measured by the shortage of manpower and by the change in the salaries offered to tempt men of even short experience. For such men £6,000 a year was frequently offered with the added bait of a partnership at an early date without capital commitment. Moreover the private solicitor seeking help had to compete with the civil service and local government. Both, but particularly the latter in 1973 and 1974, were wanting more solicitors and offering salaries which ten years earlier would have seemed fantastic. So far as business prospects went the only cloud on the horizon was the commitment of the profession, particularly in the provinces, to conveyancing business. In other areas of non-contentious business—administration of trusts and taxation in particular—solicitors had lost ground to their competitors. There was from time to time a move towards advertising the services which the profession had to offer in the newspapers and on television. Some local newspaper advertising was undertaken by local law societies. But any worthwhile publicity scheme would have been expensive and The Law Society had mainly to content itself with the provision of leaflets for distribution from solicitors' offices, Citizens Advice Bureaux and the like. It showed its concern for the problems by setting up a committee in 1966 to deal with the Future of the Profession, and the profession had the benefit of a series of articles on the subject in the *Gazette*. For the vast majority of solicitors the present seemed sufficient.

The post-1945 period had seen a complete change in the financial structure of the profession. Before that time the solicitor could normally reckon on earning an income which enabled him to save a competence for his retirement; when he did retire he could normally reckon on receiving for his 'goodwill' a capital sum amounting to between two and three times the annual income he had earned averaged over the three years preceding his retirement. Tax was not a major element. The cost of living was tending downwards. After 1955 his gross pre-tax income, as we have seen, rose and the increase became rapid after about 1965. But the rise was not enough to give the same relative margin for saving as before. Although there were tax reductions for the lower wage-earners, there were none of significance for the men earning the sort of incomes which many solicitors enjoyed. In 1974 a married solicitor with two children under eleven had to earn £12,000 a year to match even the average of 1935–1937. The men in the top bracket earning £50,000 or so had a 'take-home' of £15,000, which would have put them at the bottom of the upper decile in 1914. To attain some form of wealth it was still necessary to be fortunate in investment outside the profession.[56] Provision for retirement out of savings was more difficult than before and there was the further problem that new entrants either could not or were not prepared to pay anything for goodwill. The only relief was given by the Finance Act 1956, which enabled a solicitor to deduct from his taxable income contributions made by him to a pension scheme.[57] Inflation made any provision seem inadequate. The middle class was under pressure and solicitors were no exception.

* * * *

The extent to which attorneys and solicitors in the eighteenth and nineteenth centuries were providers of capital for the growth of British industry inevitably brought its problems. In 1868 the *Law Magazine* claimed that the profession had 'the custody of an immense percentage of the property of the State', yet there were no specific rules of professional conduct which affected the management or accounting of these funds, and at the same time in a long period of an expanding economy there were many opportunities and temptations to speculate with them. The general law had in this respect two principal weaknesses, which together facilitated speculation by a solicitor with his clients' money or muddling that money with his own and which enabled solicitors who had lost their clients' money by speculation to escape the proper consequences. First, speculation with

[56] There is an interesting account of this situation by a solicitor practising in London in *Twentieth Century* (Spring 1965, p 72): 'What I mean is one is very often in a position to know what property is going cheaply ... in addition to earnings from my practice I earn another half that amount from a few small properties I have bought.'

[57] Section 22.

clients' money for the solicitor's benefit was not a criminal offence unless it was contrary to the terms of a direction in writing given to the solicitor by the client. Breach of good faith or trust was not of itself sufficient. Secondly, solicitors, not being traders, were until 1861[58] outside the bankruptcy laws and rules, and even then bankruptcy was not in itself a ground for suspension of the solicitor's practising certificate or even for notification to the registrar of the roll. The comparatively modest incomes which many solicitors earned from their purely professional work made outside ventures all the more attractive.[59] That many succumbed to the temptation is not open to doubt;[60] most of them did so with their own moneys, but there were others who used their clients' and because the law did not forbid it considered themselves justified in doing so. They regarded themselves as bankers in respect of their clients' moneys and as entitled, like bankers, to invest those moneys to their own advantage and profit. The dangers were not much commented on until the down-turn in the economy and particularly the end of the railway boom in the 1850s. Then the warnings became frequent and insistent. In 1858 the *Law Times* commented on a particularly serious case of a solicitor's failure that it was 'only one of the many similar cases which have occurred in the past five years ... In all of them the main features have been the same': they involved 'men of respectability and having large and lucrative practices who were tempted to speculate in buildings, mines and the like and whose speculations failed';[61] returning to the matter in the following year, it stated that 'the beginning of this career of sin and sorrow and shame was the first fault of speculation beyond the walls of the office' and that 'it should be a rule with a solicitor never to engage in any business out of his profession'.[62] That view was given judicial support in 1885. Then the Master of the Rolls said that it was 'bad practice for a solicitor to enter into speculations not connected with his business'.[63] The effects were illustrated in the Board of Trade Report for 1895, which listed a number of failures by solicitors due to speculation outside their practices—one case involving £257,690 was due to unfortunate Stock Exchange speculations and another involving £70,000 was due to losses on a colliery. The warnings went unheeded. At the end of the century there was another spate of failures, generally referred to in the legal press of the day as 'the recent scandals'. One firm of the highest repute in Lincoln's Inn failed for £300,000. But the most painful of all was that of the firm of which Mr B G Lake was a partner. The sum involved was large—£170,000; but the worst feature was that Mr Lake had been President of The Law Society in 1888, the first chairman

[58] Bankruptcy Act 1861, s 69.

[59] 'Are not solicitors tempted to embark on financial and other schemes because year by year they see their incomes decrease?' (*Solicitors' Journal*, vol 45 (1901), p 275.)

[60] Reader, Professional Men, p 271.

[61] Vol 30, p 286.

[62] Vol 34, p 17.

[63] *Ex parte Salaman* (1885), 29 SJ 322.

of the Disciplinary Committee, and for thirty years a leading man in the profession. The warnings of the fifties were again repeated. The *Solicitors' Journal* in 1899 suggested that 'there ought at all events to be a strong pronouncement by the Council of The Law Society that it is the duty of solicitors to keep to their legitimate business and to refrain from speculation financing and other practices which furnish an alluring prospect of gain but are likely ultimately to lead to the bankruptcy court'.[64] At the Annual Provincial Meeting in 1902 a speaker advocated 'the crushing of the money spirit by confining our attention to strictly professional work and avoiding financial or speculative operations'.[65]

The effect of these cases on the position of the profession was inevitably adverse. *The Times* commented that 'the confidence of the public is not altogether what it was in regard to certain kinds of business as a rule conducted through the medium of solicitors'.[66] In 1903 Mr Granville Barker has a topical theme in his play 'The Voysey Inheritance', in which the plot concerned the persistent frauds of a Lincoln's Inn solicitor, which uncomfortably resembled the then recent cases. The profession which had been at such pains to improve its image and status was in danger of becoming again the butt of the novelist and dramatist. The *Solicitors' Journal* agreed that the recent events had given ground for anxiety and humiliation. In 1900 the *Law Journal* reported that 'never have the affairs of solicitors excited more public attention than during the past twelve months.... The malpractices disclosed in a number of heavy failures were calculated to create no little uneasiness in the profession itself.'[67] That unease was reflected at the Annual Provincial Meeting in 1902: 'In the past few years there have been too many cases of daring and disgraceful robberies by solicitors ... of trusts broken and great names tarnished.'[68] The problem was obvious and of long standing; the difficulty was to find a solution. In 1856 the *Law Times* had gone so far as to suggest legislation to prohibit solicitors whilst in practice from engaging in any business other than their own under penalty of suspension from the profession whilst so engaged, but that had not been followed up. Although there were many speeches and articles deprecating speculation the Council had not made any official statement on the lines suggested by the *Solicitors' Journal*. The more immediately practical steps which were considered were the exclusion of bankrupt solicitors from practice and a requirement that solicitors should keep their clients' and trust moneys separate from their own.

The problem of the bankrupt solicitor attracted a good deal of attention in the seventies, due to some extent to the interest of a member of Parliament, Sir Henry Peek. He asked the law officers in 1878 whether it would

[64] *Solicitors' Journal*, vol 44 (1899–1900), p 424.
[65] Proceedings, p 221.
[66] 27th April 1900.
[67] Vol 35, p 78.
[68] Proceedings, p 211.

not serve to protect the public if the Law List could by a suitable mark show which solicitors were bankrupts. But the law officers could not see any reason why solicitors who had been or were bankrupts should be treated in any different manner from other businessmen. In particular, if they had been discharged from bankruptcy they were in law entitled to continue their vocation. In 1879 a speaker at the Provincial Annual Meeting produced the results of the records he had been keeping since the Bankruptcy Act 1861. Between 1861 and 1877 there had been 942 solicitor-bankruptcies. One solicitor had been bankrupt twelve times and of the 942 cases there were no fewer than 130 solicitors who had failed more than once. He commented that it was a 'blot on the system that this could happen without notice or enquiry on the part of the governing body'[69] and like Sir Henry Peek suggested that at least some mark should be placed against the names of the solicitors concerned in the Law List. It was even more absurd that bankrupt solicitors should continue in practice and Sir Henry Peek suggested in 1893 that there should be legislation that 'any solicitor ... who shall have been adjudged bankrupt a second time shall be disqualified from renewing his annual certificate', but nothing came of it. The legal position was far from clear. The Law Society assumed that it had power to refuse to renew the annual certificate of a solicitor whilst he was still bankrupt in the same way as it had a discretion to refuse to renew the certificate of a solicitor who had allowed it to lapse for more than twelve months.[70] The Court of Appeal, however, ruled otherwise[71] and the Society had to seek legislation. It is an indication of the difficulties surrounding the whole problem that although the Bill passed the Lords it was ultimately counted out in the Commons. The President disclosed to the annual general meeting in 1904 that as a result there were 76 undischarged bankrupts still practising. Eventually the Solicitors Act 1906 gave the Society a discretion to refuse to renew a bankrupt solicitor's certificate, but subject to the Bankruptcy Acts he could still practise until his current certificate expired. This remained the position until the Solicitors Act 1957,[72] which provided that adjudication as a bankrupt operated to disqualify a solicitor from practice immediately by automatically suspending his practising certificate.

The more important problem of clients' money had been discussed for many years. The profession was strongly opposed to any interference in its relationship with its clients or the application to its accounting systems of rules which did not apply to other professions which had charge of other people's moneys. The heavy failures at the end of the century led the Council to call a special general meeting on 27th April 1900 at which a resolution was passed appointing a committee 'to inquire into the best

[69] Proceedings, 1879, p 142.
[70] This was in reliance on *Re an Aplication under the Solicitors Act 1843* (1899), 80 LT 720.
[71] *Re a Solicitor* [1902] 1 KB 128.
[72] Section 14.

means of protecting the profession and the public against such malpractices as have been disclosed in certain recent cases'. A strong committee including Sir George Lewis was appointed at the meeting and it was later reinforced by six nominees from the Council and six from the Association of Provincial Law Societies. The committee made a specific recommendation that the law should be amended to make a misappropriation of clients' money a criminal offence notwithstanding the absence of a written direction. There had been numerous cases where solicitors had been acquitted because there had been no such direction, and there was general agreement that this gap should be closed. Accordingly this recommendation was rapidly realised in the Larceny Act 1901. The committee also made a general recommendation: 'Many solicitors do keep a banking account separate from their own and identified as a trust account to which they place all monies in their hands belonging to their clients and in the opinion of the committee it is very desirable that as far as possible this course should be adopted in addition to the careful keeping of accounts.'

This was the vital issue. In the suspicious atmosphere of the time one leading firm in London actually circularised its clients detailing its accounting and book-keeping methods in order to allay their fears. The *Solicitors' Journal* did not think this sort of action should be encouraged. Some solicitors were dissatisfied with the committee's general recommendation and thought that the Council should seek powers to compel separate banking accounts and the audit of solicitors' accounts. The question of separate accounts in particular was much canvassed in the legal press, and the advocates of it endeavoured to demonstrate to their opponents that their fears about complicated systems of book-keeping and additional expense were ill founded. The *Law Times* in a long series of articles on office management came down firmly on the side of separate banking accounts.[73] But solicitors generally were not convinced. In 1905 a proposal was made to the Provincial Annual Meeting that separate accounts should be made compulsory, but it got no support when the President countered with a suggestion that the matter be referred to the Council in consultation with the local law societies. Nothing was done and further cases of fraud came to light. In 1906 the *Solicitors' Journal* reported that 'owing to recurring frauds by solicitors distrust has been growing among the public',[74] and finally in December 1906 the Council called a special general meeting to consider the matter. It created an unfortunate impression by holding the meeting in private and the newspaper *Truth* was particularly scathing. A motion was proposed that a Solicitors Practice Committee whould be set up to investigate and report, but the Council opposed it and it was lost. Its sponsors, however, demanded a poll and on the poll it was carried by 1,169 to 609. A committee was duly appointed.

[73] Vol 116 (1903–1904), p 146.
[74] Vol 51, p 151.

The committee did not take long to report. It was perhaps urged on by the fact that the Board of Trade was known to be contemplating legislation which would require solicitors to maintain a separate clients' account under a penalty, for the first failure to do so, of £100; suspension for a second failure; and striking off for a third. By a majority vote the committee recommended reforms which in the event have been the basis of future legislation. The first six recommendations, made with the unanimous approval of the committee, were: (1) proper accounts were to be kept and balanced at regular intervals; (2) separate accounts for clients' and the solicitor's own moneys; (3) client's money was to be applied only as directed by the client; (4) interest earned on client's money to belong to the client; (5) clients' money to be retained for the shortest possible time; and (6) where clients' money was to be kept for a lengthy period it should be paid into a separate deposit account. The other three recommendations were approved only by the majority; (7) every solicitor should have his accounts audited annually by a chartered or incorporated accountant and keep a separate bank account for clients' money; (8) on renewal of his practising certificate a solicitor who did not have a separate bank account for clients' money to file an accountant's certificate that his accounts had been properly kept and audited; (9) a solicitor keeping a separate bank account for clients' money to file a statutory declaration on renewal of his practising certificate confirming that he had done so, that his clients had received all interest earned by their money and that all clients' money had been duly dealt with and was available. The requirement to separate clients' money from the solicitor's money was generally acceptable. The *Solicitor's Journal's* view was that 'the constant recurrence of frauds by solicitors has produced a distrust in the minds of the public which it is necessary to allay by imposing rules adopted in the spirit if not in the letter by the great majority of solicitors, upon all members of the profession'.[75] It was the last three recommendations which caused dissent. They were said to be no safeguard against deliberate fraud: they would give the client 'no additional security nor would the solicitor be deterred from defrauding if he desired to do so'.[76] The idea of an accountant auditing their books was repugnant, and solicitors did not like the expense which would be involved. 'How the suggestion came to be made by practical men who know the amount of accountants' fees we are at a loss to understand' and moreover it would place the whole profession under a 'degrading obligation'.[77]

On 5th and 12th July 1907 the recommendations were submitted to a general meeting of The Law Society. The matter was of vital importance and even the galleries were full. A proposal that all the recommendations should be adopted was countered with an amendment that the first six

[75] Vol 51, p 585.

[76] *Law Times*, vol 123, p 268.

[77] *Solicitors' Journal*, vol 51, p 585.

should be accepted but the last three rejected. The amendment was carried, but the reformers demanded a poll. The first six recommendations were again accepted, but the last three were decisively rejected by 4,635 to 691. The first three recommendations were in effect adopted by the rules made in 1934 by the Council under the Solicitors Act 1933 and came into force on 1st January 1935; the second three recommendations by the rules made in 1965 by the Council under the Solicitors Act 1965, coming into force on 1st September 1965: the last three recommendations by the rules made in 1945 under the Solicitors Act 1941, coming into force on 1st January 1945. Each step was taken under pressure. Nothing at all was done before 1930, but that year there was another agitation inside and outside the profession because of another series of failures which resulted in eleven solicitors being prosecuted in twelve months. The Council proposed to the profession that it should seek legislation to enable it to compel all practising solicitors to be members of The Law Society, so that all would contribute to the compensation fund which it was planning, and to make rules with regard to the handling of clients' money. Once again the members rejected any suggestion of interference with them in this respect and the Council dropped that part of its proposals. Sir John Withers, a member of Parliament and a member of the Council, resigned from the Council to demonstrate his disgust and proceeded to prepare his own Bill, which he introduced on 9th July 1930 as the Solicitors (Clients' Accounts) Bill. The Commons had already shown their determination to have something done and the Council compromised with Sir John. Its own Solicitors Act 1933 gave it powers to make rules requiring separate accounts to be maintained for clients' and solicitors' own moneys, as had been provided for in Sir John's own Bill. The second three recommendations were adopted under the necessity created by the decision in *Brown* v *IRC* [1964] 3 All ER 119; [1965] AC 244 that in the absence of a special agreement interest on client's money belonged to the client. The third group was adopted to deal with the situation which arose primarily out of the 1934 Accounts Rules requiring separation of a solicitor's own money from his clients'. In 1938 there was an exceptional number of frauds[78] and manifestly something had to be done. The Council decided to seek powers to require production of an accountant's certificate that the rules had been complied with as a condition for the grant of a practising certificate. Notwithstanding the plain evidence, there was still considerable opposition inside the profession, and at the special general meeting held to consider the proposal only four members out of 250 present voted for it. Nevertheless this time the Council decided to proceed and the powers they sought were given by the Solicitors Act 1941. In 1945 they set up their own Investigation Department, so that if an accountant's certificate was not produced or showed that there had been a failure to comply with the rules the Society could investigate for itself. The cost of that operation in 1974 was nearly £70,000.

[78] Birks, Gentlemen at Law, p 274.

There has been a substantial improvement in the profession's financial probity. At the end of the nineteenth century the number of solicitors who were disciplined for dishonest practices was about one in a thousand of the total practising; in the 1970s the number had dropped to about half that number. In the same period the number of solicitors made bankrupt has dropped from fifty a year to not more than ten. But inevitably cases of fraud and dishonesty arise and cause loss. Such cases among solicitors give rise to particular difficulty because the loss often falls on people who are least able to bear it. The problem of whether and if so how to make good that loss as an obligation on the profession as a whole was one which for long exercised the minds and consciences of solicitors. There were many solutions offered. One was that a bond should be required from the solicitor for some such sum as £5,000 which would be available to meet in part at least losses caused if he defaulted, but that was rejected because many young solicitors would be unable to raise such a bond. The 1900 committee considered an indemnity fund, but that was also rejected. The President of the Liverpool Law Society, who had been a member of that committee, summarised the objections which then, before and later have been raised to a compensation fund: 'It was a factor in all these schemes that the insurance or guarantee fund should be provided at the cost either of all practising solicitors or of all who should be willing to join. In either case the honest practitioners were to find the money for indemnifying the victims of their dishonest brethren. All the schemes proposed seemed to me unfair to the former class and to be positively harmful because they would induce the client to repose unlimited confidence in a man unworthy of it for even if loss to the client would result he would know that he could obtain indemnity from the profession at large. The tendency therefore would be towards a relaxation of those precautions on the part of the client to which no honest solicitor ought to object and which are the surest protection against the solicitor whose want of principle or weakness lays him open to temptation.'[79]

The idea of an indemnity fund continued to be discussed. It was referred to by *The Times*[80] and it was pressed on the 1906 committee. That committee reported that several suggestions on this line had been put to it but 'nothing of general practicability has been proposed. Some of the committee are opposed to the principle involved; others, however, while they feel the matter is one of great complexity and difficulty, trust that some scheme may ultimately be devised and worked out.' This was one of the problems whose solution was made the more difficult by the fact that only half the profession were members of The Law Society. After the 1906 committee had reported the matter became quiescent, but the spate of defalcations in 1930 revived it. There was a report in *The Times* that some members of Parliament on the government side were saying that, failing

[79] Report to Liverpool Law Society: Annual General Meeting, 28th November 1900.
[80] 5th September 1904.

action to set up a fund being taken by the profession itself, it would be the duty of the government to bring in legislation.[81] The Law Society did not feel it could take any such steps unless it had the power to compel all solicitors to become members, and the agitation died down because of the row within the Society about solicitors' accounts,[82] which absorbed all the interest. The new accounts rules contributed, however, to a situation which made any further delay impossible, and eventually a Compensation Fund was established on 1st November 1942.[83] The contribution from each solicitor taking out a practising certificate was then fixed at £5 a year and raised in 1957[84] to £10, but is since 1975 at the discretion of the Council.[85] A solicitor is exempt in respect of his first three practising certificates and pays half the normal rate in respect of each of the next three. In 1965 power was taken to make a special levy not exceeding £50 in case of emergency.[86] This arose because of the losses arising from the defalcations of a solicitor named Eichholz. When this man died in 1957 it was found that he had systematically defrauded clients, mainly Jewish refugees from Nazi Germany, to the extent that the claims finally paid out totalled £525,851. Fortunately the Fund had been insured for £250,000, so that with recoveries the net cost to the Fund was £236,080. After this experience the cost of insurance was found to be prohibitive and the Council decided to carry the risk but to have power to raise additional money in an emergency. In fact the power has never been used.

Payments out of the Fund have been at the discretion of the Council and are limited to reimbursement of losses arising from the fraud or dishonesty of a solicitor in his practice and to compensation for financial hardship caused by a solicitor's failure to account for trust or other moneys. When the Solicitors Amendment Bill 1974 was before Parliament an attempt was made by Lord Gardiner to remove the discretionary element, but this was not pursued. By way of compromise the Council now has to state its reasons if it refuses to make a grant.[87] All admitted claims have been met in full, and the discretionary power has been held in reserve to deal with claims which, although technically within the scheme, do not merit an indemnity because of, for instance, the conduct of the claimant. In spite of all that was originally and persistently urged against the concept of a compensation fund, no voice is now raised in the profession against the present scheme. It is recognised that its existence and the manner of its administration have greatly contributed to the improved status of the profession and enable it to be said with assurance that persons dealing with solicitors need have no fear of loss through dishonesty.

[81] Reported *Solicitors' Journal*, vol 74, p 313. The possibility had been underlined by legislation in New Zealand in 1929.

[82] See p 103, *supra*.

[83] Solicitors Act 1941.

[84] Solicitors Act 1957, Sched 2.

[85] Solicitors Amendment Act 1974, s 11.

[86] Solicitors Act 1965, ss 15 and 16.

[87] Section 36 (1).

CHAPTER 6

Manpower and Offices

In 1960 Sir Sydney Littlewood, then President of The Law Society, told the National Conference that 'there is a serious shortage of solicitors' and that for every solicitor-applicant there were a dozen would-be employers.[1] In 1962 The Law Society estimated that there was a shortage of 5,000 solicitors. Until then the government, the public, and the profession itself had all believed that there were too many.

The early attempts to limit the number of attorneys all failed.[2] In 1455 the complaint was that 'not long before within the City of Norwich and the counties of Suffolk and Norfolk there were but six or eight attorneys at most, in which time great tranquillity reigned there; but that now in the said city and counties there were above four score attorneys the greater part of whom, having nothing else to live upon, spent their time in fomenting and encouraging little, trifling and vexatious suits to the no small damage of the said city and counties'. In 1564 the number of attorneys at Stafford Assizes caused the Bishop of Coventry and Lichfield to complain that they bred and nourished 'matters of strife and contention between party and party for their lucre sake'.[3] In 1609 Lord Chancellor Egerton complained about the number of attorneys in the provinces who stirred up 'suits and so bring water to the mill', and Lord Eure, then President of the Council of the Marches, conceded that he could do nothing to stop the increase and that there were more than two hundred attorneys practising in the counties within his jurisdiction.[4] Sir Matthew Hale, Chief Justice of the King's Bench from 1671 to 1676, attributed the heavy volume of litigation in his day in part at least to the 'multitude of attorneys practising in the great court at Westminster ready at every market to gratify the spleen, spite or pride of every plaintiff'.[5] In 1700[6] Evelyn recorded in his Diary that 'the parliament voted that the exorbitant number of attorneys be lessened (now indeed swarming and evidently causing law suits and disturbances eating out the estates of people, provoking them to go to

[1] *Law Society's Gazette*, 1960, p 482.
[2] Chapter 1, pp 11–13, *supra*.
[3] Cockburn, History of English Assizes, p 146.
[4] Ibid, p 147.
[5] History of the Common Law (Chicago ed), p 112.
[6] 4th February.

law)'. The reasoning was simple, if erroneous: formerly there had been few lawyers and few lawsuits, now there were many lawyers and many lawsuits, therefore it was the increase in the number of lawyers which had caused the increase in the number of lawsuits.

Running alongside the complaints were attempts at limitation. The situation in Norwich and its neighbouring counties was the matter of a special Act.[7] Parliament in 1606 legislated against 'the multitudes and misdemeanours of attorneys and solicitors',[8] but the Act was no more successful than earlier efforts and for practical purposes the matter was left to the judges. A series of orders of the court were made: in 1610, 1633, 1654, 1667, 1684 and 1704, but all were in vain. Limitation by the judges was bound to fail because they were financially interested in the numbers increasing. In 1651 Cock in his History of English Law said: 'Give me now leave a little to speak of attorneys which almost overrule the whole law: First the Judges though the Licensor or allower of Attorneys yet receiving great part of his extraordinary revenue from him as upon Fines.'[9] That the numbers were increasing is not open to doubt. It was a natural and inevitable result of social and economic trends. What the numbers actually were is impossible to determine. Some estimates ran into tens of thousands, but they had no basis in fact. The difficulty in forming an accurate estimate was that there was no properly maintained roll or rolls and it was therefore difficult to say whether a man practising as an attorney was properly qualified to do so. Lord Coleridge was of the opinion that by the end of the fourteenth century there were two thousand attorneys,[10] but there is no means of verifying what must have been a mere guess. In 1678 the Practick Part of the Law noted that 'the attorneys are very many not being limited to any set number' but did not venture on a figure. In 1633 there were 1,383 attorneys on the Roll of Common Pleas compared with 313 in 1578; in 1588 a Mr Richard Smith started practice as an attorney in Lincolnshire when there were only three others but in 1621 there were ten or twelve score.[11] In 1689 John Aubry estimated the total at nearly three thousand. In 1729 Parliament again intervened. Numerical limitation was still an ideal: the procedure for admission to the roll was predicated with the condition that the Act did not authorise the judges to increase the number of attorneys and solicitors, and it introduced a practical means of limitation by restricting the number of articled clerks which each attorney and solicitor could have at one time to two. The last direct reference to limitation by statute was that of the younger Pitt when he justified his annual certificate duty in 1784 on the ground that it would tend to reduce what he called the excessive number of attorneys and solicitors.[12]

[7] See p 13, *supra*. [8] 3 Jac 1 c 7. See *supra*, p 15. [9] Page 42.
[10] Quoted Christian, Solicitors—An Outline of their History, p 29.
[11] Bridenough, Vexed and Troubled Englishmen (1968), p 258.
[12] Cobbett, Parliamentary Proceedings, vol 25, cols 812–813.

The Attorneys and Solicitors Act 1729 gave for the first time some reasonably accurate statistics as to the size of the profession. In 1730 there were enrolled some 2,236 attorneys at Common Pleas and 893 in the King's Bench; in addition there were about 1,700 solicitors. Since some attorneys were on both rolls and some were also solicitors there was some duplication, and it is generally assumed that there were then 4,000 or so entitled to practise. When the first unofficial Law List—Browne's—was published in 1775 there were 1,087 London attorneys and solicitors and 2,040 country, but the list was probably incomplete. It registers no names at all for some sizeable towns where there certainly were men in practice, and no doubt then as later there were a good many who practised but did not enrol, in order to save the fees. At any rate in 1784 Pitt put the number at 4,400. Other guesses of the number in 1800 have been 4,969 by Sir Henry Fowler, as he then was, when reviewing the past century in 1901; and 5,300 by Professor Gneiss.[13] In 1821, through the Revenue returns of the stamp duties on practising certificates, it was possible to have a pretty accurate figure: 7,090. The number of practising certificates issued from that time is embodied in the following table:

Year	*Population (000,000s)*	*No of practising certificates*	*No of persons per solicitor (to nearest 50)*
1784	9	4400*	2050
1821	12	7090†	1700
1831	14	9083‡	1550
1841	16	10073§	1500
1851	18	9957	1800
1861	20	10229	1950
1871	23	10576	2200
1881	26	12688	2050
1891	29	15175	1900
1901	32·5	16265	2000
1911	36	17000 (app)	2100
1921	38	14623	2600
1931	40	15608	2550
1941	41·5 (est)	14430	2900
1951	43·75	17396	2500
1961	46	19438	2350
1971	48·75	25366	1900
1976	50 (est)	29406‖	1700

* Pitt's estimate of number who would take out certificates (Cobbett, vol 25, cols 812, 813).

† Parliamentary Papers 1833, vol 31, p 329.

‡ Ibid.

§ Ibid, 1845, vol 28, p 138.

‖ *Law Society's Gazette*, 7th April 1976.

---

[13] Verfassungs- und Verwaltungsrecht (1857), p 509.

It will be seen that what is generally regarded as the high figure of 1976 for practising certificates represents the same proportion of the population as that for 1821. Ignoring periods affected by the two Wars, the most significant years are those between 1841 and 1871. In that time the number of practising certificates increased by 503 (or about seventeen per year on average), an increase of five per cent; during the same period the population increased by almost forty-four per cent. Recruitment is inevitably affected by public opinion of the profession's actual and future financial prospects. In the 1840s and 1850s most people thought solicitors were doing badly and were likely to continue to do so. Mr Maugham, giving evidence to the Select Committee on Education in 1846, ascribed the decline in recruitment to the fall in the level of costs in common law and bankruptcy proceedings and the loss of business from the superior courts to the new county courts with their lower scale of costs; in 1854 the Metropolitan and Provincial Law Association ascribed it also to the reduction in Chancery costs then introduced.[14] It is also possible that the more difficult conditions for entry dissuaded some from trying and this would be particularly the case with the writing clerks. The changes were of course not uniform. In the Midlands and the North there were substantial increases. Between 1823 and 1901 the number of solicitors in Liverpool was said to have increased from 113 to 546 and in Birmingham from 57 to 412.[15] Yet in spite of the fact that the number of solicitors in relation to population did not increase to any marked extent even after the plateau of the 1841–1871 period, the profession became acutely conscious or at any rate completely convinced that it was overcrowded. For that reason it accepted the high rate of stamp duty on articles as a means of limiting the numbers as well as of enhancing the quality of the profession, and objected only to the annual fee, which did not affect the cost of entry. The repeated warnings, particularly at the end of the century, about the low incomes which most solicitors earned were doubtless also intended to have a dissuasive effect. When the Solicitors Act 1860 reduced the period of articles for 'ten-year men' from five years to three the *Law Times* asked: 'Why make it easier to become a solicitor when there are enough already?' From 1881 to 1901 the rate of increase was twenty-five per cent, and although this just kept pace with the increase in population there were regular complaints about overcrowding. In 1882 the *Law Times* considered that 'the profession is now flooded with young men';[16] in 1893 the Provincial Meeting was told that 'the Profession is palpably overstocked';[17] in 1896 Christian wrote: 'The profession is and always has been overstocked';[18] in 1899 the *Solicitors' Journal* noted 'the rapid increase in the

[14] Circular No 5 (1854), p 21.

[15] The numbers given in the Law Lists were somewhat less, but assistant solicitors would often not take out practising certificates.

[16] Vol 72, p 191.

[17] Proceedings, p 196 [18] Op cit.

number of solicitors';[19] and in 1906 the President of The Law Society warned articled clerks that it was 'no good to think that ... they would be sure to get a living'.[20] The justification for these statements could be found in the advertisement columns of the legal press.[21] These were full of advertisements from apparently highly qualified admitted men seeking posts as managing clerks at salaries between £100 and £150 a year; at least one offered a premium for an appointment. The chance of a partnership for those without substantial capital was very remote. At the Provincial Annual General Meeting in 1904 attention was drawn to the increase from 10,200 in 1853 to 16,265 in 1903 and some limitation on entry was mooted. It was never a practical possibility.

One aspect of the profession's nervousness about overcrowding was its attitude to allowing women to enter it. It may be that women had been appointed attorneys in the thirteenth century, but they were the wives or sisters of the litigants and not professional attorneys. In 1879 a young lady enquired of the The Law Society if she could sit the examinations and was refused.[22] There was a slight stir but it was the feminist movement of the early part of the twentieth century coupled with the availability of university education for women which brought the issue to the front. In 1912 a Mr Bell[23] read a paper to the Annual Provincial Meeting advocating opening the profession to women, but he got no support. Bills which were introduced into Parliament with the same object made no progress and the profession generally was not inclined to take the matter very seriously. The *Solicitors' Journal* commented smugly on one of them that 'we observe with relief that the Bill does not propose to open to women the way to judicial preferment'.[24] In 1914 a Miss Bebb who had had a brilliant academic career applied to The Law Society for permission to sit the examinations with a view to admission and was refused. In due course the matter came before the Court of Appeal.[25] The Law Society was faced with the problem that the Interpretation Act 1889, s 1, provided that the masculine pronoun included the feminine and that on that footing the Attorneys and Solicitors Act 1729 and subsequent legislation about admissions and education applied to women as well as to men. The matter was thoroughly investigated. The Law Society relied much on the dubious authority of the Mirror of Justices[26] for saying that women could not be appointed attorneys, and in the upshot the Court of Appeal was not prepared to upset a practice of very long standing on the strength of an

[19] Vol 43, p 583.

[20] *Solicitors' Journal*, vol 50, p 208.

[21] See Chapter 5, *supra*.

[22] *Solicitors' Journal*, vol 24, p 139.

[23] In 1939 he wrote a very entertaining book, These Meddlesome Attorneys, which gives some 'not in Baedeker' facts about the profession and The Law Society.

[24] Vol 56 (1912), p 513.

[25] *Bebb* v *The Law Society* [1914] 1 Ch 286, CA.

[26] Pages 3–4, *supra*.

Interpretation Act. The Master of the Rolls (Lord Cozens-Hardy) perhaps had not understood the matter fully since he came to the conclusion that The Law Society was 'of course a modern creation of statute'. The outbreak of war in 1914 might have been expected to postpone the resolution of the problem, but in fact it accelerated it. The profession itself remained solidly masculine in its attitude. Fears were expressed that if women were admitted to the profession it would be even more flooded than ever, because women would be driven to find work in large numbers because of the shortage of husbands due to the war and because it was expected that after the war was over many men would emigrate. In 1916 it was still hoped to discourage the reformers by expressing doubts as to whether women would in any case make successful solicitors; The Law Society's continued opposition to enabling legislation was uniformly supported by the legal press, which found the advantage of the change difficult to see. It was of course not only a matter of numbers. Many solicitors dreaded change—any change—and not a few dreaded the idea of having to do business with women colleagues. In 1919 the *Law Times*, however, conceded that 'the time is arriving when the doors of the profession should be opened to all persons irrespective of sex'.[27] The profession was not so sure, and in 1917 they attempted to gain time by urging that so important a matter should not be decided whilst so many solicitors were away on active service;[28] another attempt at legislation was made by Lord Buckmaster in 1918 and The Law Society opposed that too. When the Sex Disqualification Bill was before the House in 1919 the Society called a special meeting to decide its policy. Fifty members were in favour of the Bill, but there were thirty-three die-hards who wanted to continue the fight. In the end the Bill became law in 1919 and Miss Carrie Morrison, educated at Girton and with a first in the Modern Language Tripos, was admitted the first woman solicitor in 1922. Two other women passed the final examinations at the same time. The admission of the first woman as a solicitor might have been expected to be an event which would have been given some notice in the legal papers, particularly when one considers the trivia with which they often filled their columns. But all, including the *Law Society's Gazette*, were silent. For some time the *Gazette* listed the names of women under the heading of 'Gentlemen Applying for Admission'. At the Annual Provincial Meeting in 1922 the President ventured the witticism that women would be better employed at home bringing up future generations of solicitors of the male sex. Otherwise the only stir was caused by questions at the annual general meeting as to whether women solicitors were to be admitted as members and if so what was to be done about cloakrooms. But on 23rd January 1923 the President was able to announce that the first woman member had that day been elected, and the next month the cloakroom arrangements were duly gazetted. On that banal note ended

[27] Vol 146, p 232.
[28] Annual Report 1917, pp 26–27.

this history of masculine obstinacy. The dreaded flood of women did not materialise. Although it might have been expected that a pent-up demand would be released by the 1919 Act, only eight women had entered into articles by March 1920. In the 1920s the average annual intake was eight or nine; in the 1930s just under sixteen; in the 1940s twelve; and in the 1950s thirty. The proportion of women to men was increasing only slowly and after forty years of emancipation the intake was less than one in fifteen. Then it seems to have accelerated, and in 1975 it was 2,200, of whom only 1,500 took out practising certificates. The proportion is now about eight per cent. No woman solicitor has been a member of the Council or even proposed for membership, but the British Legal Association in 1975 elected Miss Miranda Reckitt as its Chairman.

The 1914–1918 war naturally curtailed recruitment and accelerated the losses through death so that in the years from 1909 to 1919 the number of solicitors actually dropped from 16,797 to 14,830. In spite of this fall the profession does not appear to have been under-manned after the war if one applies the test of the number of vacancies and the level of salaries offered in advertisements in the legal press at the time. Salaries for assistant solicitors did not materially change between 1919 and 1939 and in fact were tending to decline towards the end of that period. It was not until the 1950s that the profession began to find itself under strength. The work available had increased substantially after 1945[29] and the number of solicitors to do it had decreased markedly. Admissions, which had been 932 in 1938, dropped to 104 in 1942, 117 in 1944, and 180 in 1945. Over three hundred solicitors had been killed or were missing. The number of practising certificates issued dropped from 17,012 in 1939 to 13,130 in 1944. The climb-back was slow and the number of certificates issued did not reach the 1939 level again until 1951. The manpower in the private sector was affected by the attractions of appointments in commerce and industry and in local and central government. Between 1950 and 1960 the number of solicitors employed outside private practice doubled, and the trend continued. In 1962–1963 there were 581 in commerce and industy; in the next year 632. In the corresponding years there were in local and central government 1,566 and 1,592. By 1964 about one in eight solicitors was employed in this way, and the pattern was maintained. 'The solicitor in commerce and industry is in general far better off financially than even the principal in private practice' was a view formed after a careful survey in 1972[30] and by 1974 over ten per cent of practising certificates issued went to solicitors not in private practice. The competition from industry had other consequences. In 1958 the Council felt bound 'to record that the quality of entrants to the profession has been causing them some concern probably owing principally to the fact that as compared with the pre-war position

[29] Chapter 5, p 93 et seq, *supra.*
[30] By Mr R H Stanway, reported *Solicitors' Journal*, vol 116, p 245.

the opportunities offered to young men and women by industry and other undertakings are relatively greater'.[31]

The evidence of a shortage was plain to see in the mid-1950s. Employers were competing for assistant solicitors not only because there was a shortage of admitted men but because the unadmitted managing clerk (or legal executive, as he was shortly to be called) was becoming increasingly difficult to find. A newly admitted man who in 1945 might have accepted £200 a year now found that he could readily obtain ten times that amount. The advertisements for posts which had formerly been so sad a feature of the legal press were replaced by tempting offers from employers. The Law Society for the first time in the history of the profession started a recruiting campaign. It had much more to offer than would have been the case even twenty years before. The profession had a much better image as progressive and as safe and certain a way to a good income and social status as one was likely to find. The cost of entry had become trifling. Stamp duty on articles, which had been the sizeable sum of £80, was repealed by the Finance Act 1949; premiums for articles were gradually abandoned as employers saw in well-educated articled clerks a useful source of staff; more and more principals paid something (though some articled clerks thought not enough) during articles.[32] The principal expense was attendance at law school, but that was manageable. The number of clerks entering into articles increased from 998 in 1952 to 1,914 in 1972 and the rate was accelerating to 2,481 in 1974. Of course admissions and the size of the profession kept pace. In 1952 there were 588 admissions; in 1972 there were 1,713; in 1974 there were 1,894; in 1975 over 2,000. In 1951 there were 17,396 practising certificates; in 1972 there were 26,327; and at the end of 1975 there were 29,850. In twenty-five years the profession had increased by fifty per cent or about four times as rapidly as the population it served. By 1970 the old fears and doubts about overcrowding had begun to reappear. The Law Society then reported to the Ormrod Committee that it doubted 'whether the rate of recruitment even if it can be maintained is sufficient to meet the demands of the profession in the future',[33] but shortly afterwards the Council 'inclined to the view that the profession is probably not now under-manned, although there is evident need for more solicitors of good quality ... and it doubted if the profession can long continue to absorb the present rate of increase which is now approximately 1,000 a year'.[34] The Ormrod Committee decided that 'all that can be safely predicted is that more practising lawyers will be required ... and

[31] Annual Report, 1957–1958.

[32] The 'gradualness' of the process is shown by the fact that as late as 1956 the average premium on articles was 300 guineas, with 500 and 100 as the maximum and minimum. The normal arrangement was to repay the premium in the form of salary during the later years of the articles. The whole position was reviewed in the *Solicitors' Journal*, vol 100 (1956), p 426.

[33] Ormrod Report (as to which see pp 60, 63, *supra*), p 213.

[34] Education and Training Committee, October 1970, para 13.

that the increase in demand for legal services will be more than proportionate to any increase in population'.[35] The worsening of the general economic situation and the collapse of the property boom in 1974 made some people anxious about the rapid increase in numbers, but that did not deter new entrants. Indeed the shrinking of opportunities elsewhere had made the apparent security of the profession all the more attractive.

In assessing the size of the profession and considering whether at a particular time it is under- or over-manned three factors have to be taken into account in addition to the number of practising certificates issued. First, a substantial number of solicitors do not now and have not in the past taken out practising certificates although working in a solicitor's office. In 1853 it was said that two-fifths of the profession did not take out certificates because the high rate of duty did not justify doing so,[36] and if that was true then the whole picture changes because there would be some 15,000 admitted men working in the law instead of about 10,000 on the basis of the number of certificates issued. In 1974 the number of solicitors on the roll was of the order of 36,000, which was 8,000 more than the number of certificates. That figure would include some solicitors in retirement, but not many, because retired solicitors take out certificates to enable them to act as 'consultants' with their former firms and to have their names retained on the firm's notepaper. The strength of that tendency is shown by the increase in this category from 392 in 1973 to 965 in 1974. It would also include some men in central and local government or commerce and industry, but as this section took out over 3,000 certificates the number without cannot have been large. It is therefore likely that the 24,778 men in private practice with certificates were assisted by at least another 5,000 uncertificated. Secondly, the solicitor's profession in England and Wales has always relied heavily on the experienced but unadmitted clerk. In that respect it differs from the legal professions in most European countries and in the United States of America. The extent of this reliance can be seen from the estimates given from time to time of the number of persons actually employed in the law. In 1688 the economist Gregory King estimated the number engaged in the law at 10,000; but in 1732 the *Law Magazine* said that there were 50,000 so engaged, and if one deducts some 4,000 for attorneys and solicitors and another 1,000 for the Bar and barristers' clerks that would give 45,000 clerks at one level or another;[37] the economist Massie estimated that in 1759 there were 12,000 families living out of the law;[38] and in 1832 it was estimated that there were in all 23,500 in the legal profession as a whole. This last figure was calculated on the footing that there were in London 3,000 attorneys and solicitors and 7,000 clerks; in the country 4,000 attorneys and solici-

[35] Report, p 41.
[36] *Legal Observer*, vol 46, p 95.
[37] Page 240.
[38] *Economic History Review*, vol 10, p 42.

tors and 9,000 clerks. The figure for clerks was thought to be an underestimate because it was based approximately on two clerks to each employer, whereas it was said that in London many principals had twenty clerks or more and the majority had at least four.[39] The caveat was fully justified. According to statistics based on the censuses the total legal staff employed in 1851 was 32,000; in 1861 34,000; in 1871 39,000 and in 1881 44,000.[40] The 1891 census showed 14,783 persons employed in the law in London alone; the corresponding figure for 1921 was 21,770, but that was affected by the first war. In 1939 The Law Society made a survey of solicitors' staffs and the 9,633 practices whose proprietors replied were found to be employing 46,183 clerks, of whom some 2,500 were assistant solicitors. Allowing for employers who did not answer the questionnaire and assuming that of the total staffs sixty per cent would be purely secretarial or junior employees, these figures suggest a total of some 20,000 unadmitted but experienced men. The Institute of Legal Executives had at mid-1975 a total strength of about 15,000, which suggests that the normal ratio of one admitted man to one unadmitted employee able to transact work with varying degrees of supervision had been maintained. That would give a total manpower of about 55,000 in private practice made up of 25,000 solicitors with certificates, 5,000 solicitors without certificates and 25,000 employees. That in its turn gives a ratio of one to 850 of the population, which is close to the historical United States of America ratio of one to 750,[41] although on admitted personnel alone the ratio is one to 1,600.

The third additional factor is distribution. Distribution of the available manpower in a free profession presents obvious problems. The natural tendency in a free market has been for the number of solicitors and therefore staff per head of population to be highest where the business is likely to be the most lucrative and the living and working conditions the pleasantest and not where the need for their services is the greatest. In 1971 there was one solicitor to 913 persons in Bournemouth, and of the twenty towns with the highest proportion of solicitors to population only four—Manchester, Preston, Newcastle-upon-Tyne and Watford—were primarily industrial or commercial areas. The Rhondda had only one solicitor to every 22,000 inhabitants; Beeston and Stapleford only one to every 32,000. Huyton had only one solicitor's office for a population of 66,629, compared with one office for every 1,896 inhabitants in Guildford.[42] It may be that one part of the country is overmanned and another is undermanned. A not dissimilar situation had arisen in respect of type of work. Solicitors naturally preferred the more lucrative sections such as conveyancing and company law and practice and were not so readily

[39] The Extraordinary Black Book (1832), p 297.
[40] *Journal of Royal Statistical Society* (1886), pp 414–415.
[41] *Law Times*, vol 87 (1889), p 252, and Abel-Smith and Stevens, op cit, p 398.
[42] 'The Location of Solicitors', *Modern Law Review*, vol 36, pp 153–166.

available to those who wanted advice on, say, welfare problems. The profession made a serious effort to remedy this situation by voluntary schemes such as a duty solicitor rota at magistrates' courts or co-operation with local Citizens Advice Bureaux. In 1975 there were fifty duty solicitors schemes and 150 rota schemes in Citizens Advice Bureaux. The introduction of a comprehensive legal advice system under the Legal Aid and Advice Act 1972 on 2nd April 1973 was, however, the most important move. As a result so-called neighbourhood law centres were set up in areas where the private practitioner was lacking. By 1975 there were fifteen centres in the London area[43] and three in the provinces. In 1976 a centre was proposed at Hillingdon but was opposed by the local law society on the ground that existing private facilities were adequate. The Law Society supported that attitude by refusing to give to solicitors intending to work in the centre the necessary waiver in respect of the Practice Rules. The Lord Chancellor, however, persuaded The Law Society to change its mind.

Although the tendency in the post-1945 period has been towards solicitors practising in partnership and for partnerships to be larger, the profession has traditionally been made up of small units.[44] Where there were partnerships in the eighteenth and early nineteenth centuries they were generally based on family relationships. In 1875 in Birmingham the largest firm had only four partners and in the city four out of every five solicitors were sole practitioners; in 1925 the largest firm had seven partners and the sole practitioners were still three to one. Even in London firms were small. In 1925 the three most important firms in the City had only nineteen partners between them and the largest had only eight. In 1966 there were about 6,720 practices and in 1968 6,580; forty per cent of them were still run by sole practitioners and fewer than ten per cent had four or more partners.[45] The number of one-man practices did not change: in 1974 there were 2,778 men practising alone. On the other hand the size of practices increased. The statutory limitation to twenty partners was lifted by the Companies Act 1967 at an opportune moment. According to the 1973 Law List there were then in London alone over fifty firms with ten or more partners and there were five with over thirty; in Birmingham there were six firms with ten or more (and one firm with seventeen), in Leeds three, in Liverpool three, and in Manchester five. Even outside the commercial centres six-partner firms had become commonplace.[46] There was some pressure on The Law Society to make it obligatory to practise in partnership, and this was backed by allegations that where defalcation occurred it was most often in one-man practices. When the Council in 1974 made

[43] Hansard, 30th April 1975, col 163; and see also on the problem generally Smith and Hoath, Law and the Under-Privileged (1975), *passim*.

[44] In 1969 at the National Conference at Scarborough Mr Clive Jenkins described the profession as 'a cottage industry'.

[45] Prices and Incomes Board Report 1971, Cmnd 4624.

[46] Eg in Harrogate there were two, in Brighton four, in Bath two and in Bournemouth three.

a new practice rule setting standards for the supervision of offices some sole practitioners thought it was intended to eliminate them gradually. If the one-man practice does disappear it will be more likely to result from other factors. The number of such practices had been maintained by men who started up in practice on their own account because they could not get a partnership. In the post-1945 period that changed: partnerships became easier to obtain and it was generally not necessary to pay anything for goodwill.[47] Practising in partnership was in any event more attractive than being alone. It gave greater security during practice and better possibilities of provision for retirement; it enabled a degree of specialisation and therefore the possibility of a better service; and it probably had a better status.[48]

* * * *

The earliest attorneys had no offices at all. They carried their papers and such equipment as they needed or possessed in a bag—generally green—and they sought and dealt with their clients and others in the precincts of the courts or such other place as might be convenient. One of the problems of exercising any discipline over them was that often they had no fixed address and repeated orders of the judges were directed at giving them a local habitation, or an address where they could be found. In the seventeenth century at any rate they were beginning to settle. Bishop Earle wrote of an attorney 'pen-feathered he hath now nested himself and with his hoarded pence purchased an office. Two desks and a quire of paper set him up where he now sits in state for all comers.'[49] The tavern or coffee-house was used for seeing clients, and country attorneys frequently used these places not only for that purpose but for completion of conveyancing and other transactions.[50] Many used their own houses as their offices and articled clerks were used for menial domestic duties such as shopping if the business of the office was not more demanding. The library of even the best-established was not such as to take up much room. When Richard Tristram was moving office in 1751 he bemoaned the fact that a century earlier he would have been able to move all his books in a wheelbarrow. It is only in the nineteenth century that the lawyer's office becomes identifiable. The better or longest established businesses were probably still in the Inns of Chancery, but wherever they were the general opinion was that they were uninviting. Trollope said that there was no sadder place than the waiting room of a London attorney, and it was not much better

[47] Goodwill as a saleable asset had a comparatively short life. It was not until 1803 that a contract to give up practice and to recommend clients to give their business to another for valuable consideration was held to be valid (*Bunn* v *Gay* (1803), 4 East 190).

[48] Some sole practitioners gave their practices the appearance of partnerships by adding '& Co' to their names. This started in the latter part of the nineteenth century and was disliked by the more conservative.

[49] Microcosmographie (*circa* 1628).

[50] See Hine, Confessions of an Uncommon Attorney, p 69.

in the country, for even a generation later it was admitted that 'the waiting rooms of country attorneys can hardly be less forbidding'. In Hitchin they had a proper sense of social status and as late as the middle of the century they had first- and second-class waiting rooms. In 1885, in a series of articles on office management, this important part of the office was said 'too frequently to consist of a sort of pen railed off from the remainder of the clerk's office, the access of the sun's rays to it being dependent on the goodwill of a distant skylight; the wall discoloured with the dust and dirt of years ... the floor uncarpeted but certainly stained with ink; the furniture a rickety table surmounted by a fearful and wonderful bottle of water'.[51] Not all felt that their clients needed that degree of consideration. Messrs Letts Brothers with their large Holborn practice kept their clients waiting in the corridor outside the room in which three of the partners worked but to which for the sake of confidentiality only one client could be admitted at a time.[52]

The principal's room was probably not a great deal more appetising than the waiting room or the clerk's office. 'The attorney of the 1850s sits in much dingier surroundings than the solicitor of later decades,'[53] and it may well have been that old-fashioned confusion was regarded by many as a sign of respectability and of a well-established practice. 'That a lawyer should live in a muddle had become a tradition ... His patrons would have thought it perhaps suspicious and certainly out of character if he had conducted himself otherwise.'[54] Economy justified an inbred reluctance to change anything in resistance to modernisation. For many years the only piece of purpose-built office equipment regularly advertised was a 'Legal Nest' consisting of a stand with four japanned deed boxes and selling at first for six guineas but reduced later to five. A useful portable letter-copying appliance advertised in 1848 never seemed to become popular. But changes there were. In 1879 it was remarked that 'an eminent firm of city solicitors have had a telephone installed in their office by means of which they are placed in direct communication with a number of their leading clients'.[55] The legal papers commented on the proper method of using this instrument; it was recommended that it should be placed in a room where it could be used discreetly and without risk of a breach of confidence. Clearly the installation of a telephone in each room was a long way off. The first advertisements for typewriters appeared at the end of the eighties and it was not until 1919 that the *Law Times* drew the profession's attention to the convenience of sending carbon copies of drafts to the other solicitor.[56] Legal papers in the eighties published articles on

[51] *Solicitors' Journal*, vol 29, p 21.
[52] Letts, The Old House (1942), pp 45–46.
[53] Haynes, Concerning Solicitors, p 42.
[54] Crocker, Far From Humdrum, p 20.
[55] *Solicitors' Journal*, vol 23, p 959.
[56] Vol 147, p 203.

the organisation of a solicitor's office; there was a book on the subject in 1886; and The Modern Lawyer's Office appeared in 1902. American influence was beginning to make itself felt. The Rotary Neostyle was said to produce excellent copies and no office could afford to be without one provided that there was somebody who could master the knack of using the gelatine composition which it required. The Patent Pin Fastener, the forerunner of the present-day stapler, was also highly recommended. In 1902 'a few innovators' had been bold enough to use the phonograph, but it had not been largely adopted.[57] Economy also meant that the library was limited to the barest essentials and in some cases well below that level. A solicitor needed to spend at least £200 to provide himself with an adequate library and spare himself the risk of using out-of-date books, as many did, or the trouble and expense of sending clerks to borrow from friends, but many saved the initial outlay. It was 'little short of amazing what small regard is paid by a large number of solicitors not restricted as to their purchasing ability to the matter of law books',[58] and twenty books would be a largish library. Economy also meant that apart from such items as typewriters and letter-presses the office furniture was mainly assembled from the offerings of the sale-rooms or from unwanted pieces from the principal's home. Yet with all their candle-end economies before 1914 'few offices kept their expenses below fifty per cent of their gross takings'.[59]

The hours of work were consistent with the custom of the period, but just as in factories and shops so in the profession the conscience of the employer and the courage and resistance of the staff brought changes. In 1832 an employer wrote to the *Legal Observer*: 'I am sure every liberal man will allow from nine in the morning until eight in the evening are hours enough to transact business ... my object is only the health and comfort of the poor slaves of the profession.'[60] In 1843 the *Shrewsbury Chronicle* reported:[61] 'Upwards of twenty of the attorneys' clerks residing in the town met at the Cross Keys Inn ... to celebrate the joyous event of their respective employers (in pursuance of a requisition presented to them) allowing their offices to be closed at six in the evening.' Saturdays were then as now important to the staff. On 30th August 1844 the Leeds Law Society resolved that as an experiment their members should close their offices on Saturdays at 2 pm and had noted that a similar system was already operating in Manchester, Liverpool, and Newcastle. Early closing on Saturdays or some other weekday spread and local law societies and individual firms wrote to the legal papers when they adopted it as something to be proud of. A survey of sixty principal towns carried out

[57] The Modern Lawyer's Office, p 66.
[58] *Solicitors' Journal*, vol 29 (1884), p 22.
[59] *Solicitors' Journal*, vol 64 (1921), p 255.
[60] Vol 3, p 326.
[61] 29th September.

in 1854 showed that in twenty-two some form of early closing was adopted.[62] The Law Society was particularly active in the campaign and the *Law Times* acknowledged its contribution.[63] By 1860 the system was pretty well universal in the provinces, but London was a special problem because of the court sittings. Unfortunately the judges insisted on sitting on Saturday until 5 pm in the King's Bench and until 3 pm in Chancery. The Law Society persistently asked for some amelioration and in 1871 the London clerks were still complaining that because of these hours most London firms had not adopted early Saturday closing. It was not until 1876 that the courts agreed to rise at 2 pm on Saturdays and the clerks could be released.

Wages were low, but employment in a solicitor's office was considered genteel and that attracted many to it. There was little change over a long period: a clerk in Dorset in 1789 was being paid £30 a year together with his board and lodging, and he was not worse off than the good general clerk in London a hundred years later getting £1 10s a week. Office boys started at about twelve years old at a wage of seven or eight shillings a week. Their prospects naturally depended a good deal on their ability and on the sort of office they were in. When they graduated to engrossing clerks they might expect £1 or twenty-five shillings a week and when they became general or managing clerks the range might be from £1 a week to £500 a year. It was said in 1832 that some 'clerks were starving on a paltry £50; others living comfortably on £200; and others sumptuously on a £500 a year salary'.[64] A fair average was £150 a year, which was not really enough to live on if the clerk was married: 'I am a managing clerk with a salary of £150 a year yet I can hardly give my children the common necessaries of life or decently clothe them much less give them the slightest education' was one man's description of his lot in 1856.[65] The nominal salary was, however, not all the story because it was a widespread custom to pay managing clerks a commission on all the business they introduced to the office. Salaries were not necessarily higher in the larger offices and in 1871 the *Law Journal* commented on one firm with 200 clerks notorious for its low pay. The same situation applied in the provinces. In 1874 the Civil Service Commissioners found that in Liverpool one firm with over fifty clerks paid twenty-one of them under £100 a year, twenty-five between £100 and £200, six between £200 and £300 and only two over £300. Government service was better paid, and in 1881 when the new law offices were opened first-class clerks were offered £500 a year.

The senior men realised early in the nineteenth century as their employers did that they needed some form of organisation to look after their interests. In 1832 the United Law Clerks' Society was founded for

[62] *Law Times*, vol 24, p 66.
[63] Ibid, p 8.
[64] The Extraordinary Black Book, p 298.
[65] *Law Times*, vol 27, p 72.

clerks working in London and within a radius of twenty-five miles. One of its principal objects was the care of retired and sick clerks and it regularly appealed for support. The Society was much praised by important legal figures at dinners and meetings, but its annual reports do not suggest that it had much financial help. The major problem, however, was to give to the title 'managing clerk' a recognised status and, as a correspondent in 1883 put it, 'to secure to the profession respectable and competent clerks and to the clerks proper treatment at the hands of their employers'. This humble man then made suggestions which eighty years afterwards were mainly adopted: (*a*) every solicitor's clerk to pass a practical examination held at The Law Society and to receive a certificate of having done so; (*b*) the certificate to be renewed annually for a fee of 5s; (*c*) managing clerks to pass an examination 'nearly equal' to the solicitors' final examination; (*d*) the certificate to remain with the employers, who were to return it to The Law Society if the clerk misconducted himself; (*e*) a minimum salary of £2 10s for 'certified clerks'—a salary 'barely sufficient to enable a clerk to live respectably in these days of high prices and meritless rents'.[66] In 1885 another clerk suggested that there should be a register of solicitors' clerks maintained by the Inland Revenue and the list of names be published in the Law List.[67] But these were difficult matters and employers were not enthusiastic about trade unionism. Nevertheless the senior clerks proceeded with the idea of organisation. The inaugural meeting of the Solicitors' Managing Clerks' Association was held in 1892 and achieved considerable success. It had the countenance and support of leading men both at the Bar and in the solicitors' profession, and from 1897 organised lectures for its members. In 1901 there was a movement for the establishment of local Associations of Legal Assistants of which the first appears to have been at Liverpool; and it was suggested that there should be an English Institution of Legal Assistants. Presumably legal assistants were regarded as being in a higher category than managing clerks. But the movement was not taken up, and it may well have been that there was not room for two organisations drawing from the same source for members.

Women staff first made their appearance in the 1850s but were slow to be accepted. As late as 1891 according to the census there were only 112 women clerks in legal offices. The wisdom of employing them was seriously questioned because of the effect that might have on business. One thing was regarded as certain: elderly spinster clients would withdraw their business from solicitors who employed women. In other respects they had their drawbacks. Because it was axiomatic that a woman's aim in life was to get married as soon as possible it followed that they would not make a career of office work and that it was not worth taking the trouble to train them. They did not like going out of the office on errands and were less able to stand up to the proverbial rudeness of the clerks at the Law

[66] *Law Times*, vol 76, p 158.
[67] *Law Times*, vol 78, p 431.

Courts—whose lack of manners was said to be in direct proportion to their security of tenure. They did not write as well as the men did and employers did not find them such hard workers. The men clerks resented them because they increased the competition in an already overstaffed world and therefore still further decreased the wages offered. The First World War naturally changed all that.

In general, however, there were few major changes in working conditions and arrangements in solicitors' offices in the short pause between the German wars. Some modernisation of equipment and premises took place; the typewriter and the telephone had become commonplace;[68] but by and large things went their old way. In 1919 the National Confederation of Law Clerks complained that many employers had not given any salary increases and bonuses since 1914 although the cost of living had gone up by 152 per cent, and it was suggested that the matter should be referred to a Joint Conciliation Board. The Law Society for the employers would agree only if the chairman were a solicitor and on the basis that the Board should deal only with individual cases and not with a general scale. The Managing Clerks' Association asked for a minimum salary of £400 a year for its members, but the employers refused to enter into any such agreement. They contended that conditions were so varied that a scale was impossible; but quite apart from the money involved they were alarmed at the possibility of trade unionism and collective bargaining. At the other end of the staff structure—the office-boy—the starting wage was said in 1921 to be between 12s 6d and 15s per week, but the quality was also said to be poor—'hardly able to read or write or speak decently'; and the low wages paid even to experienced clerks meant that neither boys nor girls tended to regard the job as a career.[69] The repercussions of that were felt twenty and thirty years later. The period did, however, see an improvement in the status of the senior men. In the nineteenth century most clerks were merely writing clerks employed on copying, and the skilled work was largely done by the principals. Copying became more and more a job for the typewriter and the woman operator of it; the senior male clerks were more profitably employed. Their technical education and experience made them capable of handling a great deal of the work of the office under 'the general guidance of an expert principal'.[70] In some offices it could be said that they were in effective control. In the 1920s it was recognised that provision should be made for men who had devoted their lives to the profession, and after some hesitation the Solicitors' Clerks' Pension Fund was established in 1930. It started slowly, but after twenty years 786 firms had entered 2,229 clerks into the scheme and the fund had passed £500,000; in 1974 there were 5,427 clerks (of whom 938 were already receiving pensions) in the scheme and the fund was nearly £12,000,000.

[68] Provincial Meeting, 1921: Mr Armstrong's paper: the main differences between 1885 and 1921 had been caused by the telephone and the typewriter.
[69] Ibid. [70] Ibid.

After 1945 the changes became more marked. Offices were considerably improved, though even thirty years later there was still a long way to go. The commercial centres of London and other large towns were rebuilt as the result of enemy action or the enterprise of the property developer, so that for the first time in the history of the profession solicitors found themselves in purpose-built offices. Where the offices were not brand new they were in many cases refurbished. There was a determined effort to get rid of the clutter and dust of the past, and the principal's former dining table covered with files and papers was replaced by an office-desk kept as bare as possible. The old mass of papers had somehow been regarded as a sign of the solicitor's busyness; now it tended to be regarded as a sign of his inefficiency. Equipment was also drastically changed, partly because it was the fashion but mainly because shortage of staff and high wages made mechanisation necessary and economical. The larger and more progressive firms installed Telex from about 1965 onwards. The most urgent problem was that of getting trained and experienced staff at all levels but particularly of finding managing clerks. Recruitment before 1939 had been insufficient to meet the increased demand and compensate for wastage. One of the causes had been the low wages which had been paid.[71] In the post-1945 period the new entry was adversely affected by the competition from other professions and from industry and commerce and local and central government. The image of the 'managing clerk' did not help. The title 'clerk' was itself out of date; the young manager in industry and commerce was called an executive and that was applied as an adjective in numerous contexts to indicate a modern, forward-looking and energetic type of man and job. Moreover, 'managing clerk' had remained an ill-defined title. Although in many offices it was applied only to men in positions of responsibility with considerable experience and knowledge, it was given in some to men who were little better than office-boys. To give some meaning to the title The Law Society after the war introduced a scheme in co-operation with the Solicitors' Managing Clerks' Association for examinations to lead to a managing clerk's certificate, but the scheme was little used and in the early 1950s the average number of candidates was well below fifty a year. Employers gave little or no recognition to the certificates and the vast majority were probably unaware that there were such things. Accordingly The Law Society and the Association co-operated in the establishment of the Institute of Legal Executives. The Association itself ceased and the Institute started on 1st January 1963. The objectives were not dissimilar to those proposed in the 1880s. Managing clerks of sufficient experience could join the Institute as Fellows without examination, and at the end of the first year 6,530 had done so. Newcomers had to pass examinations of considerable difficulty. Recruitment was steady.

[71] It was reasonably argued during the 1960s and 1970s that solicitors' gross profits should be higher in order to enable them to pay better salaries to senior staff, not only for the purpose of keeping existing staff but to encourage recruitment for the future.

The number of students increased from 1,470 in 1963 to 4,538 in 1975; of Associates from 1,500 in 1963 to 3,630 in 1975; and of Fellows from 6,530 in 1963 to 6,629 in 1975. The maximum strength of the old Association had been only 2,600. The formation of the Institute greatly increased the status of the former managing clerks; they became another branch of the legal profession and from 1968 onwards their names appeared in the Law List. Naturally salaries reflected not only the higher cost of living but also the shortage of trained men and the better standing given by the Institute. Even in the 1950s a salary of £1,500 a year was frequently offered and £2,000 a year became recognised in the sixties as a normal rate, with much higher pay for London and for the better-experienced man. In spite of these changes the supply was quite inadequate and the assistant solicitor seemed to be in a fair way to replacing the unadmitted man, so that by the sixties The Law Society was looking to the time when the solicitor's work would be done entirely by solicitors assisted by secretarial staff, as in the United States of America and most western European countries. Perhaps the most noticeable change was the acceptance of the woman clerk. The male secretary disappeared. Warnings were given in the mid-1950s that some typists were grasping enough to ask for £9 a week together with luncheon vouchers and other unspecified perquisites, but it was not long before such a salary was as irrelevant as the wages of the thirties. In 1945 the profession finally decided that the woman clerk had come to stay and the Solicitors' Clerks' Pension Fund was in that year opened to women.

CHAPTER 7

Conveyancing

Conveyancing is the drawing of deeds and other instruments for transferring property from one person to another, and in common and even professional usage the term specifically relates to the operation of transferring land.[1] Because land is everywhere the one essential and permanent form of wealth, ownership of it has inevitably been the major concern of every jurisprudence, and that of England and Wales has been no exception. The acquisition of land, the proof of ownership of it, the defence of possession of it, and the right to transfer and charge it were all matters with which the courts whether of common law or equity were concerned from their earliest times. It is not germane to a history of the solicitors' profession to trace the development of early conveyancing procedures except to say that the more important of the devices adopted involved collusive litigation in order to bring a record of the transaction on the court rolls. The more mechanical part of the business therefore inevitably came into the hands of the attorneys, whether court officials or independent practitioners. In medieval times the volume was small, partly because of the limitations on free transfer and partly because land was held by comparatively few people. In Edward IV's reign it was reckoned that a fifth of all the land was or had been part of the royal demesne. The monastic houses were great landowners and they were accumulators of land rather than buyers and sellers. In their case and in that of the large lay owners such conveyancing as was required was done by their own staff.[2] It was the collapse of the feudal system in the fifteenth century and the dissolution of the monasteries in the sixteenth that changed the picture. The Wars of the Roses finally broke the power of the barons. When Henry VII summoned his first Parliament there were only twenty-nine temporal peers entitled to a writ of summons and even some of them were attainted. The new men were recruited from the merchant classes and they were eager buyers of land as an investment and an indispensable means to social and

[1] Technically 'land' not only means land but also includes anything permanently attached to the land, eg houses.

[2] The first precedent book which has been found dates from the reign of Edward I and was prepared by and for the use of a monastic house. It contains forty-one precedents (including one for an Oxford student's letter to his father): *Law Quarterly Review*, vol 7, p 63 et seq.

political advancement. There was a good deal of land on the market. With the confiscation of Waltham Abbey in 1540 the dissolution of the monasteries was completed and the distribution of their lands well under way. The new situation required help from Parliament, and the Statute of Uses in 1535 and the Statute of Enrolments in 1536 contributed. For the attorneys and solicitors these changes had particular significance. The concentration of the courts and the Bar at or near Westminster meant that litigation or that part of it which was worth doing tended to come to London, and the country attorney had little profit and much trouble from it. But conveyancing tended to be done locally in the nearest town to the property being transferred or charged. It became the backbone of country practice, and it is significant that the first precedent book for the use of the conveyancing attorney was Symboleography, published in 1590 and the work of William West.[3] He was an attorney of the Inner Temple but practising in Rotherham in Yorkshire, where he appeared briefly in a more public role as the adviser of the Earl of Shrewsbury when in 1583 Mary Queen of Scots was in the Earl's charge in nearby Sheffield Castle.

Although the attorneys and solicitors in every parish might be doing this work, there was nothing to prevent anyone who fancied it trying to augment his income in this way. In 1641 Sheppard's Touchstone of Common Assurances (the author is generally supposed to have been Mr Justice Dodderidge) described the men who engaged themselves in the business: 'Considering withal the mischief arising everywhere by the rash adventures of sundry ignorant men that meddle so much in these weighty matters, there being almost in every parish an unlearned yet confident attorney (not that I think all of them to be such) or a lawless scrivener that may perhaps have some law books in their houses but never read more than is on the back side of Littleton or an ignorant vicar, or it may be a blacksmith, the carpenter or weaver that have no more law books in their houses than they have law in their heads and yet as apt and able (if you believe them) either to judge of a conveyance and by the rules of law (of all of which they are utterly ignorant) to determine of the strength or goodness of a title ... or to make a conveyance to transfer the property of things from man to man.'[4]

Nevertheless there was sufficient business for the profession to call into existence a number of collections of precedents intended for its use. In 1653 the Young Clerk's Guide appeared with specimens of leases, conveyances, deeds of gift, wills and the like which the author considered would be very 'useful and necessary for all but chiefly to those that intend to follow the attorney's practice'; the third edition of the Compleat Clerk

[3] Cockburn, Rotherham Lawyers during 350 Years.

[4] Messrs Thomson, Snell & Passmore of Tonbridge trace their history to one Nicholas Hooper, a curate there in 1570, who 'made up his mind to augment his meagre stipend ... and set himself up as a scrivener, a drafter of documents, drawing up wills, charters and indentures' (The First Four Hundred, by Miss Margaret Blatcher, privately printed 1970).

justified the inclusion of similar precedents 'because the drawing of settlements of estates, joyntures, deeds of purchase and other instruments are often committed to attornies'. The courts regarded the attorney and solicitor in this respect as just another example of non-lawyers involving themselves in matters which only the Bar properly understood. It was not defamatory of an attorney to say that he 'made false writings', because drawing documents was not his business so that the words were not spoken of him in relation to his business and were no disgrace to him.[5]

In the eighteenth century the attorneys and solicitors were becoming much stronger in this field, as in so many others, and more confident of their position. When Bohun published his Practising Attorney in 1726 he described conveyancing as 'one of the most profitable and reputable branches of the business of an attorney'. By 1737 the work had run into four editions. Of the same period Roger North wrote: 'Anciently as I have been informed all conveyancing ... was done by the lawyers. Now the attorneys have the largest share.'[6] In London the Scriveners Company awoke to the fact that the attorneys were taking over much of the business which they had regarded as theirs, at any rate within the City itself. A scrivener was a tradesman who arranged loans and prepared the securities which evidenced and supported them, but in practice he did much more than that. An attorney, Nicholas Covert, published The Scrivener's Guide in the early eighteenth century. It contained precedents covering a wide range of conveyancing business and it too met a ready demand, going into four editions by 1724. No doubt it was bought by attorneys, but the fact that Mr Covert entitled his work as he did indicates the main market at which he was aiming and the scope of the scriveners' work at the time. To protect that business the Scriveners Company in 1749 summoned an attorney named Alexander to appear before the Lord Mayor's Court to answer an allegation that he had contravened a City by-law that 'no person shall follow any art, trade, occupation, mystery or handicraft without being free of the city'. The attorneys' concern was two-fold: they wished to be able to continue their conveyancing business unrestricted and they did not wish to have to become members of the Scriveners Company, which would have given them the status of tradesmen and placed them under the jurisdiction of tradesmen. The Society of Gentlemen Practisers resolved to support Mr Alexander, but he was convicted, as was almost inevitable in a case of this nature tried before a City jury. The conviction did not deter the attorneys from continuing their conveyancing business in the City, and accordingly the Scriveners brought prosecutions against a number of them. The Gentlemen Practisers undertook the defence, which was conducted with eighteenth-century finesse. The struggle was long and arduous; the essential step was to obtain an order that the cases should

[5] *Auditor Curle's Case* (1623), Win 40.
[6] Autobiography, chap xi, pp 140–141.

be tried before a jury who were not freemen of the City. The case of Mr William Smith was chosen as a test case and in December 1760 he appeared before the City recorder and a special jury. The recorder put the issue to the jury in this way: if they were satisfied that drawing deeds was the proper business of an attorney then they should find for the defendant, but if they were satisfied that it was the proper business of a scrivener they should find for the prosecution. The jury found for the defendant[7] on 11th December 1760 and the event was celebrated with a dinner. Counsel showed their sense of the solidarity of the profession when faced with intruders by refusing to accept any fees, and the Society presented each of them with a piece of silver suitably inscribed. There was no further dispute with the Scriveners, for whom this litigation seems to have been fatal. Jack Ellis, who often dined with Dr Johnson, was said to have been the last of them carrying on their normal business. For the profession their significance remains that an applicant for a faculty to practise as a notary public within the jurisdiction of the Company (mainly the City of London and Westminster) must take up the freedom of the Company. Scriveners were not included in the list of professions entitled to draw deeds in the Pitt legislation in 1804.

If there were those who wished to inhibit the attorneys, the attorneys themselves were concerned about what they considered now to be unfair competition. On 8th February 1763 the House of Commons received one of the most important petitions in the history of the profession. The petitioners were 'attornies and solicitors residing in the Cities of Bath and Wells, and in the counties of Somerset, Wilts, Hants, and Gloucester, and other Cities and Counties within that part of Great Britain called England' and they commenced by reminding the House of the Act of 1729 which permitted only attorneys and solicitors to sue out process and of the duty which they had to pay to the government. They then went on to say that they apprehended that 'the preparing of Conveyances of all sorts has, Time immemorial, been as much the Business of Attornies and Solicitors, as commencing or defending Suits at Law or Equity, but that Part of the Petitioners' Practice hath of late years been greatly reduced by the Interference of Schoolmasters, Parish Clerks and others, not skilled in such Matters and that the Petitioners apprehend that by passing the said Law, the Legislature intended that the Business and Profession of an Attorney and Solicitor should be conducted by men who had by their education gained knowledge and experience therein and which would prevent the Disorder and Confusion which the property of men would be subject unto under a contrary direction; and therefore conceive that the mischief in this Particular is equal to any provided against by the said Act: And therefore praying the House to permit a Bill to be brought in for restraining persons from drawing writing or ingrossing or perfecting any Deed, Conveyance, Assignment, Lease, Articles of Agreement, and any Writing or

[7] Gentlemen Practisers' Minutes, p 286.

Instrument whatsoever to be ingrossed on Stamps who shall not be a barrister at law, or an Attorney or Solicitor, legally admitted according to the Act above mentioned or Persons immediately employed, or who shall not be of the Scriveners Company in the City of London' or employees of the Bank of England and other companies when acting in the business of their employers.[8] The competitors referred to were of course almost the same as those mentioned by Sheppard a hundred years earlier.[9] The petition was noteworthy in two other particulars. It emphasised the public interest as well as that of the profession in preventing unqualified men dealing with property transactions; and it specifically reserved the right of the petitioners to employ about this business men who were not admitted. The petition was referred, as most petitions affecting legal practice and procedure were, to a committee which included all the gentlemen of the long robe. As the Bar then regarded the attorneys and solicitors as interlopers in this work almost as much as the attorneys and solicitors so regarded the schoolmaster and the parson it is not surprising that the petition did not result in any legislation.

The matter was, however, about to be resolved. In 1782 the younger Pitt went to the Treasury and started a chain of events of immense significance to the profession and particularly in relation to conveyancing. In 1784 the Stamp Act imposed stamp duties on deeds prepared by attorneys and solicitors but, probably by inadvertence but possibly because of the greater difficulty of collection, not on deeds prepared by others. This was serious enough because it penalised those who employed attorneys and solicitors in conveyancing matters. In 1785 Pitt found that he needed another £20,000 to offset revenue lost as a result of a change in the tax on shops. He told the House of Commons that to find that money he proposed to resort to a subject on which many had run before him and therefore he was not apprehensive of its being objected to. It was a tax on attorneys. The announcement was received with loud cheers.[10] With that encouragement Pitt, who had by that time retired from practice at the Bar, spoke with irony of 'certain Practitioners in the Law' and expressed the hope that 'perhaps the tax might in some degree diminish the number of those gentry but in so doing the public would be much benefited for at present they were too numerous'. So far as he could ascertain there were 3,000 of them in the country and 1,400 in London, so that with the former at £3 a head producing £9,000 and the latter at £5 a head producing £7,000 he was in a fair way to recouping the money he had lost on the shops.[11] The attorneys and solicitors were therefore now to pay what for many was a substantial fee to practise in competition with men who paid none and whose clients were exempt from stamp duty on their transactions.

[8] House of Commons Journals, vol 29, p 445.

[9] See p 126, *supra*.

[10] Parliamentary Debates, vol 62, 3rd Series, p 175.

[11] Cobbett's Parliamentary History, vol 25, cols 812–813.

They reacted at once. On 7th March 1786 three petitions were presented to the House of Commons by practitioners in the courts of law and equity on behalf of themselves and their brethren. The petitioners made a number of points: first, that the fees they were allowed to charge had been fixed at a very distant period and were 'in consequence of an advance in the price of all the necessaries of life become an inadequate compensation for their trouble'; secondly, that the stamp duties which had been imposed lessened their profits because they had to lay out the money to pay the duties and then recover them without interest from their clients; thirdly, that the recent annual duties had further increased their burdens; fourthly, that the 1785 Act 'did not extend to a description of persons who call themselves conveyancers who in respect of the liberality of their fees and their immediate re-imbursement of sums expended are better able to bear the burthen of taxation' than the attorneys and solicitors; and fifthly—and in the context perhaps the most important point—that 'for want of a positive law restrictive of the practice of conveyancing many illiterate and unqualified men have intruded themselves into that branch of the profession to the great prejudice of the public, by the promotion of litigation and the disgrace of the profession of the law'.[12]

The petitions were unheeded. Pitt, having found a useful new source of revenue, tapped it further. In 1795 he imposed a £100 stamp duty on articles of clerkship in London and one of £50 in the country; in 1797 he imposed a duty of £8 on admission certificates. In 1804 he decided to double the annual fee and raise the duty on articles of clerkship. On Friday 6th July he sent to the Gentlemen Practisers a copy of the schedules to the new Stamp Act embodying this and other proposals affecting the practice of the law; on 9th July he received 'a copy of resolutions entered into last Saturday by several persons calling themselves a Law Society'.[13] The resolutions were against the proposals and Pitt saw a delegation from the Gentlemen Practisers. He was not prepared to withdraw his proposals, though he modified them by making the increase effective only after a man had been in practice three years. He also agreed to adopt a draft clause submitted to him by the Gentlemen Practisers which provided in effect that there should be a penalty of £50 on 'every person who shall for or in expectation of any fee gain or reward directly or indirectly draw or prepare any conveyance of or deed relating to any real or personal property or any proceedings in law or equity other than and except serjeants at law, barristers, solicitors, attorneys, notaries, proctors, agents or procurators having obtained regular certificates and special pleaders, draftsmen in equity and conveyancers being members of one of the Inns of Court' and having taken out the prescribed certificate and paid the fee. No reference to this clause was made in the debates, although the proposals generally were bitterly fought by Sheridan in particular. He 'condemned the annual

[12] House of Commons Journals, vol 41, p 301.

[13] Cobbett, op cit, col 963.

licences required for attorneys as illegal and oppressive; there were good and bad in all professions and why should they be selected for this burden; why might it not as well be laid on physicians and merchants?'.[14] It would have been inconsistent for the opposition to have objected to a provision which at any rate gave something to the attorneys in return for the special taxation imposed on them.

It was this new provision which created the so-called conveyancing monopoly, which ever since has been the subject of considerable controversy, in particular as to whether the provision was introduced and continued because it was needed to secure the revenue or because it was necessary in the public interest. No contemporary statement in or out of Parliament was made as to the object. The revenue connection is manifest from the fact that the provision was introduced in a Stamp Act, was until 1921 enforceable only at the instance of the Inland Revenue, and was part of fiscal legislation until the Solicitors Act 1932. But there were other cogent reasons for Pitt agreeing to introduce the penalty. The arrogance of his speeches on the Bill in relation to lawyers in general and the attorneys in particular is evidence that he would feel no need to make any concession to them which the public interest did not warrant. The loophole in the existing Stamp Acts was the exemption from duty of documents prepared by laymen and that could have been readily closed. However much the attorneys and solicitors might protest about the certificate duty, they would have no alternative but to pay it. But Pitt would have readily seen and conceded that it was reasonable to extend to conveyancing the same restriction as had for five hundred years applied to litigation. If, as had never been doubted, it was in their own and the public interest that litigants should be represented only by qualified men, it was logical that men involved in the equally or more important business of buying and selling land should also be represented only by qualified men. There was in this respect the additional reason that, however perfect English land law might be in theory, it was defective in practice. 'We believe it may be confidently asserted that of the real property of England a very considerable proportion is in one of these two predicaments: either the want of security against the existence of latent deeds renders actually unsafe a title which is yet marketable or the want of means of procuring the formal requisites of title renders unmarketable a title which is substantially safe.' That was the view of the Real Property Commission in 1830, and the *Morning Herald* in 1846 said that 'there is scarcely a title marketable'. The situation was certainly not better in 1804. Limitation of the business of conveyancing would not cure that condition for many years, but it would be a step in the right direction.

The Gentlemen Practisers may well have thought that they had achieved a satisfactory compromise, but from the outset the annual certificate tax was a matter of the greatest annoyance to many in the profession. As early

[14] Ibid, col 1013.

as 1806 a Mr Charles Ilfley of New Inn published a pamphlet in which he contended that the 'tax is entirely indefensible on any just principle'. He was answered in another pamphlet entitled 'Defence of Attorneys' which stated what became the classic defence: the tax was calculated to 'render the profession more respectable and eventually to cause the members of it to rank higher in the estimation of society, inasmuch as it will have a tendency to drive out of the pale of the profession the vile pettifogger, to whom alone is attributable all the obloquy which the publick from a want of due diferimination attaches to the whole body'. It added two further defences of a less permanent character: first that 'it would be dangerous in times so perilous as the present to embarrass the measures of the Government by raising any objections to the payment of it' and secondly 'to defend the profession against the insinuation which has been thrown out as to the possibility of our being roused to war against the Constitution under any circumstances however pressing'.[15] The end of the war in 1815 left only the 'respectability' defence for a tax which was in that year raised for the London man to £12 from £10. As the circumstances in which the tax had been imposed receded into forgetfulness the opposition to it began to grow. The campaign for repeal formally started with petitions by The Law Society in 1842 and 1845, but for some time it did not seem that there was much drive behind it. The Annual Report for 1845 told members that the Council could not 'hold out much prospect of success'; that for 1846 assured them that the matter had not been 'lost sight of'; and that for 1847 referred to 'several considerations having induced the Council to defer the effort in the present session'. When the *Law Times* started publication in 1843 with its predominantly country attorney support it seized on this matter as one in which it could do something practical and at the same time attack The Law Society and Mr Maugham. It asserted that 'the plain fact is that there is no sincere desire on the part of the leaders of the profession in London to be rid of the tax. It falls lightly on them. £12 makes but a small hole in incomes of two or three thousand a year and the leviathans of the law have a notion it helps to keep out rivals—it deters their confidential clerks from getting into the profession.'[16] There was some truth in that assertion. Mr Maugham in his Treatise on Attorneys had already stated his understanding that the duties were intended to improve the respectability of the profession and he might be assumed therefore to approve them. The *Legal Observer*, which was in effect the mouthpiece of the Council, carried some letters from men who warned 'the profession, if it gets rid of the tax it must relinquish its privileges'[17] and related the continuance of the tax directly to the conveyancing monopoly. Although the annual certificate duty was quite illogical, the Council felt it best to go slowly and was particularly anxious lest the cam-

[15] *Gentleman's Magazine*, February 1806, p 153.
[16] Vol 10 (1845), p 384.
[17] Vol 23, p 519.

paign might result in a reduction of the stamp duty on articles, which nobody wanted. At any rate the early pressure came mainly from outside The Law Society. In 1842 there were no fewer than thirty-three petitions from towns throughout the country against the tax; in 1844, the Metropolitan and Provincial Law Association organised a mammoth petition said to have been signed by a majority of solicitors and presented to the House of Commons by Sir Thomas Wilde, a former attorney and a future Lord Chancellor. In 1848 a meeting was organised by the *Law Times* in London and was respectably attended. The *Law Times* reported that on their way to the meeting a number of provincial attorneys called on Mr Maugham to find out what The Law Society was doing. Whether this was so or not, the fact is that the Society became much more active and the *Legal Observer* much more emphatic in its opposition to the duty. The campaign had the support in the House of Commons of Lord Robert Grosvenor, one of the members for Middlesex. In 1850 he obtained leave to bring in a Bill to repeal the annual duty with a majority of 155 to 136, but the Bill was deferred until the next year; in 1851 leave was again given, but the Bill was abandoned. The *Law Times* was beside itself. Victory had been so close, so inevitable, almost announced, and now 'the surrender was unconditional'. Political pressure was put on members of Parliament, and it was all the more effective because many of the attorneys were also election agents. Petitions piled on petitions. Advice as to how to make and present them was given in the legal press. Except for *The Times*, the non-legal press was strongly for repeal, though it was doubtful if it would be achieved. When Mr Disraeli was Chancellor of the Exchequer in 1852 he was encouraging, but his party's position was too uncertain for him to be specific. By 1853 leave to bring in a repeal Bill had been given no fewer than six times but without result. In that year Mr Gladstone became Chancellor of the Exchequer and he soon made it clear that he was heartily sick of the whole argument, knew the whys and wherefores so well that he did not need to hear any more deputations, and was going to put an end to it. He told the House when he presented his Budget: 'The profession said: "Take the tax off the annual certificates of those who are in the profession; leave those who have to enter to pay precisely the same".' He did not think that was right, and with £50,000 to spare he had decided to allocate it by reducing the certificate duty from £12 to £8 and from £8 to £6 and the stamp duty on articles from £120 to £80.[18] It was the very result which the Council had feared. The *Law Times* described it as 'the heaviest blow and the greatest discouragement which the profession had been subject to for many a year'.[19] The truth seemed to dawn on the profession that it had better be content with what it had through wiser counsels obtaining fifty years earlier. The *Law Times* had to confess it had changed its mind; the Council found that its enquiries as to taking the matter further

[18] Hansard, vol 125, 3rd Series, col 1407.

[19] Vol 21 (1853), p 178.

met with very little encouragement from the country; the topic which had for four or five years appropriated so much space in the legal press now scarcely rated a mention.

Whether the penalty on unqualified conveyancers was of much practical importance in the nineteenth century is open to doubt. Enforcement was in the hands of the Inland Revenue and was by way of the cumbersome procedure of an action for the fine in the High Court on the information of the Attorney-General. The Annual Reports of The Law Society suggest that he could be moved to take action only on the presentation of the most cogent evidence, and the Council could do little more than warn those who wished to complain of encroachments that they must have their tackle in perfect order if they were to have any prospect of action. Although such cases would have been of the greatest interest to the profession, there are few if any reported in the legal press, and it is reasonable to suppose that there were not enough undertaken to be of any significance. It was not until the Finance Act 1921 made the infringements punishable summarily that The Law Society could take action of its own initiative. Probably the most effective deterrent until then was that the profession itself, without any minimum fee rule, was prepared to do this class of work at such a low price that there was scarcely any scope or need for the amateur or semi-professional. In 1874 Lord Cairns told the Select Committee on the Land Titles and Transfer Bill that 'some solicitors told me that they had cut up a piece of land into 300 or 400 parcels to build some houses for working people upon ... and they made a charge including every expense to the purchasers and the charge would be as low as 10s and in a great many cases 20s'; in 1889 a solicitor in Hastings was reported to be prepared to act for vendors at 5s per cent; and in 1893 the Birmingham Law Society said that in its area building plots were conveyed at a cost to the purchaser of £2 2s plus stamp duty. Of the permitted competitors the certified conveyancer was treated as a serious vexation. The Inns of Court allowed more men than had been expected to become members solely for the purpose of being 'certified' and without any intention of being called to the Bar. It had also been expected that the certified conveyancers would, as members of the Bar usually did, confine themselves to drafting. Instead they often carried on ordinary conveyancing business. The attorneys protested at this competition from men who were free of any discipline and exempt from the most burdensome of the taxes imposed on themselves. As early as 1785 there had been a petition to the House of Commons that 'the gentlemen practising under the Bar should be restricted to their legitimate province'. The Gentlemen Practisers resolved to thank a Mr Charles Barton of the Inner Temple for deprecating in his book The Elements of Conveyancing 'the practice of conveyancers of assimilating with their own the business of the solicitor'.[20] The Law Society in 1846 suggested that no new certificates should be issued, leaving the existing certi-

[20] Minutes, p 180.

fied conveyancers to continue; in 1851 and 1852 there were protests to the Benchers; in 1860 the Solicitors Act required new entrants to obtain an annual certificate from the Benchers. The position of the existing practitioners was not affected, but this provision appears to have solved the problem. In real terms it was much smaller than the protests suggested. According to the Law Lists there were only thirty-nine conveyancers in 1790; forty-two in 1840; thirty-seven in 1870; ten in 1890; and in 1910 there were only two. Of these the survivor was Mr Whitty Chandler, who died in 1927 in Bournemouth, where he had practised in his latter years. Certified conveyancers died with him, and in the Solicitors Act 1949, which repealed the 1860 Act, they were not mentioned.

Manifestly the profession's main competitor was the Bar. In this instance there could be no arguments based on lack of skill, want of authority customary or statutory, damage to the public, and the other reasons repeated endlessly in complaints against other competitors. If the Bar was excluded from ordinary conveyancing business it was by its own choice and practice. The full realisation of the situation which had been created seems to have occurred about the middle of the nineteenth century. In 1849 it was said that 'the great improvements which have of late years taken place in the education of attorneys and solicitors must necessarily have the effect of rendering them more qualified to perform the onerous and multifarious duties which have now by long custom devolved on them'[21] and in 1862 that their practice extended 'over a much wider field than the terms of attorney or solicitor strictly import, encroaching in a great degree on the formerly exclusive province of a barrister'.[22] *The Times* in 1851 fulminated against the Bar rule which required the intervention of an attorney or solicitor in conveyancing matters and the payment of two men for work which one man could have done. In 1857: 'In the conveyancing department it is well-known how vast a proportion of country business is engrossed by attorneys at the present day' and as 'respects the relative position of the two branches of the profession there has undeniably been a vast loss of business to the conveyancing barristers';[23] in 1851 a member of the Bar wrote: 'Every private individual who has bought or sold a house … must have an attorney. When anything concerning property is to be settled or unsettled, it is he who dictates what is to be done.'[24] The practicality of the matter was that the lay client had by Bar usage to instruct an attorney or solicitor before he could obtain the services of counsel; in conveyancing business it became less and less necessary to consult counsel; as a result the whole of the business was transacted in the attorney's office and counsel saw nothing of it. This was difficult terrain. The self-denying Bar rule was severely questioned[25] and was not uniformly observed. In

[21] Pulling, Law of Attorneys, p 160.
[22] Ibid, 1862 ed, p 10.
[23] *Law Magazine and Review*, p 241.
[24] Johnston, England As It Is, p 170.
[25] Chapter 9, *infra*.

1881 The Law Society reported to the Inner Temple the case of counsel who had on the instructions of a lay client prepared an abstract of title, perused a draft conveyance, and answered requisitions on title. The Benchers severely censured the barrister and cautioned him as to his future conduct.[26] On the other hand the Attorney-General as head of the Bar in 1888 made a statement which affirmed the right of counsel to accept instructions direct from the lay client in non-litigious matters.[27]

The matter resolved itself on the basis of a demarcation of functions. The Annual Statement of the Bar for 1902–1903 said that 'a barrister should not act for both parties as the sole "lawyer" in a conveyance of property, either attending or not attending completion, nor should he act as such for one of the parties personally, sending or receiving the draft conveyance, abstract of title etc'.[28] There were two further rulings in the Annual Statements for 1919 and 1924 that 'it is contrary to professional etiquette for a barrister to carry through conveyancing matters by sending requisitions, examining documents and attending completions whether for remuneration or not, which business is ordinarily done by a solicitor'. Practical conveyancing was the work of solicitors and drafting documents was the work of counsel. Solicitors interpreted 'practical conveyancing' as 'the ordinary work of making searches and preliminary enquiries, preparing or investigating abstracts of title, correspondence, sending in and answering requisitions, perusing conveyances and carrying out completions'.[29] That was in any event work which the Bar was not equipped to do, and because the demarcation was on this factual basis it appears to have been generally accepted until in 1949 in the Annual Statement of the Bar an exception was made in respect of barristers who were clerks to local authorities. The solicitors were seriously concerned, although the number of barristers affected was then small. The ruling had, however, the danger to solicitors that if barristers who were local authority clerks could do solicitors' work there would be a temptation for local authorities to appoint them and so impinge on what was practically a solicitor-monopoly. The Law Society suggested a compromise in 1952 that when a barrister-clerk was doing the practical work of conveyancing he should do it *qua* clerk and not *qua* barrister. This was rejected. The Bar contended that s 48 of the Solicitors Act 1932 (which specifically reserved the right of barristers to draw or prepare Land Registry transfers and to lodge documents at the Land Registry) was irreconcilable with The Law Society's contention. But The Law Society regarded the whole matter differently. 'To us this is a vital matter of principle. The fact that the number of barristers who may be affected by it is small is quite immaterial. Potentially

[26] *Law Society's Gazette*, vol 51 (1954), p 120.

[27] This right was restated in the Bar Annual Statements in 1919 and 1924, but with the qualification referred to later as to conveyancing.

[28] *Law Society's Gazette*, vol 51 (1954), p 120.

[29] Ibid.

the number is enormous.'[30] There were further negotiations and ultimately the Bar Council in 1955 withdrew the rulings of which The Law Society had complained.[31] The only concession was an agreement that barristers who had been employed by local authorities before the 1949 rulings were withdrawn might still do practical conveyancing.[32] Perhaps because nobody said anything officially about it, barristers in the civil service doing solicitors' work escaped formal attention.[33]

The amount of conveyancing business of any sort which came to the Bar was in any event decreasing. The land law reforms of the mid-nineteenth century and later greatly simplified conveyancing and made reference to counsel less and less necessary. The introduction in 1883 of an *ad valorem* scale for fixing the permitted charges on a conveyancing transaction[34] may also have made it less attractive to solicitors to instruct counsel since their own charges could not be any higher even if they did so.[35] When a barrister in 1920 repeated the claim that there was nothing in law to prevent him accepting instructions direct from a lay client in conveyancing business the *Solicitors' Journal* commented that it did not really matter very much in practice whether the claim was right or wrong: 'Counsel get less of the easy straight-forward work than in the old times but that is as it should be. It is the only justification for the conveyancing Bar.'[36] The erosion of the Bar's share in the conveyancing work was gradual and apart from the furore of the 1850s attracted little attention. It certainly needed no accelerating pressure from the solicitors. They were in any event much more concerned with the threat from 'officialdom' which they saw in the persistent attempts by one government after another to introduce a system of compulsory land registration.

Officialdom in the nineteenth century was anathema to all right-thinking men conducting their own businesses and it was all the more so when it seemed to endanger their livelihood. At the end of the eighteenth century it is likely that conveyancing was a useful adjunct to profits earned from other professional work but not much more.[37] By the middle of the nineteenth century the picture had changed. 'If the scheme for registration of titles to be produced next session is anything like that which has been described in the newspapers, half the solicitors in the country must be prepared to shut up their offices. Three-fourths of the business of the profession in the provinces—all indeed which is worth having—comes from

[30] *Law Society's Gazette*, vol 51 (1954), p 125.

[31] Law Society's Annual Report, 1955–1956, p 21.

[32] Annual Statement of the Bar, 1959, p 25.

[33] *Solicitors' Journal*, vol 101 (1957), pp 6 and 7.

[34] Solicitors' Remuneration Order 1883.

[35] Abel-Smith and Stevens, Lawyers and the Courts, pp 213–214.

[36] Vol 64, p 71.

[37] Robson, The Attorney in Eighteenth Century England, p 163. Mr Christopher Wallis' accounts show that in 1804 out of £2,130 profit only £230 came from conveyancing; and in 1805 the figures were £1,610 and £150. But in any event his profits were largely from 'extra-professional' business.

conveyancing.'[38] A directly contrary view was expressed in 1862: 'It is notorious that conveyancing is the least remunerative of the employments ... of a solicitor',[39] but that was a lone voice and nobody at the time or since has supported it. All the indications are that conveyancing had become the most important part of the profession's business. The profession rightly or wrongly was convinced that land registration would in the long run mean that conveyancing would be done by officials and be lost to the profession. Its opposition to the introduction of the system was understandably bitter.

There was nothing new about the idea of a land registry or registry of deeds. Bills with this purpose in view were introduced in 1529 and 1535;[40] Cromwell attempted to deal with the 'ungodly jumble' of English land law and put forward a scheme for a Universal Register of Titles to the Barebones Parliament in 1653 but 'the sons of Zerniah' were too strong even for him;[41] Lord North was said to have prepared Bills in the same sense in the latter part of the seventeenth century;[42] during the period 1685 to 1700 there were at least six attempts at legislation. Roger North lamented the failure of his own design, which he considered 'the best ... that ever was advanced for the establishment of English titles', and continued: 'Let posterity reflect what advantages might have been to them from it if their predecessors had suffered it to pass.'[43] Eighteenth-century lawyers were so pleased with English law in its every aspect, and after them Lord Eldon in his long term as Lord Chancellor—from 1801 to 1806 and from 1807 to 1827—was so adamant against every change, that it was not until 1830 that the earlier ideas were revived. A commission was appointed to report as to the state of real property law and reported in 1830. It was satisfied about the law itself, but recognised the defects in conveyancing practice which made titles unmarketable, and specified one of the causes as the want of security against latent deeds. A solicitor named Fonnereau practising in London suggested the solution: 'A registry of the property—a registry which should in itself be evidence not of a deed but of a title—would be highly beneficial by accomplishing finality and cheapness of transfer as well as security of title.' There had long been deeds registries in Yorkshire—the one in the West Riding was established in 1703, that in the East in 1707 and the third in the North in 1735; and the Middlesex Deeds Registry was set up in 1708. The first proposals which were based on the recommendations of the Registration and Conveyancing Royal Commission of 1857 were very different: they involved a title registry and they were embodied in the Land Transfer (or Land Registry) Act 1862.

[38] *Law Times*, vol 28 (1857), p 209; in 1966 fifty-four per cent of the profession's gross income came from conveyancing.

[39] *Solicitors' Journal*, vol 6 (1862), p 353: at the time this paper favoured registration.

[40] Holdsworth, History of English Law, vol 4, pp 572–574.

[41] Ludlow, Memoirs, vol 1, p 333.

[42] He was Attorney-General in 1671 and Chief Justice of Common Pleas in 1674.

[43] Autobiography, p 188.

It was these which had caused such anxiety in the profession. The new Land Registry opened in October 1862 with two barristers as its Chief and Deputy Land Registrars. The *Solicitors' Journal* considered that it would be 'no less the interest than the policy of lawyers to accept loyally and turn to the best account what the legislature had passed' and that 'at least for many years to come solicitors will be the gainers rather than the losers by the new system of land transfer'.[44] The *Journal* was still regarded as expressing the views of the Council of The Law Society, and the country solicitor for forty years or more suspected that the Council favoured title registration. At any rate the profession did not take to the new system. In its time the Registry only took on 488 first registrations and at one time it was said that these were running at no more than eighteen a year. The failure could not, however, be attributed to the hostility or apathy of the solicitors. Lord Cairns afterwards confirmed that it was no 'opposition of solicitors which caused the failure of the Act of 1862',[45] and the Royal Commission of 1869 set up to enquire into the operation of the Act reported that there was no foundation for the allegation that the body of solicitors were 'hostile to the system'.[46] There was no compulsion to register, and not many solicitors saw any reason to do so voluntarily. Those who did were not encouraged by the procedure at the Registry. The two registrars were determined not to accept any but perfect titles, and there were cases where their examination of titles took as long as two years and seven months to complete. Notwithstanding the kind words used by Lord Cairns and the Commissioners, the Royal Commission suggested that if title registration was to succeed there should be some element of compulsion, and it was this recommendation embodied into Bills introduced in 1873 by Lord Selborne and in 1874 by Lord Cairns which roused the profession to full-scale opposition.

The Associated Provincial Law Societies met on 30th April 1874 at Manchester to consider the 1874 Bill. The meeting was attended by representatives from Bolton, Gloucester, Leeds, Liverpool, Manchester and Newcastle-upon-Tyne, and they passed resolutions calling for the establishment of district registries, the postponement of compulsion until the system had been shown by experience to be satisfactory, and the restriction of registry business to solicitors. The Council of The Law Society had also considered the Bill and agreed that there should be no compulsion: 'A large majority of the Council and they have reason to believe of solicitors generally throughout the country are of the opinion that registration should not be made compulsory until experience for a much longer period than three years has tested the efficiency of the system. Several solicitors, however, consider that compulsory registration is necessary for effectually testing the efficiency of the system.'[47] That proviso was to assume major

[44] Vol 6, p 859.
[45] *Solicitors' Journal*, vol 18, p 393. [46] Para 20.
[47] Observations on the Land Titles and Transfer Bill 1874, p 7.

importance later on. Compulsion was a vital issue, and the Solicitor-General like many other politicians and public men resented the opposition of the solicitors to the proposed changes: 'Who objects to the amendment of that state of affairs?—the solicitors.' Nevertheless the 1874 Bill was withdrawn and the subsequent Land Transfer Act 1875 did not introduce compulsion.

But the idea of a national land registration system had not been abandoned, and in the 1885 election it was a major issue. It was hardly possible to pick up a newspaper without reading a statement by 'some candidate for parliamentary honours as an article of political faith that there must be a diminution in the cost and delay in the transfer of land'.[48] The politicians had no doubt as to who stood in the way of achieving that goal. The President at the 1885 Annual Provincial Meeting said: 'We have for electioneering and party purposes been represented as a set of harpies who render the transfer of land at a reasonable price impossible'; and the Duke of Marlborough said of solicitors that 'it is this profession which has signalised itself in history by fastening on this country even down to the present day one of the most fatal inheritances of middle-age feudalism namely an incomprehensible business language'.[49] But the profession was not deterred and organised a parliamentary opposition for the first time, and this may have helped to defeat in 1890 the Bills which were introduced in 1887 and 1889. The Land Registry was also not pacific. In 1889 it published notes containing phrases which the profession could not but regard as hostile: 'A vendor will hardly ever require a solicitor and most purchasers of average business ability will be able to do their own work also'; 'The fees now charged are fixed at about one-fifth of the scale costs which a solicitor is allowed to charge for conveyancing with unregistered land'; and 'Where registered land is sold or mortgaged as a whole the transaction may be completed by the parties themselves in a quarter of an hour'.[50] The notes produced a storm of protest from solicitors; refuge was sought in the excuse that their issue had not been authorised; and finally they were withdrawn. But the suspicions remained: 'Notice or no notice it will doubtless pursue its anti-solicitor campaign.'[51] When Lord Halsbury became Lord Chancellor in 1895 he determined to push land registration through and introduced the Bill which became the Land Transfer Act 1897. His predecessor Lord Herschell had tried again in 1893 and had received on 27th April 1893 a strong deputation from local law societies urging him—but without success—to refer the matter to a Select Committee. The profession was 'determined to oppose it to the bitter end',[52] but there had already been suspicions that there had been some negotia-

[48] *Solicitors' Journal*, vol 29 (1885), p 322.
[49] *Law Journal*, vol 20 (1885), p 575.
[50] See *Weekly Notes*, 1889, p 69, and *Solicitors' Journal*, vol 33 (1889), p 293.
[51] *Solicitors' Journal*, vol 33 (1889), p 344.
[52] *Law Notes*, vol 14 (1895), p 151.

tions for a compromise. When the 1897 Bill was being considered fourteen major local law societies met to decide on their attitude. The feeling ran high. It was openly stated that the meeting had been called so that The Law Society could say that it had abandoned its opposition to land registration because of the opinion of local law societies; it was pointed out that The Law Society had passed no resolutions on the Bill at all. The event lent some support to these rough North Country assessments. The Law Society withdrew its opposition and the Bill became law. The President explained to the Provincial Annual Meeting in 1897 that after consultation with the provincial law societies the Council had decided that 'the proper course would be to facilitate an Act for a trial of the scheme, confined to a limited district, and if the county council of that district did not object'.[53] Compromise was for many solicitors the equivalent of surrender if not of treachery, and the comments were bitter. 'Little wonder therefore if on this change of front becoming known the provincial solicitors felt stranded and helpless, the more so as the ability and industry of the Council in past years has been so great as to lull the provincials into inactive and grateful appreciation';[54] 'No one who has observed the course of recent events can doubt that as regards the protection of the profession against officialdom the central Society has ceased to be an effective agency';[55] and 'The Incorporated Law Society have become the pensioners of the government of the day'.[56] Lord Halsbury, the author of the Bill, was virulently criticised: 'The whole object of the Bill is the creation of officials at the expense of solicitors without the slightest advantage to the public. If the Bill passes Lord Halsbury will have succeeded in creating a system of political patronage which will hand his name down to posterity as the most cynically nepotic Lord Chancellor ever seated on the Woolsack.'[57]

The Council soon found itself in difficulties; it was 'hoist on its own petard'[58]. It had expected that the experimental area would be Yorkshire, but the Government decided on the County of London. As there were no local law societies in that area it fell to the Council to oppose the proposed Order in Council. The Yorkshire solicitors would have none of it and mounted a strenuous and in the end successful opposition. The leader of the House of Commons thanked them for 'the energy and public spirit [the County of York] had shown and for the steps it had taken in the advance of a rational solution of the problem'.[59] It was an issue which threatened to disrupt the profession and its organisation, all the more

[53] As reported *Solicitors' Journal*, vol 41, p 797.

[54] Mr Arthur Middleton in a letter to the *Solicitors' Journal*, 26th February 1898.

[55] *Solicitors' Journal*, vol 42 (1897–1898), p 92.

[56] Ibid.

[57] *Law Notes*, vol 16 (1897), p 111. This paper was published by the law tutors, Messrs Gibson & Weldon, and was widely read, particularly by articled clerks.

[58] *Solicitors' Journal*, vol 41 (1897), p 691.

[59] Ibid, p 692.

because to the country solicitor the whole business seemed to prove that the Council was interested in London and nothing else. In 1899 the local law societies in Yorkshire with two exceptions broke away from the Associated Provincial Law Societies, which they thought too much under the influence of the Council. The Yorkshire Union's objectives were first to resist encroachments and secondly to oppose undue increase in officialism. They rejected The Law Society: 'The palpable undeniable fact is that in this matter at any rate the Council of the Incorporated Law Society of the United Kingdom did not and does not represent the profession of the country.'[60] The membership of the Society, which had been growing steadily, for a time declined. In 1899 the net increase was only thirteen, in 1900 there was a decrease of 201, and in 1901 a net increase of only three. Worse still was to come. The Council had emphasised the experimental character of the new Registry; the period for the experiment was to be three years and the Council had believed it had an undertaking from the government that if the experiment had by that time not been a success the Registry would be closed or at any rate that there would be an enquiry into whether it had been a success or not. But the events did not support that interpretation. The expansion of the Registry staff did not seem consistent with a temporary experiment. The expenditure on salary and other services increased from £7,863 in 1897 to £38,393 in 1901. Certainly the government did not accept that it had given any undertaking. In 1902 it succeeded in extending registration to the City of London notwithstanding strong professional opposition. 'The long fight for a system of registration which is to make simple things in their nature complex has ended in London at least against the attorney. The Land Registry is open and full of officials. So the next generation of auctioneers and accountants or the next but one may hope to manage those dealings with land which have hitherto been the function of the solicitor.... So the attorneys may close their offices.'[61] The profession has never lacked prophets of the doom which every change in the familiar order of things seems bound to bring.

Although London had been lost, the struggle against further extension continued. When the so-called experimental period ended[62] the Council pressed the government at any rate to desist from making any new compulsory areas until there had been a full enquiry into the way in which the system had operated in London. The pressure was maintained by protest meetings and petitions. In 1905 the government announced its decision not to press for any further extensions in the immediate future[63] and in 1908 it appointed a Royal Commission to investigate the working of the Act. When the Commission reported in 1911 it was on the whole favour

[60] *Solicitors' Journal*, vol 44 (1899), p 169.
[61] Christian, Leaves of the Lower Branch (1909), p 275.
[62] The profession calculated the date to be 18th July 1901.
[63] The announcement was made by Mr Gerald Balfour to the Leeds Law Society and reported to a special general meeting of The Law Society in 1905.

able to the existing scheme and it recommended extension nationally. The profession therefore had to reconcile itself to the fact that compulsory land registration had come to stay, but it had the advantage that extensions could still be made only piecemeal on the initiative of the local authority for the area involved. This meant that opposition could be mounted on a local level and it also introduced the advantage that almost every local authority chief officer was a solicitor. The campaign was fought with bitterness on both sides. In 1911 the Lord Chancellor (Lord Loreburn) said that solicitors mulcted landowners of four millions a year in fees and accused the profession of standing in the way of land registration because of their aversion to learning a new system;[64] the most voluble of the solicitors, a Mr J S Rubinstein, published no less than seventeen booklets with titles such as 'The Land Transfer Scandal' and 'Nemesis', and in one he 'urged that the existence of the Land Registry is a standing menace to the country' and did not hesitate to use the then prevailing anti-German feeling and say that 'officialdom and compulsion are the idols at whose shrine the Germans worship'.[65] There were no further extensions before war interrupted, but solicitors saw with concern that the Land Registry buildings were being considerably enlarged and witnessed with mixed feelings the Chief Land Registrar[66] unfurl the Union Jack above them on 1st December 1913.

When the Birkenhead real property legislation was being considered in 1923 the Lord Chancellor promised The Law Society that there would be no change in the existing extension system until the expiration of ten years from the date when the new Acts came into force, that is not until 1st January 1936. There were two small extensions, namely to Eastbourne in 1926 and to Hastings in 1929; and to the County of Middlesex in 1937 and to Croydon in 1939. In 1942 the so-called Scott Committee[67] followed its predecessors in recommending compulsory registration for the whole country and suggested it should be done within five years. The Rushcliffe Committee set up immediately afterwards to report on the practicability of this time-limit favoured extension of compulsion by stages. It was, however, not until 1950 that the first order was sought. Surrey was chosen and the three local law societies involved called for an enquiry. They strongly opposed the order and their grounds were not markedly different from those which had been used in the 1880s and 1890s. Land registration meant an extension of bureaucracy and State monopoly. Again the question of costs was vital. Whatever the advantages of land registration, the profession opposed it so long as the fees for dealing with what was called registered land were markedly different from those paid on unregistered conveyancing. The order was nevertheless made[68] and this may have

[64] *Solicitors' Journal*, vol 55 (1910–1911), p 661.
[65] The Land Transfer Scandal, pp 61 and 63.
[66] Sir Charles Fortescue-Brickdale.
[67] Committee on Land Utilization in Rural Areas (Cmd 6378).
[68] SI 1952 No 395.

discouraged other local societies from opposing orders proposed for their own areas. But there were in any event persuasive factors in favour of the acceptance of registration. In 1953 the fees were increased so that the differential was only about one-third.[69] The problem of the profession was to overcome a serious shortage of trained staff in face of a rapidly increasing volume of conveyancing work. An abstract of title in respect of a large area being developed by division into numerous units could represent a major task for even the most experienced conveyancer, and would certainly cost a great deal to prepare. With registered title the solicitor could for a few shillings obtain what were called office copies of the title with plans; his opposite number was spared the chore of examining the deeds; and both had the guarantee that the title was good and marketable.[70] Moreover on a large development there was the great advantage that the Land Registry kept a map of all the sales off, so that there was an immediately available accurate map showing the up-to-date position. Local law societies no longer sought the help of 'Chancery Lane' when an extension order was proposed. Papers like the *Solicitors' Journal* expressed the opinion that 'unregistered conveyancing is wasteful and unsuited to the needs of the present day',[71] and the profession accepted that this was so. By the mid-sixties the majority were only too glad when an extension order was applied to their area and until then they generally advised their developer clients or indeed clients who had large estates or complicated titles to register voluntarily. The Law Society favoured extension as quickly as possible. The irony was that in the property boom of the early seventies the Chief Land Registrar had to restrict voluntary registrations. The old fear of bureaucracy and officialdom disappeared, partly because the profession had come to accept these as part of its life, but also because the Land Registry, at any rate after 1945, was singularly free from official attitudes. Solicitors pushed from their minds the danger which had seemed so real to their Victorian predecessors that simplification of conveyancing might be the forerunner of their own redundancy. In the meantime registration left them with no loss of profit as compared with the old system; apart from its savings, the differential in costs, such as it was, disappeared with the abolition of scale charges in 1972.[72]

The more pressing problems for the profession in the post-1945 period were conveyancing costs and the defence of the monopoly. The two problems were closely inter-related. It was an opinion widely held outside the profession that conveyancing costs were too high, which attracted intruders and instigated government enquiries into both the level of costs and the justification of the monopoly. Conveyancing costs had been a matter of great concern to the profession since 1843, when their bills for this

[69] *Solicitors' Journal*, vol 97, p 85.
[70] See on this Dr Gilchrist Smith in *Solicitors' Journal*, vol 101 (1957), p 13.
[71] *Solicitors' Journal*, vol 105 (1961), p 307.
[72] Solicitors' Remuneration Order 1972 (SI 1972 No 1139 L 14).

class of business became liable to taxation in the same way, by the same officials and on the same principles, as litigation bills.[73] Probably not many clients required their bills to be taxed or tried to hold their solicitors to the level of charges which would be allowed on taxation,[74] but in the absence of any other method of charging it was necessary to calculate fees on the basis of time spent and words written and read, and in theory at any rate the same fee was chargeable whether the work was done by an expert or a tyro. Whether the bill was to be taxed or not, the solicitor had to deliver one and inevitably had to set out in exhausting detail each item of work done. It was generally thought that this alone contributed greatly to the odium attaching to the profession and to its reputation of pettifogging. *The Times* described it as 'the odious system of paying for brain-work by the yard'.[75] The alternative was called the commission system, that is to say a scale of charges fixed by the amount of the sale price. The commission system was increasingly advocated from the mid-1850s onwards, and in 1870 the Council prepared a scheme which it submitted to the profession through the local law societies. It was not until 1880 that it adopted a much more elaborate scheme for submission to the Lord Chancellor as a necessary ancillary to the radical property law reforms then under way. It was a case where public and professional interest coincided. The Council thought that 'remuneration by commission or percentage is calculated to raise the character of the profession and will be acceptable to the public';[76] *The Times* thought that from the client's point of view it was requisite that he should 'be able to reckon without difficulty and as nearly as may be with absolute certainty what he must add to the price asked to represent the costs of the purchase. The scheme of The Law Society left no doubt on this head.'[77] The principle was adopted in the Solicitors' Remuneration Act 1881. Unfortunately the committee set up to make the order could not leave well alone and introduced unnecessary complications into the Society's scheme. The President refused to sign it and it was regretted that 'the signature wanting is that of the representative of the class which the order specially affects'.[78] Nevertheless the Solicitors' Remuneration Order 1883 became the guarantee of the profession's prosperity until 1972. By then the wheel had come full circle.

The fees fixed by the order were adjusted from time to time to take some account of the changes in the value of money. In 1925 they were increased by a third and that lasted until the financial crisis of 1931, when the increase was reduced to a quarter; it reverted to a third when things got better in 1936; in 1944 the increase was increased to one-half but was considered by solicitors to be quite inadequate to compensate them for a three-

[73] Attorneys Act 1842.

[74] See the evidence of Sir George Stephen to the Select Committee in 1846, ans 1982.

[75] Quoted *Law Times*, vol 74, p 214.

[76] Annual Report, 1881.

[77] Quoted *Law Times*, vol 74 (1883), p 214.

[78] Ibid.

fold rise in overheads, and they pressed for something much more substantial. They were handicapped by their own reticence about their affairs, and The Law Society had no figures on which any reliance could be placed. In the absence of such figures from the profession the Lord Chancellor asked if he might obtain some from the Inland Revenue, but the Council did not feel it had authority to agree. In spite of this, the Lord Chancellor produced statistics which showed that the average incomes of solicitors before tax in 1948–1949–1950 were more than double what they had been in 1938–1939, and the Council shifted its attack to non-scale remuneration.[79] The profession was in any event entering upon a period of comparative prosperity and its problem became rather one of defending what it had got than of increasing it. The *ad valorem* scale was particularly favourable in the middle price brackets, and that was now the range in which most properties were bought and sold. There was more than enough work to go round and the under-cutting which had been widespread between the wars was unnecessary. In 1936 the Council had made a practice rule under the powers conferred on it by the Solicitors Act 1933[80] which in effect made it a professional offence for a solicitor to hold himself out as prepared to do conveyancing work for less than the fee prescribed in the scale laid down by the local law society for the area in which the property conveyed was situated. At first local scales were generally less than the maximum permitted by the Remuneration Order—generally they were eighty-five per cent of it—but the pressure was towards making local scales the same as the maximum because it was illogical for the profession to complain about the level of its fees whilst charging less than the law permitted. As the Master of the Rolls in 1950 refused to approve a practice rule which would have made it a professional offence to charge less than the scale fee whether or not there was a local scale in operation, there was also urgency in the completion of the local law society network. By 1962 that was achieved and by 1964 there were only four out of the 117 local societies which either had no local scale or fixed less than one hundred per cent of the permitted charge as their local scale. For practical purposes outside London—the Holborn and Westminster Societies were two of those without a local scale—the maximum charge and become the minimum which a solicitor could properly make. The practitioner found it easy to explain to clients that, whatever his own wishes might be, he had no alternative but to charge the maximum. There were some other adjustments which increased the scale fees. The 1953 Order removed the previous top limit of the scale—£100,000—and this became of increasing importance with the rise in property prices; and in 1960 the scale at the other end, that is in respect of transactions involving less than £1,000, was increased.

The profession came under heavy fire on account of its policy in relation

[79] *Supra*, p 93.
[80] The Solicitors' Practice Rules 1936 (SI 1936 No 1005).

to costs and the level of conveyancing charges during the 1960s and early 1970s. It did not have many friends. The *Estates Gazette* said in 1962 that 'in our opinion the skilled work of solicitors' conveyancing departments is heavily underpaid',[81] but almost without exception the press and what were by then called 'the media' were hostile. The young married couple buying their first house with their joint savings and a building society mortgage were the favourites of the critics. The property they would be hoping to buy would be costing £3,000 and with a building society mortgage the legal costs amounted to over £70; before the war the same property would have cost £400 and the solicitor's costs would have been £6 or £7 for the same amount of work. The fact that 'the price was fixed' was particularly disliked because public opinion was moving strongly against price maintenance. A monopoly has never been a popular concept, and a monopoly operated so as to exclude competition from outside and price-competition from within was inevitably open to attack. The monopoly itself appeared to be seriously threatened by the activities of a Mr S G Carter who in 1960 founded the National House Owners Society in Harrow for the purpose of carrying out conveyancing transactions without using a solicitor and at something like one-half of the scale charges. In 1965 he was prosecuted for preparing conveyances and transfers for fee, gain or reward contrary to the Solicitors Act 1957. He was convicted, was fined £250, and had to pay 100 guineas costs. He appealed, but his appeals except on one technical issue were dismissed. Mr Carter represented himself as a crusader, and he had substantial support outside the profession. The maximum fine which could be imposed for each offence was £50 and was not higher in respect of subsequent convictions. Proving an offence was a difficult matter and inevitably Mr Carter and any others who might imitate him would have a long run before they were convicted. The NHOS, as it was called in the profession, flourished and could afford to take the risk. In 1967 the Director of Public Prosecutions prosecuted him for further breaches, and again Mr Carter was convicted and his appeals were dismissed. The Law Society was faced with a difficult decision. Further prosecutions only gave the NHOS more publicity and enabled Mr Carter to play the part of the small man challenging the large corporation. Clearly fines were not a deterrent. Mr Carter had in any event started using what was called the 'honorary conveyancer' device. The Act only prohibited the drawing of deeds and similar operations for fee, gain or reward by an unqualified person; all other steps in the conveyancing work could be done by anybody at a fee. Accordingly Mr Carter appointed one of his friends to do for nothing that part of the work which was prohibited to the unqualified if paid. Mr Blower, who was appointed, had no knowledge of conveyancing and the device was a palpable attempt at evasion. The problems facing The Law Society were, however, such that one experienced commentator wrote: 'It is clear that The Law Society would break com-

[81] 8th September.

petitors like Mr Carter if it could (and equally, that in all probability in this particular case it will fail).'[82] Nevertheless in 1968 The Law Society tried again. Because fines had been useless it applied to the High Court for an injunction to restrain Mr Carter from committing further breaches.[83] The action was settled in 1971 on Mr Carter giving an undertaking not to offend again, but he reappeared on the scene in 1972, by which time NHOS had been changed to House Owners Co-operative Ltd and registered as a friendly society. In 1973 three agents of NHOS, namely Messrs Blower. Hickmott and Duke, were prosecuted and convicted on a total of fifteen charges; the total fines were £750 and the costs £450. By this time, however, Mr Carter had been eliminated. He had quarrelled with some of his agents and as a result information as to his method of operation, particularly in relation to the finances of the NHOS, was revealed. He was interviewed on Granada Television on 15th January 1973. It was disclosed to a very wide public (as the profession had long known) that seven of the NHOS employees were ex-solicitors who had been struck off the roll and ex-solicitors' clerks who had been convicted for offences involving dishonesty. There were also problems about the Society's accounts, long overdue, and £75,000 of members' money and out-of-date pamphlets. The programme ended with the words: 'We can only hope that by the next Annual General Meeting, whenever that is, Sydney Carter will put his house in order. Until then we advise any home buyer to think very carefully before deciding to join the cut-price society of Sydney Carter.'

Although this was fatal to Mr Carter, he had opened up attractive possibilities. He claimed that in ten years he had helped 5,000 clients. Others were not deterred by the prospect of proceedings from trying their hands. The Property Transfer Association was a splinter from the NHOS and it used the 'honorary conveyancer' device. Its three principal officers were convicted at Worcester in June 1974, but that did not stop it from carrying on its business. The National House Owners Co-operative Society was claiming in 1975 that its business was expanding and a member of Parliament named Weetch became its chairman. Another firm known as Homes Organisation had by that time four offices and eight associated offices. On a completely different tack were two other companies using the title insurance method widely known in the United States of America. Stewart Title, a subsidiary of an American title insurance company, started in business in 1974 with considerable publicity and for some time had Lord George-Brown, a former cabinet minister, as its chairman. National Conveyancing Guarantee Ltd, based on York, had in 1975 nine other offices. The monopoly again became the subject of questions in the House of Commons and articles and correspondence in the press, particularly *The Times*. There were demands for a Royal Commission and proposals for legisla-

[82] Zander, Lawyers and the Public Interest, p 178.

[83] The action was by the Attorney-General on the relation of The Law Society. The terms are reported at *Solicitors' Journal*, vol 115, pp 890–891.

tion. The monopoly was limited to the preparation of the deed effecting the transaction; every other step could be taken by a layman. The abolitionists' argument was that with the rapid spread of title registration the preparation of the deed was a simple matter—something which was no more than high-grade clerical work carried out in many cases in a couple of minutes. There was a certain familiarity about the debate. In 1975 Mr Weetch tried to introduce a Bill with the object of abolishing the monopoly; a Mr Drummond had done the same thing in 1850. The complaints and fears of the profession at the encroachments of the unqualified in the 1960s and 1970s had already been expressed in the 1840s: 'In the country at this moment there are a considerable number of persons neither certificated nor attorneys prosecuting a thriving practice greatly to the detriment of those who to fit themselves for their profession have spent a considerable time in study.'[84]

In the meantime the problem of conveyancing costs was being resolved. The profession was subject to a mounting volume of adverse criticism. The *Solicitors' Journal* on 27th March 1964 wrote: 'Something must be done about the present conveyancing fees scale ... the question is becoming one of urgent public discussion and one we cannot ignore.' On 7th April 1964 a private member's Bill was introduced by a Mr Edwards reducing scale charges by one-half and prohibiting increases in the future. On 10th April 1964 the *Solicitors' Journal* wrote that 'the attacks continue'. It was widely reported that the Secretary-General had been given a warning by the then Prime Minister (Mr Wilson) that the government was considering giving local authorities power to transact conveyancing business and that costs were a material factor. This particular canard was disposed of on 14th May 1964 when the government stated that it did not think it would help to involve local authorities in business which had nothing to do with their public responsibilities, but the possibility remained. Most members of the profession, though not all, felt strongly that their scale fees were amply justified. They frequently complained that estage agents' commissions on sales were much more than their own costs and that under the then prevailing conditions they had more work to do in a transaction than the estate agents had. The official view was rather that conveyancing was a highly technical matter not made any easier by the recent planning legislation, and that if the costs were to be reduced then the English land law would have to be simplified. In any case, the argument ran, the solicitor's profit was not excessive considering his responsibility. The Law Society, however, thought it right to set up a special committee to consider the problem. This seemed to some solicitors to smell of a compromise or an admission, and just as in 1897 when The Law Society was thought to have weakened in deference to the Council's friends in the 'Establishment' there was a strong protest. For the first time for a hundred years another association was formed on a national basis to represent the profession.

[84] Polson, Law and Lawyers, vol 2, p 312.

The British Legal Association was set up in the course of 1964 (the date of its formal establishment seems to have been November 1964) although by March 1965 it had only 133 members.[85] In 1966 it claimed to have 2,250 members or ten per cent of the profession. It received support when in 1965 The Law Society's special committee issued its report. The committee recommended the adoption of what was called 'The Title Certificate' scheme. In general terms the scheme was based on the theme that it was wasteful for a title to be examined for its full period (then thirty years) on each occasion when there was a dealing, and that it should be sufficient for each solicitor to investigate the title back to the date when it had been certified by another solicitor as good and marketable. It was in effect a combination of the private conveyancing system and the land registry. Because the title investigation and therefore the responsibility would be less, the committee recommended that the scale costs should be reduced by one-quarter. The Council adopted the report, and at first the reaction of the profession through local law societies was favourable. But when it was realised that one-quarter off gross receipts might mean a substantial loss of income the profession saw considerable technical difficulties, and it soon became clear that the scheme was not acceptable.[86] Fortunately the government decided that the best solution was an acceleration of the land registration system and it took a very optimistic view of the time that would be required to make it applicable throughout the country. The Lord Chancellor was not in favour of introducing another conveyancing system at this late stage and accordingly the Council was able to let the proposal drop.

The government persisted, however, to vex the profession with regard to its costs. It had in 1967 referred the question to the Prices and Incomes Board set up under the Prices and Incomes Act 1966. The Board published its first report in 1968.[87] The figures which it published about solicitors' incomes then and in its subsequent reports in November 1969 and March 1971[88] showed that the profession was not likely to get much satisfaction from its recommendations. The Board, it is true, recommended that there should be increases in county court costs and in conveyancing where the transactions were at prices of £2,000 or less, but these were unimportant when set against its other proposals. The price of property had increased so that most houses were changing hands at £4,000 or more; the Board recommended that the scale charge in this bracket should be reduced by six per cent. In many cases the same solicitor acted for both seller and buyer and was not only entitled to charge the full scale fee against both but required as a matter of professional conduct to do so; the Board recommended that the fee in these cases should be one and a half times the scale

[85] *Solicitors' Journal*, vol 109 (1965), p 325.

[86] Ibid, p 817: 'The profession's reaction can be described in a word: disenchanted.'

[87] Report No 54, Cmnd 3529 (1968).

[88] Cmnd 4217 and 4624.

fee divided equally between both parties, or a reduction of twenty-five per cent. The whole structure of conveyancing costs depended in the opinion of most solicitors on the rule that the full scale fee must be charged; the Board recommended that it should be made clear that the scale fee was a maximum and that solicitors should be entitled to reduce their charges below that fee where they thought the work did not justify charging according to the scale. Solicitors were incensed. They seemed to be under attack from all sides. They seemed to be singled out for dissection and to be threatened with a major reduction in their incomes at a time when everybody else was getting increases. The question was: why should they of all professions be the only one whose fees were regulated by an outside body? Conveyancing charges were regulated by a statutory committee acting under the Solicitors Act 1957 and consisting of the Lord Chancellor, the Lord Chief Justice, the Master of the Rolls, the President of The Law Society and the president of a local law society nominated by the Lord Chancellor. The dual role of the Lord Chancellor was criticised. He was the head of the judiciary but he was also a politician, and conveyancing had become a political issue.

In June 1970 there was a change of government and accordingly a change of policy. The Prices and Incomes Board was wound up on 31st March 1971. There was of course also a change of Lord Chancellors. There was some amelioration in the matter of costs in respect of the lower value transactions[89] and scale charges were retained for transactions of up to £30,000. Then came a proposal from the Lord Chancellor that scale charges should apply only up to £10,000, with charges for transactions above that figure fixed according to the work done and other factors.[90] Even the Prices and Incomes Board had not gone beyond suggesting the scale should end at £20,000. Solicitors were alarmed at the new proposal because it seemed to be leading to a total elimination of scale. They were almost unanimous that scale was best in the interests of the public and the profession. In 1967 it was reported that 'after a thorough investigation and careful study of this whole question the Council resolved that the scale system of remuneration for conveyancing is the best method of charging and should be retained'.[91] The main argument in favour of scale, as in 1883, was that it enabled a client to know exactly what his costs would be before he embarked on a transaction. When the Lord Chancellor's proposal was received the *Law Society's Gazette* declared that 'to remove this certainty would in the long run bring about sheer human misery'.[92] Less dramatically the presidents and secretaries of local law societies, having

[89] The Solicitors' Remuneration Order 1970 increased as from 15th February 1971 the scale charges on transactions up to £3,000.

[90] These were the seven factors on which so-called Schedule II costs were based (p 96, *supra*).

[91] *Law Society's Gazette*, vol 64, p 295.

[92] Ibid, vol 69, p 1.

considered the proposal, decided that 'scale fees have prevailed for ninety years and should be retained'[93] and the Council told the Lord Chancellor that it had 'maintained for many years that a scale basis of remuneration in conveyancing matters is best in both the public and the profession's interests'[94] and remained of that opinion. But the voices against scale were becoming more readily heeded because the profession was utterly tired of its affairs being the subject of comment in the 'media' and of its remuneration being constantly under review by a statutory committee. In March 1972 the Lord Chancellor (Lord Hailsham) invited Mr W O Carter (as he then was), the President of The Law Society, to see him[95] and in April 1972 made the suggestion that scale should be abandoned and that the Council should consider making a practice rule prohibiting the same solicitor acting for both parties in a conveyancing transaction. The Council accepted the suggestion. The profession learned of the decision by letter from the President[96] and there were strong protests that on so vital a matter there had been no consultation.[97] Inevitably there were prophecies of disaster and there was a good deal of anxiety as to how the system would work in practice. The *Economist* expressed the hope that having got rid of scale it would now be possible to get rid of the conveyancing 'monopoly', and not a few solicitors saw that danger. But the property market was booming. Sellers were making large profits and legal fees seemed insignificant in relation to the other sums involved. Everything was costing more and there was no sign that the public was asking solicitors to charge less than they had done before. The policy of the Council had been fully justified. It had 'with dignity and patience pressed the case of solicitors for proper remuneration in conveyancing matters'[98] and it had succeeded. Abandonment of scale meant release from the statutory committee. It meant submission of bills for taxation if the client so required, but it rarely was required.[99] As if by magic the topic seemed to disappear from public view; the sheer human misery which threatened in January 1972 the sellers and buyers of properties costing £10,000 or more either did not happen or was ignored; the importance of certainty about finance which had produced so much earnest thought and written and oral eloquence suddenly vanished. At a stroke the profession which had been born in chains was free.

[93] Ibid, pt 2, p 1.

[94] Ibid, p 386.

[95] Something of the background is given in Lord Hailsham's The Door Wherein I Went, p 267.

[96] *Law Society's Gazette*, vol 69 (1972), p 381.

[97] Eg from the President of the British Legal Association—*Solicitors' Journal*, vol 116, p 377.

[98] *Conveyancer and Property Lawyer*, vol 35 (1971), No 2, p 69.

[99] Instead of asking for the taxation of a bill by one of the court taxing masters the client can ask for it to be submitted to The Law Society, and this is the usual course. Although the number is increasing, in 1974 only 1,185 certificates were issued.

There was running through all the debates on land law reform in all its aspects the allegation that solicitors were opposed to any changes in the existing system because of their self-interest. Lord Crewe, speaking on the Conveyancing and Real Property Bill in 1913, summed up this contention: 'the lion in the path of would-be reformers' was 'the indomitable opposition of solicitors'. The Law Society on the other hand claimed that solicitors 'have always supported and in many cases initiated law reforms for the benefit of the community at large without any regard to the interests of their own profession as such';[100] Lord Birkenhead after his property legislation of 1925 was achieved agreed that 'the claim of The Law Society to have initiated reforms for the benefit of the community at large is completely justified';[101] and commentators outside the profession have concluded that 'the solicitors gave continuous support to many of the property law reforms'.[102] There was some truth in both points of view. Solicitors had more practical experience of conveyancing than any other profession and they were able to suggest reforms and to see the dangers in practice in reforms suggested by others; they would have been more than human if their ideas had not been affected by their own pecuniary interests. Inevitably they preferred to keep things as they were until they were completely satisfied that a change was needed and they were more difficult to satisfy when a proposal for change seemed likely to affect their pockets adversely. The reforms of 1881 could be accepted with equanimity because during the previous ten years the *ad valorem* system of charging had been carefully worked out and had achieved acceptance as fair to both profession and public; extension of land registration could be accepted in the 1960s because the two systems of charging had been approximated and because the cost and difficulty of non-registered conveyancing had increased; in 1973 the *ad valorem* scales and minimum fee rules could be abandoned because inflation and general economic conditions made it advantageous to do so. But there was nothing unreasonable in that. As *The Times* (never an outspoken friend of the profession) said in 1883: 'As long as solicitors were paid by the length of deeds they could not be fairly asked to assent to legislation by which it was hoped to reduce deeds to the narrowest possible limits.'[103] In any event reform of land law and conveyancing procedures was so vital a matter that it could not be entertained lightly. In 1830 the Real Property Commission reported that the law of real property in England and Wales required 'very few essential alterations' and solicitors had the conviction that the reformers were primarily concerned in changes which left the profession with the responsibility and the 'headwork' but heavily reduced their remuneration. Positive conveyancing reform coupled with a change in methods of charging became a major

[100] Memorandum to the Lord Chancellor, 1921.
[101] *Law Times*, vol 151, p 429.
[102] Carr-Saunders and Wilson, The Professions, p 53.
[103] Quoted *Law Times*, vol 74, p 214.

occupation of The Law Society in the early 1870s, and in 1879 the President made that the main topic of his presidential address. He was able to say that the Society had submitted to the Lord Chancellor thirty proposals for reform so that the profession's considered views could be taken into account in framing the then pending reform legislation. 'By such exertions whether successful or unsuccessful the just influence of the Society is maintained and the best answer is given to the vulgar assertion that solicitors are, from interested motives, averse to the improvement and simplification of the law.'[104] From the foundation of the Society in 1825 down to the present day there have been a constant scrutiny of and suggestions in relation to all property legislation. If their object has been primarily obstruction they were singularly unsuccessful. In the seventy years following the 1830 Real Property Commission's finding that little reform was needed no fewer than 138 measures on the subject reached the statute-book. Some of them have been promoted by the Society, including the fundamentally important Trustee Act and Land Charges Registration and Searches Act of 1888.

So the profession survived the attacks on it and the monopoly was preserved. Conveyancing business remained essential to the viability of the profession, particularly in the provinces, and without it the public might lose the services of the profession. Occasionally in the legal press and elsewhere there were fears and opinions expressed that solicitors were unwise to rely so much on a situation which could be changed by statute. 'An era is coming to a close—the era of the conveyancer. And it is no bad thing for the profession that this era should end.'[105] The profession was urged to extend its business into other areas and to try to recapture business which by neglect it had lost to others, particularly accountants and banks. In 1966 The Law Society set up a committee to consider the Future of the Profession and since then frequent articles have been published in the *Gazette* on the subject. But these opinions and fears had all been expressed before. Time and again the profession had been warned of the impending doom of the end of the monopoly. Generally speaking it remained content with the present and was prepared to let the future take care of itself.

[104] Law Society Annual Report, 1879, p 9.
[105] *Solicitors' Journal*, vol 108 (1964), p 371.

CHAPTER 8

Litigation and Legal Aid

Until the nineteenth century the primary function of attorneys and solicitors was reasonably well defined. It was to attend to the pre- and post-trial formalities of civil litigation and of criminal proceedings. Civil litigation was for practical purposes confined to the courts at Westminster or to nisi prius at assizes, and although there were numerous local courts these were by and large concerned only with very small claims. Criminal work followed the same pattern. For the country solicitor conveyancing was at an early date more important and more lucrative than civil litigation or crime, but for the London man the situation was reversed. It was this distinction which lay at the root of the suspicion with which the country solicitor viewed The Law Society. 'The Law Society regards mainly the interests of one branch of the profession, nay if the whole truth be told of a few twigs of that branch'[1] was the opinion of the *Law Times* in 1848 and for years afterwards. It was a journal mainly supported by country solicitors and always active in their interests, particularly in relation to conveyancing, which it and they suspected would be sacrificed to what it called 'the great London houses'. The fact was that for many years conveyancing was to the Council a matter of secondary importance. From 1840 for many years two other leading objects of the Society monopolised to a great extent the attention of the committee. These were the centralisation of the courts of justice and the simplification of legal procedure and legal education. It was not until 1879 that the Council took a positive interest in conveyancing, and litigation was for long its first consideration.

That it should be greatly concerned with the centralisation of the courts in some more convenient place and style than those at Westminster naturally followed. As early as 1835 it made informal representations, but these and similar ones repeated in 1836 met little encouragement. A Select Committee of the House of Commons was appointed in 1841 to consider the matter and it reported in 1842. All the evidence it had received was in favour of concentrating the courts and offices on one site. The site was suggested in 1846—'west of the Institution and extending from Carey Street to the Strand'. This of course suited the profession very well indeed, and for the next twenty years the Council persisted in its efforts to get it accepted. In 1865 the Act was passed to enable the site to be bought

[1] *Law Times*, vol 10 (1848), p 46.

and the buildings erected, but inevitably there were further delays. It was not until 1874 that building was started and not until 1882 that they were finished. Unfortunately that was after the death of Mr Field, a solicitor to whom much of the credit was due; his efforts are acknowledged by his statue in the courts. The courts were opened with great ceremony by Queen Victoria on 4th December 1882; a loyal address from the solicitors was handed to the Queen by the Lord Chancellor and subsequently Mr Thomas Paine, the President, went to Windsor to be knighted; provision was made for 120 solicitors to have seats.

In civil business the most important event of the nineteenth century was the establishment of the county courts by the County Courts Act 1846. The *Law Times* called it 'the great reform measure of the last half-century'.[2] The county courts were set up to collect small debts limited at first to £20 but in 1850 to £50. Debt-collecting was a large part of the profession's business because credit was freely—even rashly—given by tradesmen as a means of attracting and keeping custom, particularly the custom of the nobility and gentry. For a couple of hundred years the dun and the bailiff in possession hardly carried any stigma or social disadvantage. The King's eldest son's house was infested with shabbily dressed men hoping to collect something on account of his debts; Count Alfred D'Orsay, the beau ideal of the early nineteenth century, had for long periods to keep house to avoid arrest for debt; Disraeli, when a rising politician and before a judicious marriage, was forced to use subterfuge and trickery to be rid of those who were dunning him; Charles James Fox was as notorious for his insolvency as Burke and Sheridan, and banker Coutts noted that his promissory notes were worth nothing. The less prominent were equally improvident. The result was a substantial business for the attorneys and the Bar. Legal newspapers made a prominent feature of weekly lists of bankrupts and insolvents. A common business for attorneys was to take assignments at a discount of book debts partly for the profit they made if the debts were paid but mainly for the costs they could earn. One of the official assignees told Sir George Stephen 'that it is perfectly incredible the extent to which you find small bills from £20 to £50 discounted by attorneys' and he estimated that the amount ran into millions of pounds.[3] Any change which might adversely affect this business was therefore of vital importance, particularly to the London man. When the Bill was being debated in 1846 a large meeting was held in London to consider the implications; the immediate consequences were dreaded; when in 1850 the jurisdiction was extended never had there been 'so many blank faces; it was impossible not to feel some hint of the alarm which was expressed on every side'.[4] High Court business undoubtedly suffered; it was one of the reasons given for a reduction in the taxation on attorneys by Gladstone in 1853 and

[2] Vol 8 (1847), p 363.
[3] Select Committee on Legal Education. 1846, ans 1997.
[4] *Law Times*, vol 15, p 77.

for the slow rate of increase in the number of attorneys in the middle of the century. In 1867, 127,702 writs were issued in the High Court but only 55,783 in 1881; in the latter year over a million plaints were issued by county courts and the money recovered there was nearly ten times as much as in the High Court. Clearly a great deal of work had left London for the provinces. For the Bar the consequences were worse. 'Hundreds nay thousands must go out of the profession or be starved out'[5] was one considered opinion. In their case the matter was the more serious because the County Courts Acts gave to the attorneys a right of audience and settled in their favour for this purpose the then much-debated question of whether counsel might appear in court if he were not instructed by an attorney. The Bar was concerned at the possibility of a class of specialist advocates being created among the attorneys who would be instructed to conduct cases in court by other attorneys. That concern was resolved in 1852 by the provision that an attorney could appear only if he had the general conduct of the action, and that situation has been preserved ever since. The attorneys had their own problems. The limited fees, the opportunity for creditors to do their own collecting as a result of the simpler procedure, the opening for the unqualified to encroach, were all factors which made life more difficult for them. It was the competition from the unqualified—mainly men who called themselves accountants—which was the main source of complaint, and the inability of The Law Society to control it was a recurrent grumble, particularly from those attorneys who were not members.

The profession's reaction to the county courts was variously assessed according to the standpoint of the observer. It may well have been the bitterness which the Bar felt at this first major intrusion which prompted some of the aspersions on county court attorneys which at the outset appeared in the legal papers, particularly those favoured by the Bar. Attention was drawn to the advocacy of 'some of the most successful attorney advocates' and the question asked 'whether their loud shop-boy manner sharp and incisive as it may be would not be tolerated at the Bar? As attorneys they are eminent, as barristers they would collapse.'[6] They were said to 'keep a tout or touts at the public-house which is always found opposite or next door to the court'.[7] There was probably more truth at the time in the statement that 'attorneys themselves do not as a rule make much out of their county court practice. Such practice in any country town amongst the attorneys is always looked down on as third-rate or of the lowest class. The best offices indeed except in a few cases will not touch it.'[8] And it was probably still truer that attorneys withdrew from county court practice as soon as they had other business to do. These assessments received support thirty years later from the President of The Law Society.

[5] Cox, The Advocate, p 7.
[6] *Law Magazine and Review*, vol 4 (NS) (1875), p 89.
[7] Ibid, p 88. [8] Ibid.

Giving evidence on behalf of the Society in 1878, Mr Burton was asked what he thought of solicitors as advocates, bearing in mind the evidence of some of the county court judges that there are 'solicitors who are fully competent to conduct cases before the county court'. He replied: 'I do not know that I know enough about it, but for myself I do not believe it',[9] and he later added: 'I do not think the solicitor is capable of conducting cases as well as a barrister.'[10] As to the standing of the county court practitioners Mr Burton's view was that 'it is not a matter of dignity but a man of position cannot go into the county court'[11] and that the county court quite apart from the practice was a place one really could not go to because of the people one met there.[12] He himself had only looked into a county court twice in thirty years, and Mr John Hollams (as he then was) told the same enquiry that he had never been inside one. For lesser men, particularly in the provinces, it was a different story, and if The Law Society until the end of the century resisted any extension of the jurisdiction of this rather vulgar court the large provincial societies like Liverpool and Leeds strongly supported it. It was true that the scale of fees was low,[13] but the net result was probably better than having the case tried in London or at assizes. The assessment of the profession in the county court made by the county court bench was naturally varied. The new appointments were not always happy ones, and men who had been neglected by attorneys at the Bar no doubt felt some satisfaction in showing their authority over the profession when elevated to the bench. But by and large the bench and the attorneys got on very well and the judges expressed the opinion that the attorneys managed very well.[14]

From the point of view of the profession in the provinces the important fact was that the county courts were a success. In the first seven years no fewer than 3,575,205 cases were entered there and it was clear that they were meeting a real need. Their jurisdiction was accordingly gradually increased: in 1850 to £50; in 1903 to £100; in 1938 to £200; in 1955 to £400; in 1970 to £750; and in 1974 to £1,000. In addition Parliament added significantly to the importance of the county courts. They were given jurisdiction in bankruptcy in 1869; in 1880 in cases arising under the Employers' Liability Act, which later became in 1897 the Workmen's Compensation Act and in its day one of the most fruitful sources of litigation; in 1890 in the winding up of companies with a capital of not more than £10,000 and a registered office in the district of the court; in 1915 in cases of whatever value arising out of the Rent and Mortgage Interest Restrictions Acts;

[9] House of Commons Committee on County Court Bill No 2, ans 4406.

[10] Ibid, ans 4482.

[11] Ibid, ans 4221; he repeated the opinion at ans 4355.

[12] House of Commons: Judicature Commission, ans 6181.

[13] At the outset the maximum fee was 15s, increased to 40s in 1849. In 1886 the fee for conducting a case in court was one guinea and the fee was the same if one retained counsel As late as 1936 the fee allowed for conducting a case on trial without counsel was £2 2s

[14] *Supra.*

in 1930 in appeals under the Housing Act; and in 1967, most important of all, in matrimonial cases. Although the increases in the maxima for normal business were partly set off by the decline in the value of money, the total result of all these measures was that a large part of all civil litigation could be transacted from start to finish by solicitors without the intervention of counsel or for that matter of London agents. As the county court acquired new jurisdictions it tended to lose its original character of a small debts court and its status greatly improved. Most provincial firms found it necessary to handle county court business. In spite of the prohibition in the 1852 Act against one solicitor instructing another to act purely as an advocate, there were from an early date solicitors in each county court who specialised in advocacy before it. By 1857, according to the *Midland Counties Herald*, 150 attorneys had appeared in the Birmingham County Court, but practically all the business was conducted by three men who did nothing else. Nevertheless the 1852 prohibition was irksome and there were some highly technical interpretations put on it so that there was even a doubt as to whether a solicitor could instruct an assistant solicitor, employed by him full-time, to appear as an advocate. There was a great deal of pressure on The Law Society to have the prohibition removed, but nothing was done. It may be that the Council thought it best not to push the Bar too far.

Immediately they had a right of audience in the county court a good many solicitors thought it right that they should appear robed. It gave them a certain dignity and it had the practical advantage of identifying who were the lawyers present and who were not. As early as 1847 the practice started in the West Country; in 1851 there were reports of it at Driffield and York; in 1858 it seemed to have become pretty general and a number of county court judges, anxious to improve the status of their courts, encouraged and some insisted on it. One firm of gownmakers in Chancery Lane had already sold sixty. Nobody knew what was the correct gown to wear, or whether one should also wear bands. Some suggested that a form of headdress should also be adopted. The practice varied from place to place and at least one solicitor was temporarily arrested because he came without a gown and refused to wear one. The Law Society was asked for guidance. It was not sure, but ventured the opinion that wigs might be uncomfortable in hot weather in some of the cramped rooms in which county courts were held. In 1905 it expressed the opinion that 'it was desirable that solicitors appearing as advocates should be robed' and communicated this opinion to the judges. They did not give notice of it to the profession except through the Society's Handbook, which came into the hands of only half the solicitors practising. This added to the embarrassment of those who did not wear gowns, because the judges said that their professional body had ruled that they should. The point was publicised in the legal press as a result of the misfortunes of these men and in that way became known to all solicitors and generally followed.

In criminal work the situation had been that at assizes attorneys were not heard,[15] but at quarter sessions the position was that 'the advocates at sessions who by inherent right or by the practice of the court are entitled to take upon them the causes of others and to prosecute for the Crown are barristers and attorneys. At sessions where a sufficient number of barristers attend it is usual to give them sole audience and the attorneys are consequently not heard in person. At sessions where the Bar do not attend, as in most boroughs and cities, it is usual to hear the attorneys as advocates; and though it may be doubted whether they are in strictness entitled to prosecute indictments it is customary and certainly convenient to allow them that privilege. In cases where the Bar have not been accustomed to attend but two or more barristers wish to do so, it is usual for them to intimate their desire to the chairman and request that they may have pre-audience; and if this request be granted the attorneys cannot afterwards be heard in their presence unless they should all be retained on one side.'[16] It was a matter for each court of quarter sessions to decide for itself,[17] but it was not an easy situation for the attorneys who wished to practise at quarter sessions, because the chairman or recorder was invariably a member of the Bar. There were some brave spirits. At Woodbridge in 1831 an attorney asked to be heard because none of the counsel present would accept a brief marked with the usual fee; another spoke of the like experience; they were asked to offer the briefs again in open court and when these were refused by counsel the attorneys were given audience.[18] At Doncaster the rule was that the Bar had exclusive right of audience if four attended; in 1852 when only three were present a local attorney asked to be heard but was refused; the local press thought with some justice that he had been badly treated. The attorneys were gradually excluded so that by 1967 there were only seven sessions where they had audience—Doncaster, Holland (Parts of Lincolnshire), Barnstaple Borough, Cornwall County, Penzance Borough, Caernarvonshire County and Anglesey County—although there were a handful more where they had the right if less than four counsel were present. They were not greatly concerned and it did not seem worth a quarrel with the Bar. During the latter part of the nineteenth century crime was decreasing. In 1895 and 1896 there was only one prisoner to try at Poole and in the same years white gloves were presented at Lincoln and Plymouth. There was no legal aid until 1903 and even then it was meagre. In 1874 a resolution was passed at The Law Society's annual general meeting that solicitors should have audience at quarter sessions, but nothing came of it or appears to have been done

[15] There appear to have been occasional exceptions, eg in 1587 Edward Makyn, an attorney, pleaded on an indictment at Essex Assizes on behalf of Peter Lewes, the Vicar of Burnham, on a charge of barratry, the prosecution being conducted by the Attorney-General (Emmison, Elizabethan Life: Disorder (1970), p 144).

[16] Merrifield, Law of Attorneys (1830), pp 434–435.

[17] *The Queen* v *The Justices for Denbighshire* (1846), 15 LJQB 335.

[18] *Legal Observer Supplement*, 1831, p 124.

about it; in 1894 a resolution in the same sense was rejected at the Annual Provincial Meeting; in 1967 when The Law Society was assembling its evidence for submission to the Beeching Committee on Assizes and Quarter Sessions only sixty-four out of the 111 local law societies troubled to reply and of those who did twelve expressed no interest either way and only thirty-seven were strongly in favour; when the British Legal Association asked its members for their views on the matter for submission to the Monopolies Commission only twenty-seven per cent replied. There was one important exception. After 1872 quarter sessions were also the confirming authorities for licences granted by licensing committees for public-houses and hotels. This was lucrative business because generally a brewer was involved. Accordingly The Law Society pursued this aspect vigorously and was able to report in 1905 that when quarter sessions was sitting as a confirming authority solicitors had a right of audience in forty counties and forty-two boroughs. There was another exception, unimportant in itself but indicative of the Bar's tenacity. When quarter sessions were given jurisdiction in rating appeals solicitors wished to have a right of audience in this business; the matter was compromised by giving them it at county but not at borough quarter sessions and by limiting it to cases where the rateable value did not exceed £100. When quarter sessions were abolished by the Courts Act 1971 solicitors were given a limited right of audience primarily in relation to appeals from magistrates' courts in cases where the solicitor appearing has also appeared in the court below.

At what were for long called petty sessions the attorney's position was even more equivocal than at quarter sessions, for he was entirely dependent on the practice of the court. Until 1848 he had no right to attend on behalf of the parties where the decision of the justices was final;[19] 'on a preliminary hearing he has no right to be present and if permitted it is only a matter of courtesy and in that case he cannot interfere in the proceedings in any way whatsoever without the permission of the magistrate'.[20] He was in much the same position as the advocate now is when appearing before a coroner. His right to represent parties at petty sessions was given statutory backing in 1848,[21] but some magistrates still maintained that they had control over the practice of their own courts and as late as 1894 one text-book writer supported that attitude.[22] In 1886 one bench sought to exercise a disciplinary function and threatened a solicitor with exclusion if he did not stop touting for business.[23] But these were exceptional courts, and petty sessions became the base on which many a young solicitor established his practice. Cases there were reported in detail in the local press and the solicitors whose names appeared most often and with the most success had an advertisement which had hitherto been available only to

[19] *Collier* v *Hicks* (1831) (reported *Legal Observer*, vol 2, p 135).
[20] Merrifield, op cit, p 431. [21] 11 & 12 Vic c 43, s 12.
[22] White on Solicitors (1894), p 58, relying on *Collier* v *Hicks*.
[23] *Law Journal* (1884), p 159.

the Bar. To them went people of substance who found themselves involved at petty sessions and who thought that on this occasion they needed a solicitor perhaps a little more alert than the man who did their conveyancing business. The work at petty sessions began to cover a much wider field than it had done a hundred years earlier and this meant that people had to go into these courts who at one time would never have contemplated the possibility. The motor-car contributed an increasing amount of work; family law and problems came in 1878 with the power to make separation and maintenance orders and extended in 1926 to include adoption of children; licences to sell intoxicants and the whole paraphernalia of the control of the liquor trade became increasingly important after 1879; the enforcement of the welfare and public health legislation of the period was a matter for the magistrates.

The aggregate effect of the expansion of the jurisdictions of the county courts and petty sessions and of the social and economic changes of the period meant that there was a vast amount of work available to solicitors in the places where they practised for which they had no need of the help of either counsel or London agents. But most continued to regard it as not being worth while, and it was certainly not very remunerative. In 1920 it was said that 'among the poorer practitioners are the police court and county court solicitors',[24] and most were glad to leave the work when their success at it enabled them to do something else. Until 1949 legal aid was insignificant or even non-existent. In 1922 it was held that there was no '*in forma pauperis* system in the county courts'[25] and the Finlay Committee appointed in 1925 to consider the problem followed the evidence of The Law Society and recommended that this should remain the case. The recommendation was accepted, so that when the Rushcliffe Committee reported in 1947 it could laconically say that 'no system has ever existed in the county court for the assistance of poor persons engaged in litigation in that court'. In petty sessions the position in practice was not much different. Petty sessions had since the Poor Prisoners' Defence Act 1903 been able to grant legal aid in summary trials, but by and large justices did not think much of that sort of thing and very few if any orders were made. If the justices decided to commit a prisoner for trial they could, if the nature of the defence disclosed required it, grant a legal aid certificate which entitled the prisoner to counsel and solicitor. The solicitor, for instructing counsel and attending the trial, was entitled to a fee of two guineas with some carefully scrutinised out-of-pocket expenses; if the judge certified that the case had been one of exceptional length and difficulty the fee could be as much as £5. The Poor Prisoners' Defence Act 1930 which followed the Finlay Committee Report slightly ameliorated the solicitor's position. The justices were empowered to grant a legal aid certificate to a defendant

[24] Haynes, Concerning Solicitors, p xxv.

[25] *Cook* v *Imperial Tobacco Co Ltd* [1922] 2 KB 158, in which the history of the matter is fully reviewed.

who they thought needed legal aid because of the gravity of the charge he faced or because of exceptional circumstances but who had insufficient means to pay for it himself. The justices nominated the solicitor from a panel of those who had indicated their willingness to serve, but they took into account the defendant's wishes. The solicitor was entitled to a fee of £3 3s plus £1 11s 6d for any day after the first, but to prevent costs being inflated nothing was allowed for appearances on applications for bail or on remand. Travelling and other proper out-of-pocket expenses were allowed. The justices remained unenamoured of this procedure and very few certificates were issued: the total for England and Wales in 1939 was a mere 327. On committal a defence certificate might be issued and the solicitor's fee for all the work involved was £4 14s 6d with out-of-pocket expenses—this could be increased to £9 if the judge found the case was of exceptional length or difficulty. It can hardly be wondered at that the profession generally preferred to do other work and that poor prisoners' defences were undertaken mainly as a charity.

This situation was completely changed by the Legal Aid and Advice Act 1949. Probably no piece of legislation has so affected the solicitors' profession as this one; the costs which now are paid to solicitors under the Act and its successors cannot be precisely stated but run at the rate of more than £10,000,000 a year. In the courts at Westminster there had been some provision for poor litigants since 1494, but it is doubtful if much use was made of it. When the Rushcliffe Committee on Legal Aid reported in 1945 it said that some such system had existed for 'probably more than 150 years' in the courts which had been absorbed into the Supreme Court, so that it does not seem that the earlier system had been well known. The profession was certainly not intended to have any financial reward for its services. The pauper (he was a man worth not more than £5) was specifically relieved of all fees and costs unless he recovered at least £5. If he did then in the King's Bench he could get no order for costs against his opponent since such an order was by way of indemnity, and as he had no legal liability to pay fees or costs there was nothing against which to indemnify him. In that situation the solicitor was likely to get very little, for the court fee might be as much as £4. In Chancery the position was better and an order might be made against the unsuccessful opponent of the pauper. But in 1883 it was ruled that the King's Bench practice should prevail and that solicitor and counsel were to receive nothing but their out-of-pocket expenses. In a further attempt to avoid vexatious cases coming before the court, an applicant for pauper status had to provide a certificate from counsel as to the merits. 'By this time not only did an opinion of counsel have to be obtained but a solicitor also had to be found who was willing to prepare an affidavit and a case to counsel and thereby run the risk of being chosen by the court to conduct the case free of charge.'[26] The only amelioration was that the financial limit was raised to £25.

[26] *Law Quarterly Review*, vol 61, pp 87–88.

The courts' determination that solicitors (and counsel) should do this work at their own expense was further exemplified in the first regular scheme for legal aid in the Supreme Court, which came into operation on 1st January 1914. The financial limit was raised to £50, or £100 in exceptional circumstances. The conducting solicitor was expressly forbidden to take any fee, profit or reward from the poor person for the 'enquiry, report, or the conduct of the proceedings'. As to out-of-pocket expenses, the solicitor was permitted to receive 'remuneration' out of such fund as the Treasury might create for the purpose of paying them. Apparently the hope was that the fund would be mainly supported by charitably minded citizens supplemented by the Treasury. In fact no fund was ever created, so that there was nothing available to pay even out-of-pocket expenses. Nevertheless some use was made of the scheme, though applications were carefully scrutinised. In 1918, 305 applications were made in the King's Bench and Chancery Divisions and seventy-seven were granted; inevitably the main weight of business was in divorce—4,101 applications and 2,218 granted. But only 1,074 cases got as far as petitions being presented and only 486 were tried.

This was not satisfactory and in 1919 a committee was appointed under Mr Justice P O Lawrence to consider the working of the scheme. It found that one of the reasons why there was such a discrepancy between the number of certificates granted and the number of petitions filed was that the poor persons could not find the out-of-pocket expenses to enable them to start proceedings. These expenses were normally £10, made up of £5 actual out-of-pockets and £5 for the solicitor's office expenses. The solution the committee discovered was to forbid the solicitor to claim anything for office expenses. It was impressed with the fact that some solicitors had actually managed to make a profit out of the existing scheme; one solicitor had 523 and another 401 active cases in one year. Such a thing could not be allowed. In addition the solicitor was expressly forbidden to take a fee; his reimbursement for out-of-pocket expenses he had to receive from the Poor Persons Department and not direct from the client. The result was that whereas previously there had normally been no profit, now there was an actual loss, so that solicitors became increasingly reluctant to accept poor persons cases and the situation became chaotic. The Lord Chancellor in 1922 appealed to solicitors to join the scheme and asked the President of The Law Society to support him. Some 2,000 solicitors responded, but in 1925 Mr Justice P O Lawrence's committee found that many solicitors were reluctant to do so because they found the actual work distasteful. By the end of 1924 there were 412 divorce cases waiting for solicitors to accept them. It was clear that the existing scheme had broken down. Not only were many people unable to get representation but others were driven to instruct solicitors who would take on their actions on a purely speculative basis and thus to create the 'ambulance-chasers'. The need was to ensure a scheme which provided honest advice and assistance and commanded the support of the profession. The Law Society had already in 1913 resolved that it was desirable that it should publicly show its interest and its willingness to co-operate in providing legal aid for people who could not afford normal fees and in 1923 it decided to submit to the Lawrence Committee a scheme for the Society and the provincial law societies to take over the whole business. Applications for certificates would be submitted not to individual solicitors but to committees appointed by the Lord Chancellor on the nomination of The Law Society and the provincial law societies. The Lawrence Committee recommended that this offer should be accepted and that the cost, estimated at £3,000 a year, should be paid by the Treasury. The recommendations were accepted and implemented. For years The Law Society kept well within the grant in spite of the increased volume of work and higher level of expenses; as late as 1944–1945 the estimated cost was only £14,500. The new arrangements were a success and the backlog of work seemed in a fair way to being cleared. In the first twelve years of the operation of the scheme 68,000 applications had been received and dealt with. The bulk of the cases were matrimonial[27] and the Matrimonial Causes Act 1937 greatly enlarged the grounds upon which divorce could be sought. That inevitably brought with it a flood of new cases, and there were difficulties in finding solicitors to take them up. In 1939 the Associated Law Societies of Wales refused to deal with any more poor persons cases until their members were given reasonable remuneration. Nevertheless The Law Society had demonstrated that the profession was able to deal with the problem far more effectively than any other agency, and that was an achievement of the greatest importance. As to individual solicitors (and barristers) the Rushcliffe Committee after the war commented: 'We feel we ought not to pass from this subject without adding our tribute to that frequently paid by the judges but too little appreciated by the public to the work done for poor persons by barristers and solicitors. They do not merely work without reward but in the case of barristers often and in the case of solicitors always at cost to themselves.... Every poor persons case undertaken by a solicitor represents a substantial financial burden to him.'

The Law Society was again called in to help in 1942 when the divorce problems of the services, coupled with the acute shortage of solicitors, had created a situation beyond the capacity of the existing scheme. It established a Services Divorce Department which handled cases which could not otherwise be tackled or where the 'poor person's' contribution was less than £10. Then in 1944 the Lord Chancellor appointed the Rushcliffe Committee to consider legal aid and advice in all its aspects. It might have happened that at a time when there was a Labour government legal aid might have been treated as other social services were and made the responsibility of a government department. But The Law Society was the only

[27] In 1937 forty-seven per cent of all divorce cases heard in the courts were poor persons cases.

organisation with any practical experience and it had succeeded where government-controlled schemes had failed. Moreover, on the committee were two strong representatives—Mr Gillett and Mr Littlewood, as they then were—backed by the experience of the Society's secretary, Mr Lund (as he also then was). The committee recommended a comprehensive system of legal aid and advice extending over a much wider range of people than the old scheme and to be operated by the legal profession. For practical purposes that meant The Law Society. The recommendations were accepted and embodied in the Legal Aid and Advice Act 1949. The Law Society entered on this enormous task with energy and skill, and by and large the view expressed by the Lord Chancellor's Advisory Committee at the end of the first year has remained valid ever since: there was 'nothing to blame and much to praise in the way The Law Society have tackled their arduous task'. It was perhaps the most important event in the history of the Society and of the profession. For the solicitor it has meant that all clients, whatever their means, are on the same footing from the point of view of costs and has therefore enormously increased the volume of business. The scheme was naturally strongly supported from the start and by 1954 9,711 solicitors or about half the profession were on legal aid panels. Legal aid was introduced in stages. It was available in the Supreme Court from the start, and that included divorce, which constituted the largest part of the business. It was extended to the county courts from 1st January 1956, and poor prisoners' defence cases were brought in as from 1st January 1960 so far as remuneration was concerned. In civil cases the ordinary level of fees applied, less an allowance of ten per cent, and in criminal cases new scales were introduced as from March 1960. The pre-war fees had been increased by fifty per cent in 1953 and there was a further increase in 1959, but they were still inadequate. As from 1960 a solicitor in a summary case might be paid between six guineas and £47 10s with a daily rate of nine guineas; and on cases committed for trial the fees ranged from eight guineas to £78 15s 6d. The financial benefit to the profession has been considerable, though it is not possible to state it with any precision. In 1964–1965 when the flow of work had settled down 95,904 legal aid certificates were issued in civil matters, and on an average of £40 a case that represented nearly £4,000,000 in costs. In the magistrates' courts in 1974–1975 the total payments for solicitors' costs, for their disbursements and for counsel's fees were £9,100,000. The escalation of the cost had begun to cause anxiety and criticism, but the profession maintained that the fees it was allowed were inadequate.

The introduction of legal aid even on this scale had not changed the profession's attitude to litigation. In general they preferred other work, and on an average not more than one-third of their gross income came from it. It is probable that it would be a loss-maker if it were assessed by itself (except for the specialists and those dealing with major commercial cases). In many firms it is regarded as a service which has to be provided.

But quite apart from the profit motive they remain convinced, like Christopher Wallis in the eighteenth century, that it is litigation which 'perplexes and requires much attention'. In 1966 one assessment was that 'there are a few solicitors who specialise in advocacy and a greater number who specialise in the conduct of litigation but it is a safe generalisation that the actual conduct of most litigation is left to common-law clerks and is not dealt with by their principals. The majority of solicitors despite our descent from the attorneys and solicitors and despite our official title of "solicitor of the Supreme Court" shun litigation in all its forms.'[28] It is a far cry from the days when the most frequent reproach was that the profession was the principal instigator of lawsuits.

[28] *Solicitors' Journal*, vol 110 (1966), p 25.

CHAPTER 9

Relationship with the Bar

In 1614 the Benchers of the four Inns of Court issued the following order: 'For that there ought always to be preserved a difference between a counsellor at law which is the principal person next unto serjeants and judges in the administration of justice and attornies and solicitors which are but ministerial persons and of an inferior nature, therefore it is ordered that none henceforth, no common attorney or solicitor shall be admitted to any of the four houses of court.' It was a militant and aggressive statement of the policy of the Benchers first publicly announced some sixty years earlier[1] and continued for the next three hundred. In the circumstances of the sixteenth and seventeenth centuries the attorneys and solicitors were not able to resist the execution of that policy, which resulted in their losing their right of audience in the courts of record and their membership of the Inns of Court. The first signs that they felt able to make a stand came in the eighteenth century. In 1761 the general meeting of the Society of Gentlemen Practisers directed their committee to consider and report their opinion as to the most proper method to be taken to discountenance and prevent barristers by themselves and their clerks transacting business which properly belonged to the other branch and had the courage to suggest that offenders should be prosecuted at the expense of the Society;[2] in 1764 the committee considered what action should be taken to contest an order of the Inns that attorneys and solicitors should not be called to the Bar unless they had ceased to practise for two years; and in 1765 it was decided to apply for a mandamus if the Benchers refused to admit to an Inn a student who had otherwise conformed to the rules but who was in conflict with the 1764 order. It does not appear that much came of these gestures, but when in 1766 a Serjeant Davy was reported to have told a jury that 'You gentlemen who are on the outside of the curtain do not see the tricks and management within; we that are on the inside see the whole, and I will take it upon me to say, that out of the many mistakes that happen in the management of causes, nineteen out of twenty happen by the ignorance of attorneys', the Society decided that 'any counsel at the Bar making use of such like reflections upon the attorneys in general ought not to be employed as counsel by any member of

[1] On this subject generally see pp 17–19, *supra*.
[2] Minutes, p 104.

the Society'.[3] The threat worked, although it took Serjeant Davy a little time to bring himself to apologise and to assure the Society that he did not mean to reflect on the profession, which on the contrary he had always held 'in the most esteem and gratitude'. The Society was generous enough to accept this *amende* and later briefed Serjeant Davy; he refused a fee, so that in the end all was well. Where there were no internal jealousies the profession could show a united front. When the Scriveners' litigation was proceeding[4] the barristers who represented the attorneys at the request of the Society declined any fees and were presented with suitable silver. Erskine greatly helped the Society in its efforts for better remuneration for attorneys and his success was signalised by a resolution that his name should be a standing toast at the Society's dinners.

The attorneys and solicitors in the nineteenth century were acutely sensitive about their social status and their reputation.[5] They found the contrast between their situation in this respect and that of the Bar particularly irksome and this was one of the constant themes in any discussion of their status. It undoubtedly embittered their attitude to more directly professional aspects of their relationship with the Bar. It was made all the more difficult to bear because the Bar seemed to make a point of it. 'We allude to a foolish jealousy that exists in many quarters between the Bar and the attornies. With whom the fault lies we will not take upon us to determine; probably there is error on both sides. Perhaps the Bar is over-nice and the attornies may be over-sensitive.'[6] Certainly 'one of the problems was the distant attitude of the Bar'.[7] The social difference was of long standing. The Inns of Court from the late sixteenth century to the mid-nineteenth century received as students the sons of the nobility, partly because a legal education was a useful training for a man who might have to manage large estates and partly because the Inns became centres of entertainment for the young, the rich, the noble and the talented. Coke himself signed the order in 1603 which provided that 'none be hereafter admitted into the society of any house of court that is not of gentle descent'. In the mid-seventeenth century at least four out of every five men entered in the Inns came from noble families or at any rate from the gentry. There were of course those like Serjeant Chauncy who complained that 'these mechanics ambitious of rule and government often educate their sons in the seminaries of the law whereby they overstock the profession and make it contemptible', but even that was a very different matter from the tradesmen who, having failed at everything else, became solicitors. At the beginning of the nineteenth century, notwithstanding the progress they had made, the attorneys were 'separated from the barristers by a social

[3] Minutes, p 114 (1766).
[4] See p 128, *supra*.
[5] Chapter 11, *infra*, *passim*.
[6] *Law Times*, vol 1 (1843), p 38.
[7] Ibid, p 65.

abyss',[8] and even fifty years later barristers still carried much more weight socially.[9] The social background of the barristers had a very practical significance. The Bar even in the Tudor period dominated the House of Commons, and that continued down to the late nineteenth century. In the nineteenth century as a whole about one-quarter of all members of Parliament had been called to the Bar and moreover called at so young an age that they had time to develop a political career. The cause was that the Bar was recruited from families which had seats at their disposal; the result was that for some six hundred years or more no voice critical of the Bar was heard in the House and no statute was passed which subjected it to any control or in any way limited its functions.[10] Patronage was directed by members of the Bar in office to those in practice; a member of the Western Circuit, William Pitt the Younger, when he was at the Treasury issued a minute that in government legal appointments barristers should be preferred to solicitors.[11]

The enormous prestige of the judiciary in England, to which only the Bar could aspire; the preponderance of the Bar in political life; the enormous interest taken by the public in daily newspaper reports of *causes célèbres* in which barristers appeared as able and courageous fighters for the lives and reputations and fortunes of their clients; the more select but nevertheless considerable interest among educated and influential people in the constant flow of reminiscences and biographies of barristers and judges; all these were factors which socially and professionally sustained the status of the Bar in contrast with that of the attorneys and solicitors. 'The eminent successes open to lawyers of the two branches secure for the Bar a brighter *éclat* and wider respect than solicitors possess as a professional fraternity.'[12] For them there were no high legal offices available to crown a career or comfort a retirement; the newspapers did not mention their part in the *causes célèbres*—except perhaps when Sir George Lewis was acting—and when solicitors were mentioned it was generally in connection with some misdemeanour or worse of which they were accused; in the whole period only two solicitors wrote their memoirs,[13] and only one was the subject of a rather dull biography;[14] the legal reminiscences of the Bar so rarely mentioned solicitors that the average reader might have remained ignorant of the fact that they existed.

[8] Halévy, History of the English People, p 22.
[9] Best, Mid-Victorian Britain, pp 271–272.
[10] Save 9 & 10 Vic c 95, s 2, which excluded counsel from the county courts except by leave of the judge; and cf Observations on the Oppression and Grievances of Solicitors and Attornies (1838), p 23: 'It has been said that no Minister has dared tax the Barristers so heavily as the Solicitors because the former are so powerfully represented in Parliament and could annihilate any official who should make the attempt.'
[11] *Monthly Law Magazine*, vol 4, p 47.
[12] Jeafferson, A Book about Lawyers, vol 2, p 329.
[13] Sir John Hollams and Sir George Stephen.
[14] Mr E W Field.

The difference in social and professional status persisted long enough for Lord Birkenhead to mention it in his memoirs and to be a fact of life down to the present day. 'Most professions expect and are entitled to be judged by the heights or status attained by their outstanding members. This is not to discount the general impression conveyed by the ranks. Nevertheless the natural and human tendency is to judge a school by the achievements of its best pupils, a regiment by its awards, a club by the social or official standing of its members. On this basis, the impartial albeit cursory observer of the English legal scene is entitled to reach certain conclusions about the standing of the solicitors' branch of the legal profession which, though probably mistaken, are hard to refute on a comparative honours board tally. To a certain and perhaps large extent the availability of top legal posts tends to reflect the status of the profession within the structure of the legal system and even perhaps socially.'[15] On every count other than the Bar's monopoly of legal appointments the professional and social distinction had by the mid-nineteenth century lost its justification. In a professional sense the initiative taken by The Law Society in the matter of examinations and education was vital. In 1846 when legal education was being investigated it was quite clearly shown that the Inns of Court had ceased to perform any educational function at all, and their subsequent resistance to the introduction of an educational system till late in the century degraded—to use a word applied by a contemporary—the standing of the Bar; until 1872 a man could become a barrister without taking any law examinations at all. It was absurd to accord superiority to a branch of the profession which could be entered by eating a number of dinners. The social distinction was becoming equally anomalous. It had long been artificial. The three greatest Lord Chancellors after the Restoration were all sons of attorneys: Somers, Hardwicke and Macclesfield. One of the most frequent complaints or observations in the mid-nineteenth century was that a large proportion of the Bar was composed of the sons or relatives of solicitors; for whatever reason they were among the most successful counsel so that it was said that 'eminent judges have brothers or near relatives in the inferior branches of the law'. At the end of the century Lord Selborne summed up the matter: 'From a social point of view to treat barristers as if they ought to belong to a different caste from solicitors, whose sons, brothers, or sons-in-law many of the most successful and honourable among them were, would be simply absurd.'[16] The two branches were in any event by this time being recruited from the same classes of society and from men who had had the same sort of education. In a severely practical age, moreover, the hard truth was recognised that the solicitors were dealing with the bulk of the country's legal business and had the handling of much of its wealth. It was increasingly pointed out in the professional and general press that it was absurd to treat a

[15] Law Society Archives: Memorandum on Official Appointments 1965.

[16] Memoirs Personal and Political, vol 1, p 53.

profession whose members were engaged in the most important affairs of the first families and the wealthiest corporations as inferior to another many of whose members could hardly get any business at all or were concerned with the prosecution of petty offenders at the Old Bailey.[17]

Against this background there were throughout the nineteenth century and beyond a number of major issues between the two branches. The demarcation issue related primarily to conveyancing and rights of audience. The others were patronage—in its widest sense of eligibility in law and fact for judicial and other legal appointments—the rules relating to transfer from one branch to the other, fusion, the etiquette of the Bar, and the right of counsel to accept instructions directly from the lay client. It was the last of these issues which caused the most heart-burning and aroused a great deal of public interest and on occasion some plain speaking from the general press. As has been seen, it was an issue which affected the conveyancing question, but it was also fundamental to the whole relationship between attorneys and solicitors on the one hand and the Bar on the other. There was a good deal of uncertainty. The law was stated by Lord Chief Justice Campbell in 1850 in these terms: 'There certainly has been an understanding in the profession that a barrister ought not to accept a brief in a civil suit except from an attorney; and I believe it is for the benefit of the suitor and the satisfactory administration of justice that this understanding should be generally acted upon; but we are of the opinion that there is no rule of law by which it can be enforced.'[18] The attorneys' standpoint was clearly stated by the Gentlemen Practisers in 1800: 'It was a highly improper practice for counsel to receive clients and transact their business independently and without the intervention of an attorney.'[19] But that may have been an exaggeration or at best a reflection of the standard which was accepted in the higher ranks of each side of the profession. There was no response from the members of the Society to whom a circular was sent with a view to preventing 'in future a practice so highly prejudicial to the interests of attorneys and solicitors'; and some non-members to whom the circular had been sent returned it 'in the most unhandsome manner'.[20] The Bar certainly did not see the matter in such simple terms as the committee of the Gentlemen Practisers. In 1824 when faced with a boycott by attorn ys on the Northern Circuit Brougham announced that he would accept instructions direct from laymen and his Bar Mess could find no circuit rule which prohibited him from so doing; and when he was faced by a similar threat in 1830 because of his suggestion of establishing local courts he made the same counter-threat with the maximum publicity in the House of Commons, on 10th November 1830. In 1845 barristers were still taking instructions direct from lay clients at the

[17] For instance, the *Saturday Review*, quoted in *Law Times*, 12th December 1857.

[18] *Doe* d *Bennett* v *Hale* (1850), 15 QB 171.

[19] Minutes, 27th June 1800.

[20] Ibid, 2nd June 1802.

Central Criminal and Bankruptcy Courts;[21] in 1868 a country attorney reported that 'several barristers in his district' were also taking instructions without the intervention of an attorney.[22] In 1869 the *Law Magazine and Review* stated that it had 'never been doubted that in conveyancing or criminal cases a barrister may by common law be directly retained by the client and as it has been laid down that he cannot withhold his services when a retainer is tendered it seems to follow that before this doctrine can be narrowed by a condition that such tender shall be made only through an attorney, some long-established rule of professional etiquette or immemorial usage to that effect must be shown to exist. We do not know of any such rule nor can we find trace of any such.'[23] Sir Richard Webster as leader of the Bar gave his opinion on 19th July 1888: there was 'no objection to a barrister seeing and advising a lay client without the intervention of a solicitor upon all points relating to the lay client's own personal conduct or guidance or the management or disposition of his own affairs or transactions'.[24] As the lay client would normally wish to consult counsel on his own rather than another's affairs, this ruling gave a considerable latitude. But even so the Bar was at pains to show that, whatever the practice might be, in its precise terms the principle was of recent origin, certainly not older than the latter part of the eighteenth century. In 1862 Serjeant Pulling in his standard work on the Law of Attorneys gave the most balanced view: 'During the last century the practice was gradually introduced of barristers requiring the intervention of attorneys and solicitors in cases which came professionally before them . . .; and such is the practice now generally followed though the legal right of barristers to dispense with such interventions is unquestionable.'[25] When the matter was being much discussed in the 1870s the comments from the Bar were: 'Even during the last century it was not fully established';[26] 'The practice such as it is is comparatively modern';[27] 'The practice of taking instructions direct from the client was followed by the most eminent members of the English Bar up to a recent time.'[28]

The custom or rule (and there do not appear to have been many practising barristers prepared to test it) was not without its critics inside and outside the profession. It was designed, said a contributor to the *Law Magazine and Review*, to bring a barrister under what Sir Robert Phillimore had called 'the malignant influence' of the solicitors and to 'compel the litigant to pay two sets of costs for work which might in most cases be far more efficiently performed by one'.[29] *The Times* had earlier been

[21] *Law Times*, vol 5, p 470.
[22] Ibid, vol 45, p 59.
[23] Vol 36 (1868–1869), p 291.
[24] *Law Times*, vol 85, p 176.
[25] Page 12.
[26] Charley, Legal Profession (1873), p 166.
[27] Lefevre, Discipline of the Bar, p 19.
[28] *Law Magazine and Review*, vol 52 (1874), p 840.
[29] Vol 13 (NS) (1887–1888), p 193 et seq. The editor expressly disclaimed the views so expressed but published them so as to give a full coverage.

at its most thunderous in condemnation of the rule and of the Bar for observing it. 'By obliging the client in the first instance to place himself in the hands of the attorney it has vested in him the patronage of the profession; it is only through the goodwill of that powerful class that a barrister can hope to succeed.... The attornies have very naturally become conscious of their power and have brought their own relations to the Bar as the future recipients of those good things whose distribution etiquette has forced upon them.... The Bar is ceasing to be a profession and becoming an inheritance.'[30] The rule should be abolished to save 'the toll which the British public has hitherto been prepared to pay'.[31] The acceptance of the rule by the Bar was described as a 'voluntary abdication'.[32] The *Cornhill Magazine* in 1863 pointed out the fallacy of the economies which it was claimed would be achieved by direct access. Taking the case of leases, which were often quoted as examples of the 'toll' which the public had to pay, it said that in order to make the lease 'worth having it is necessary to have the title examined, searches made in various registers, original deeds compared with copies and all manner of questions discussed in which the expediency of standing on a strict legal right is at least as important as the question of the existence of such right. If the barrister is to do all this besides drawing the lease and settling the phraseology of particular clauses, he must of course be paid for it, and then the client gains nothing except that he pays one man instead of another. If he does not what is the lease worth?'[33] From time to time individual barristers wrote to *The Times* to protest, and when the county courts were being set up in 1846 some of them thought that they would be benefited if they could accept instructions direct. There were not wanting voices warning the Bar of the dangers. 'We have refused to do without attorneys; and the consequence is that the attorneys are doing without us' and moreover 'to attorneys the present system is wholly advantageous. It gives them the patronage and the position of vantage in the profession.... It debars them from nothing but the higher walks of advocacy which they have neither the leisure nor inclination to pursue. And, while it takes nothing from them that they care to have, it leaves them free to usurp all that they are able to accomplish.'[34] It was suggested that the Bar etiquette was determined by the senior men who were well established with the attorneys and had everything to gain by keeping on good terms with them. For whatever reason the Bar conceded the point without any positive action from the attorneys. The hard fact was that if the Bar had taken instructions direct from clients it would have become indistinguishable from the attorneys and solicitors and would have ceased to exist as a separate profession.[35]

[30] On the whole subject see *The Times*, 1st and 7th November 1851. [31] Ibid.
[32] *Law Magazine and Review* (1857), p 254. [33] Page 111.
[34] *Law Magazine and Review* (1857), pp 255–256.
[35] Counsel may accept instructions direct from patent and parliamentary agents; and in criminal cases from prisoners in court under the dock brief system, though this is now obso-

Whether that was desirable was the subject of debate inside and outside the profession throughout the nineteenth century, and the debate still continues. In 1825 Mr Maugham expressed the opinion that 'it does not seem possible, even if it were desirable, for attornies in the present times to fill both offices with the vigilance and skill which are essential to the interests of suitors and which by the division of labour are now so effectually bestowed'.[36] In the 1850s articles such as those in *The Times* on the alleged wastefulness of having to consult two lawyers when one might do naturally raised the fusion issue. It was considered in 1852 by the Society for Promoting the Amendment of the Law and more significantly by the Commissioners appointed in 1854 to consider the legal education being provided by the Inns of Court. The Commissioners were aware that 'the profession of attorney had very much risen in importance and respectability compared with what it was 200 years ago';[37] moreover it knew that The Law Society was providing legal education for the attorneys and their articled clerks whereas the Bar was doing nothing. It seemed to the Commission that both branches were to be highly educated and trained in the same subjects and in that event it wished to know why the lay client should have to employ both. Mr Cookson, an attorney, replied: 'The two branches of the profession always have been and in my opinion ought to remain distinct.'[38] Nobody supporting the dual system has since added very much to that statement. The issue became more urgent as a result of a statement by Mr Justice Hannen in 1867 at a dinner of the Solicitors' Benevolent Association. He said that 'he did not hesitate to express the opinion that the two branches of the profession might be amalgamated'. He believed 'it was peculiar to England that the two branches of the profession were separated and not only peculiar to England in its largest sense but peculiar to this country; for in almost all our colonies the two branches have been amalgamated. He was not aware of any inconvenience which arose from it; and there could be no better training for a young barrister than to devote himself to the business of a solicitor.' Naturally a statement in these terms from a High Court judge aroused a great deal of professional interest. A meeting of neighbouring law societies was held in Leeds to consider the matter, but significantly the resolutions they passed at the end of their meeting referred primarily to the Bar's monopoly of appointments and to the funds in the Inns of Court and Chancery which the Bar had and which the meeting considered 'were originally common to both branches'.

---

lescent if not obsolete as a result of legal aid. The Law Society has been vigilant to prevent further exceptions, eg in favour of foreign attorneys working in London. In 1928 The Law Society expressed its disagreement with a Bar ruling that instructions might be accepted direct from local authority clerks who were not solicitors (Annual Report, 1928, p 29), though this is sometimes done.

36 Treatise on the Law of Attorneys and Solicitors, p 9.

37 Report, 1854–1855, BPP vol 18, qu 1571.

38 Ibid, ans 1581.

The issue was before the Annual Provincial Meeting in 1874. Although there were some solicitors who were enthusiastic, the bulk of the profession preferred the existing system. It was from outside the profession that the pressure came. In 1880 the *Economist* wrote that 'all that fusion will do will be to save expense, to make communications between lawyer and client direct, and to prevent the arrangement under which the solicitor is enabled to shift his responsibility on to counsel and counsel by his privilege to drop it altogether with the result of leaving the client's interest often totally unprotected against negligence or stupidity'.[39] *The Times* in 1884 returned to the charge and maintained that fusion would cheapen litigation. It pointed out that in one year (1881–1882) out of 714 cases in London where damages had been awarded there were only 160 where the amount had exceeded £200, and considered that it was absurd that for such small sums each party should have to employ and pay two lawyers.[40] In 1888 Sir Edward Clark QC, the then Solicitor-General, speaking to the law students in Birmingham, expressed the personal opinion that amalgamation would be to the benefit of the public and that it was hard that a man had to pay two lawyers instead of only one. 'At enormous cost the knowledge which the solicitor has is conveyed to another person in order that he may put to the court the matters which probably the solicitor knows much better and could explain just as well.'[41] The majority of the profession was not convinced. Motions in favour of fusion were rejected at the Annual Provincial Meetings in 1884 and 1888. At the latter meeting a resolution was passed by a substantial majority that there was 'no sufficient reason for seriously entertaining any scheme having for its object the amalgamation of the two branches of the profession'. Apart from the profession's natural conservatism and justifiable reluctance to upset a system with which it was familiar, fusion had few attractions for the smaller firm or sole practitioner, particularly in the country. A separate Bar placed at their disposal specialists and particularly specialists in advocacy without cost to themselves; and moreover, specialists to whom they could not lose their clients. Fusion might be attractive for many of its solicitor-supporters because they thought it would ease their way to judicial and other appointments; but judicial and many other appointments were for many in the country such remote possibilities as to count for nothing in the argument.[42]

The matter rumbled on until after the 1914–18 war and was then revived in 1919 at a special general meeting of The Law Society at which the argu-

[39] 21st January 1880, pp 70–71. The comment on shifting responsibility arises from the long-established doctrine that because counsel had no legal claim to his fees he had no legal liability for negligence (*per* Lord Kenyon in *Fell* v *Brown* (1791), 1 Peake's Rep 96); a solicitor properly instructing a suitable barrister and acting on his advice was and is similarly exempt.

[40] 5th January 1884.

[41] Delivered 15th January 1888 and reported *inter alia* in *Law Journal*, vol 23, pp 49–52.

[42] Proceedings, pp 22–26.

ment was advanced that it was 'in the public interest as a means of reconstruction that there should be a complete fusion' of the two branches. There was a majority of ninety-five to twenty-nine for fusion, but a poll was demanded. The importance which the profession attached to the question was reflected in the size of the poll. Over sixty per cent of the members voted and the motion was overwhelmingly defeated by 3,531 votes to 1,820.[43] The attitude of The Law Society was consistently hostile. It opposed a Bill with the purpose of fusing the two branches introduced in 1921 by a Mr Charles Percy and supported by, among others, Sir William Joynson Hicks, an eminent London solicitor,[44] and continued its opposition when the Bill was re-introduced in 1922. In the crisis years of 1930 and 1931 *The Times* revived the debate[45] but without achieving anything, and the next major statement was in an Addendum which a minority added to the Report of the Evershed Committee in 1953. The committee had been appointed by the government in 1947 with a wide authority to consider Supreme Court Practice and Procedure and specifically measures for reducing the cost of litigation,[46] and the minority expressed the opinion that fusion ought to be 'considered forthwith by an appropriate body constituted for the purpose with appropriate terms of reference. The view is held by some that fusion would result in a reduction in the cost of litigation. Whether or not this is so we do not know but the division of the profession into two distinct branches is one of the most obvious peculiarities of our system which invites criticism and requires to be rationally and convincingly justified.'[47] Nothing came of this recommendation.

Although The Law Society was officially opposed to fusion its spokesmen repeatedly referred to the issue. In 1957 the President said: 'My own [view] and I believe that of the great majority of solicitors and possibly even of barristers are opposed to fusion';[48] in 1959 it was discussed at the National Conference and most speakers were against it;[49] in 1965 the President said it 'would harm the public interest';[50] in 1968 the Young Solicitors Group, having set out the arguments for and against fusion, came to the conclusion that 'no conclusive argument can be sustained to effect a change'.[51] Fusion was a fleet in being the existence of which the Bar was not to be allowed to forget, and when need arose the possibility of it putting to sea was always there. In 1960 the President said that he

[43] Annual Report 1919, p 34.
[44] He was Postmaster General 1923, Minister of Health 1923, and Home Secretary from 1924 to 1929, when he became Viscount Brentford.
[45] 13th November 1930 and 26th June 1931.
[46] Cmnd 8878: 1952–1953 BPP, vol 14.
[47] Ibid, Addendum, p 316, No 11.
[48] National Conference, reported *Law Society's Gazette*, vol 54, p 620.
[49] *Law Society's Gazette*, vol 56, p 750.
[50] *Financial Times*, 12th July 1965.
[51] *Law Society's Gazette*, vol 65, p 24.

had no wish to see a fusion of the two branches but unless the Bar did something to improve its position it might happen.[52] But until then the issue could be safely left to the theorists and the reformers. For them 'the scales come down in favour of unification',[53] and even if, as in Victoria legislation, effecting fusion would make no difference in practice it should still be adopted here so that the individual could suit himself. Sadly 'it must be said that to some members of the profession many of the obstacles to a logical solution of the professional problems of the day stem from the rigid maintenance of that division in every respect'.[54] But when in 1970 the Lord Chancellor (Lord Gardiner) showed signs of not implementing the recommendations of the Beeching Committee that solicitors should be eligible for appointment to some of the new judicial posts then proposed and that their rights of audience should be enlarged, the Bar was given a sharp reminder. 'If the two branches fail between them to meet the public interest, the clamour for outright fusion will gather strength and might in due course result in irresistible pressure for changes which history would record with regret' and 'there has been growing pressure from certain quarters for the fusion of the two branches of the profession'. If the Bar resisted the solicitors' 'reasonable' demands (and are not one's own demands always reasonable?) 'ill considered pressure for fusion must inevitably gain strength and might well in due course overbear the truly valid considerations against so radical a change'.[55] In 1970 there was a change of government, and the Courts Act 1971 and the Administration of Justice Act 1973 gave to solicitors most if not all that they had asked for and fusion became again a minor problem. Officially 'neither branch of the profession believed in fusion' and membership of the European Economic Community did not require it.[56] It reappeared on the agenda of the National Conference in 1974, but there was nothing new to be said about it. A motion in favour of fusion was proposed by Lord Goodman but was defeated.[57] The profession was generally no more enthusiastic than the Bar. It was more interested in a system which it knew and which worked reasonably well than in one which might be more logical but which could certainly raise problems of which nobody had yet dreamed.

[52] *Law Society's Gazette*, vol 57, p 179.

[53] Mr Michael Zander's Lawyers and the Public Interest (1968), at p 326. This work sets out fully the arguments on either side as well as tracing the development of the argument.

[54] F C Shepherd, *Law Society's Gazette*, vol 60, p 203: Mr Shepherd is (or then was) a part-time lecturer at Manchester University.

[55] *Law Society's Gazette*, vol 67, p 736.

[56] The Attorney-General in the House of Commons, 20th December 1971.

[57] The debate is briefly reported in the *Guardian-Gazette*, 30th October 1974; there was a so-called 'Declaration of Bath' made after a meeting of representatives of the Bar Council and The Law Society 21st to 23rd November 1975 in which it was stated *inter alia* that 'the interests of the public are best served by a legal profession divided into two branches of equal status but with different and complementary functions' (reported *Guardian-Gazette*, 17th December 1975, p 1245).

Transfer from one branch to the other was another awkward problem. The Benchers combined with their policy of excluding attorneys and solicitors from the Inns of Court the supplemental one of making it as difficult as possible for them to become barristers. In 1764 the Inner and Middle Temples ordered that no attorney or solicitor or clerk in the Chancery or Exchequer should be called to the Bar until he should have actually discontinued practice for two years. In 1793 the Benchers of Lincoln's Inn resolved not 'to hear the exercises of any gentleman who had been admitted an attorney or a solicitor until his name had been taken off the Roll or to hear the exercises of any gentleman acting as clerk to an attorney or solicitor'.[58] In 1808 Lincoln's Inn resolved not to call any attorney or solicitor to the Bar till his name had been off the roll for two years nor any man who had acted as clerk to a solicitor or attorney until he had ceased to act for two years. In 1825 Lincoln's Inn and the Middle Temple, followed by the Inner Temble and Gray's Inn in 1828, resolved that no *recipiatur* for entering into commons should be granted to any attorney or solicitor whether the owner of chambers or not. This, of course, was almost an absolute prohibition, since it meant that an attorney or solicitor wishing to transfer had to cease practice and in effect earning a living at all before he entered the Inn and then had the normal period to pass before call. The rules were in practice relaxed and it was possible for attorneys or solicitors to be called after the gap of two years had elapsed. But in 1844 the rules were made more stringent. The Benchers then ordered that 'no attorney at law, solicitor ... shall be allowed to keep commons for the purpose of being called to the Bar ... until such person being an attorney shall have taken his name off the rolls'. The position in the middle of the century was therefore that, although three years were sufficient to keep the usual number of terms, an attorney had to cease to practise the law professionally for a total of five years. The reason for the rule was never formally stated, but it was generally understood to be to prevent the attorneys and solicitors who transferred from bringing with them the advantage of their former associations; or that 'the attorney who is accustomed to hold immediate intercourse with suitors would carry with him too much of their personal feeling to fit him for the position of barrister and to secure the confidence of the court'.[59] The restriction greatly irked the lower branch. They felt it was absurd if not worse to insist on these conditions when to qualify as attorneys or solicitors involved a much higher standard of professional knowledge and training than was required of the Bar.

In 1875 The Law Society formally protested to the Bar that it was not only against the public interest but also against 'the just expectations of the solicitor class' that these restrictions on transfer should be continued.[60] This was followed by an approach to the Inns to lift or ease the restrictions;

[58] Black Books, vol 4, p 111.
[59] *Legal Observer*, vol 34 (1847), p 434.
[60] Law Society Annual Report, 1875, p 10.

the Inns appointed a committee but no change was recommended. The Law Society thereupon decided that it would be politic to show that it believed in simplifying transfer, whether or not there was reciprocity, by seeking legislation changing the rules applying to barristers wishing to become solicitors,[61] and after 1877 barristers of five years' standing could be admitted as solicitors merely by passing the final examination and without any interval between leaving the Bar and being admitted.[62] The Bar did not accept the olive branch, and that shrewd man of business Sir John Hollams in 1878 moved an amendment in the House to the Bar Education and Discipline Bill to enable a solicitor of five years' standing to become a barrister on passing the Bar finals. The Bar took fright and dropped the Bill altogether. The next move was an approach by The Law Society to the Lord Chancellor (Lord Cairns), whom they persuaded that if necessary the Bar rules should be changed by legislation. His discussions with the Inns had not reached a conclusion by the time that there was a change of government. His successor (Lord Selborne) had to tell The Law Society that the Inns had not made up their mind. Accordingly at the next annual general meeting of the Society in 1880 it was resolved that 'the time had passed for seeking at the hands of the Benchers a modification of the rules' and that legislation should be sought.[63] Lord Selborne spoke plainly to the Inns, and rather than have legislation the Benchers agreed to reduce to one year the waiting period for solicitors of five years' standing. This of course was not reciprocation, and the Annual Provincial Meeting in 1888 urged that this should be requested, though it rejected fusion.[64] The Inns of Court then agreed that a solicitor of five years' standing could take the final Bar examination without keeping any terms provided he gave twelve months' notice; he was not to be under an obligation to give up practice as a solicitor whilst his notice was running. In 1910 the Bar sought to reverse this decision and to impose an embargo on practice during the period of the notice, but The Law Society refused to agree to a change of the rule, which it not unreasonably pointed out had been settled twenty-one years earlier after negotiations extending over fifteen years.[65] The year's notice was reduced in 1928 to six months after further representations to the Inns. This still left the considerable financial obstacle that the normal one year's pupillage had to be served, and during the first six months of that the entrant was subject to the same rule as other Bar students that he could not take any form of paid work from solicitors. This was further eased from 1st October 1969. Solicitors of three years' standing with adequate advocacy and court experience need only do six months' pupillage.

[61] Annual Report, 1876, p 6.
[62] Solicitors Act 1877, s 12.
[63] Annual Report, 1880, p 4.
[64] Report, p 113.
[65] Annual Report, 1925, p 34.

Quite apart from the technical obstacles to transfer, the attorney or solicitor who had turned barrister was not made very welcome. He was an intruder and the attitude of the Bar to him was summarised in the words used by Foss in his Lives of the Judges in respect of Thomas Wilde. Wilde was the son of an attorney and practised as an attorney, but in 1850 he became Lord Chancellor as Lord Truro, having as Foss put it overcome 'all the obstacles in the way of one who, as it were, intrudes himself into a higher branch of his profession'.[66] Nevertheless there were many who made the transfer with conspicuous success and not a few who attained the highest judicial offices.[67]

The monopoly which the Bar enjoyed in respect of judicial and other appointments was the most frequent of all the complaints which were made by attorneys and solicitors. It was something which touched the profession in its pride as well as in its pocket. No attorney ventured to criticise it until the mid-nineteenth century, but then the profession was flexing its muscles and gaining in confidence. Persistent comments began to be made on the absurdity and unfairness of the system, and attempts were made to change it. In 1873 Mr C E Lewis, a solicitor then recently elected member of Parliament for Londonderry, coined the phrase 'the reign of Barristerdom' as descriptive of the monopoly and urged his brethren to overthrow it. But the monopoly was vital to the Bar's survival. Who would take all the financial risks of going to the Bar if he did not have the assurance of a safe and comfortable haven? Accordingly the Bar, however pusillanimous it might be in relation to some of the disputed areas, was resolute in defence of this one. No sooner were the attorneys and solicitors conscious of their better status as a liberal and prosperous profession than the strife began. 'Internal jealousies, the constant accompaniment of such a state of things, are rife with us, which is shown in the struggle growing up (we see no good reason for disguising it) between the two principal divisions of the legal profession for position and profit, or, as the profane would say, for place and plunder. The Attornies desire to participate more largely in the dignity, the patronage, and the professional recognition which has hitherto been accorded to Barristers. The Barristers find not only these important matters but their very life blood, their revenues, without which neither life nor honour can live, in the world as at present constituted, encroached upon by the growing importance, justified by the improved intelligence, activity, and respectability of the Attornies.'[68] In 1868 the position was stated by a Mr Jevons, speaking to the Leeds Law Society, to be: 'All the higher judicial officers at home and in the colonies, county court judges, commissioners in bankruptcy, records, and judges of all inferior courts of record, examiners in Chancery, associates, stipen-

[66] Lives of the Judges, vol 9, p 306.

[67] There are too many to give a complete list; at the present time the most eminent are Lord Widgery LCJ, Megarry V-C and Payne J.

[68] *Law Review*, 1849, vol 10, pp 148–149.

diary magistrates, and revising barristers, are exclusively appointed from members of the Bar; who besides monopolise a number of other appointments ... There are some other offices ... to which barristers and attorneys are both eligible but the majority of which are conferred on barristers. The only offices exclusively given to attorneys are the offices of chief clerk to the Chancery judges, taxing masters in Chancery, and registrars of the county courts. Attorneys and solicitors are declared by statute incapable of being appointed county magistrates and although legally eligible as borough magistrates it has been the practice of late to refuse to appoint them.[69] Attorneys and solicitors are, in fact, equally fit with barristers for many of the offices to which barristers are exclusively appointed and from their greater acquaintance with the practical details of the profession are better qualified for many of such offices.'[70] In 1877 there was a particularly bitter paper read to the Annual Provincial Meeting by a Council member named Follett[71] and the Bar expressed concern that such views could be held by a man who might one day be President. By a quirk of fate Mr Follett was next year removed from the debate by being appointed solicitor to the Customs and Excise, a post formerly given to a barrister. It was not only that the Bar was accused of having an unfair share already; some solicitors thought the Bar was not to be trusted in the allocation of the numerous new posts being created at the time. Mr Charles Ford (he was a doughty fighter, as the Council well knew from his campaign against them in respect of the Law Club[72]) wrote that the Bar was 'constantly encroaching upon their weaker brethren by rushing in on them in unguarded moments and obtaining legislation in their own favour by introducing sections into Acts of Parliament.... For instance, in the present Land Titles and Transfer Bill an attempt was made to exclude hard-working solicitors from the offices which will be created by the establishment of district registries.'[73] In 1880 the *Economist* pointed out that 'solicitors had to make very considerable sacrifices to support the existing state of things. The prizes of the Bar are perhaps the greatest to be found in any profession in the world. Yet none of these is open to solicitors.'[74] In 1888 the Annual Provincial Meeting was told during the fusion debate that 'there is no calling except one where one branch is admitted within the sacred precinct of honour whilst another is kept shivering outside'.[75] In 1896 the list given by Mr Christian in his Short History of Solicitors[76] was the same as that given by Mr Jevons thirty years before. A slight improvement was achieved in 1922 when the Lord

[69] The practice was in fact of long standing; the Home Secretary (Sir George Grey) wrote to the Lancaster justices in 1855 that he thought 'it right to adhere to the rule which has hitherto been generally adopted that practising solicitors should not be placed in the commission'.

[70] *Law Times*, vol 45 (1868), pp 409–410.

[71] Proceedings, pp 98–107.

[72] See p 34, *supra*.

[73] *Law Times*, vol 57 (1874), p 80.

[74] 21st January 1880, pp 70–71.

[75] Proceedings, p 95.

[76] Page 231.

Chancellor agreed that so far as possible solicitors should be appointed to the solicitorships of government departments,[77] but somehow the possibility never seemed to become a reality. The Law Society continued to press the point, and in 1927 the Lord Chancellor wrote to them to the effect that appointments would be made in future on the basis of merit alone and with that the Council was 'obliged to rest content'.[78] So far as judicial appointments went it seemed that the dictum in the Mirror of Justices that attorneys could not be judges[79] must remain for ever valid. It was true that in the Small Debts Act 1845 attorneys were eligible for appointment as judges of the courts set up by that Act, and one of them, a Mr James Stansfield of Halifax, actually was appointed. The courts were almost immediately abolished and replaced by the county courts, and the County Courts Act 1846 preserved the attorneys' rights, which for practical purposes meant those of Mr Stansfield, who accordingly became county court judge of the Halifax area. But he was unique. In 1870 a Mr Merriman introduced a Bill to make solicitors eligible for judicial offices, but nothing came of it. In any event the profession was not so enthusiastic about this as it was about non-judicial appointments. A proposal that solicitors should be eligible for county court judgeships was rejected by the Annual Provincial Meeting in 1894. There was a slight movement in 1938 when solicitors were made eligible for appointment as chairmen of quarter sessions, but it was only a gesture. Thirty years on, only one solicitor occupied that office compared with sixty-three barristers; and only four were even deputies compared with 200 from the Bar. It was not until 1971 that any real progress was made.

The Second World War may have made changes easier. At any rate it was possible to report in 1945 that posts as important as the Director of Public Prosecutions, the Public Trustee and the Chief Land Registrar had for the first time gone to solicitors.[80] The office of stipendiary magistrate, always previously reserved for the Bar, was opened to solicitors of seven years' standing by the Justices of the Peace Act 1949, but no solicitor was in fact appointed until 1956 when Mr Pugh was appointed at Huddersfield; the next appointment was not made until 1960 and almost twenty years after the Act was passed there were still only three solicitor-stipendiaries. In the House of Lords in the debates on the Administration of Justice Bill in 1960 and 1961 there was support for the wider use of solicitors as a source of judges from Lord Chorley (a barrister) and for the appointment of solicitors to the county court bench from Lord Ogmore (a solicitor). Lord Ogmore pointed out the absurdity of the situation in which 'many business men come from all over the world and have their agreements drawn in London because of the great expertise of some of

[77] Law Society Annual Report, 1922, p 34.
[78] Law Society Annual Report, 1927, p 40.
[79] Selden Society ed, p 44.
[80] *Law Society's Gazette*, vol 42 (1945), p 33.

those firms in the City. Yet those men have no chance even of being made county court judges ... All they can hope for is to be metropolitan magistrates.' The Law Society began to increase the pressure. In 1961 the *Gazette* complained that to exclude ninety per cent of the legal profession from consideration for judicial office was 'one of the least satisfactory consequences of a divided profession'[81] and Sir Thomas Lund in 1963 said he could not accept that the Bar had 'a monopoly of the wisdom and other qualities which go to make a good judge'.[82] There was outside support. As the Bar became busier the question arose whether it could continue to supply men of the right quality for the increasing number of posts which had to be filled and still maintain an efficient Bar. *The Times* in 1961 questioned whether it could, but Lord Kilmuir, then Lord Chancellor, told the House of Lords on 15th November 1961 that he had no doubt it could. It was a *reductio ad absurdum* of the position that when pressure of work in some county courts made it necessary to appoint deputies these had generally to be taken from barristers who had little or no work to do and who therefore probably had little or not enough up-to-date practical experience, in preference to solicitors who would on all other counts be more suitable but were ineligible because they were solicitors. The pressure of work in the courts was, however, such that it was clear that some radical changes were necessary, and the government appointed the so-called Beeching Committee to enquire into the arrangements for the administration of justice at assizes and at quarter sessions outside Greater London and to recommend what reforms were needed. When the Report was published in 1969[83] it drew attention to the anomaly that whereas solicitors had since 1938 been eligible for appointment as chairmen of quarter sessions they were not eligible to be appointed county court judges; the anomaly was the more serious because an important recommendation of the committee was the amalgamation of the two benches. The committee by a majority were in favour of making solicitors eligible for appointment as circuit judges and recorders.[84] The committee by a majority rejected the argument that it was unfair to remove a monopoly from one branch of the profession without looking at all the monopolies enjoyed by both. The matter appeared to be resolved in favour of the solicitors, but to their astonishment and anger the Lord Chancellor did not intend to include this recommendation in the Courts Bill. The issue was allied to the more important one of right of audience,[85] and the press was delighted at the possibility of seeing a public trial of strength. In the event this did not happen, though many angry words were said before the issue was settled. A change of government brought a new Lord Chancellor in Lord Hail-

[81] *Law Society's Gazette*, vol 58, p 530.
[82] Ibid, vol 60, p 134.
[83] Cmnd 4153.
[84] The committee's reasoning is contained in paras 245–248.
[85] *Supra*, pp 158–162.

sham and the Courts Act 1971 made solicitors of ten years' standing eligible for appointment as recorders—their function being to act as 'part-time judges of the Crown Court and to carry out such other judicial functions as may be conferred on them by this or any other enactment';[86] when a solicitor has been a recorder for at least five years he becomes eligible for appointment as a circuit judge 'to serve in the Crown Court and county courts and to carry out such other judicial functions as may be conferred upon them under this or any other enactment'.[87] The Act, as amended by the Administration of Justice Act 1973, makes a solicitor of ten years' standing eligible for appointment as a deputy circuit judge, but however long he serves in that capacity he does not become eligible for promotion to circuit judge unless he has served five years as a recorder.[88] The number of solicitors appointed under these powers to the middle of 1975 was thirty-six. It was a start and it raised the profession's self-respect.

One other matter affected the relationship between the two branches: the rules made by the Bar to regulate the conduct of its members, that is to say Bar etiquette. The rule with regard to acceptance of instructions only from solicitors naturally had the support of solicitors, who were concerned only to see that it was not infringed and that it was if possible strengthened. Other aspects of Bar etiquette, or to use a later description, restrictive practices, were not so welcome. Partly it was a social matter. Bar etiquette forbade anything which might savour of currying favour with solicitors. 'In the eighteenth century Pratt remained a long while briefless because he would not invite solicitors to his dinner parties nor dance with their daughters; and Wedderburn on the other hand built up a large body of clients by canvassing the City solicitors for briefs.'[89] But the solicitor's main concern was with the Bar practices which affected him in his daily work and, as he saw it, also affected his client's interests. The Bar had its own rules made by itself without reference and not subject to any outside jurisdiction or interest. Underlying the Bar etiquette was the concept that barristers were volunteers accepting an honorarium for their services but not under any legal obligation to provide them or perform them carefully. The solicitors found it inconvenient that they could not discuss fees with barristers but had to do so with their clerks. They found it inconvenient and often harmful to their clients and therefore embarrassing to themselves that barristers returned briefs at the last minute, or were not present in court when cases were called on, or in the case of leaders not present when the cases were being heard. They found it unreasonable that because of a Bar rule that a junior barrister should be paid two-thirds

[86] Courts Act 1971, s 21 (1) and (2).

[87] Courts Act 1971, s 16 (1) and (3).

[88] Courts Act 1971, s 24 (2) (*a*), as amended by Administration of Justice Act 1973, s 15. In 1976 the Lord Chancellor indicated his intention that the period should be reduced to five years.

[89] Halévy, op cit, p 22.

of the fee paid to a Queen's Counsel appearing with him in a case their clients should have to pay the junior barrister much more than he would have expected to be paid if he had been appearing alone and bearing the whole brunt of the matter himself. The solicitors could or felt able to do little until the 1960s, when public opinion was becoming increasingly critical of all monopolies and restrictive practices and when their own were favourite targets. The Law Society was at the time led by men of particular ability and character and did not feel itself in any way inhibited from criticising the Bar's rules, many of which it considered to be out of date and in need of urgent change. A committee was appointed in 1962 to consider the question of 'Counsel Fees and Kindred Matters' and it treated its terms of reference as enabling it to look at the whole problem. In 1964 The Law Society sent to the Bar Council the memorandum which the committee had prepared and the Council of The Law Society had adopted. The memorandum did not mince its words or show any recollection of the inferior station to which its authors' predecessors had been relegated in 1614. The Bar practices were in many cases, it alleged, 'relics of a bygone age' and, originating as they did in 'medieval and earlier times, are ripe for change'. If the memorandum was not very sound historically, its meaning was clear. It dealt with the matters which had rankled for so long. It wished to have an end of the 'honorarium' fiction and with it among other things the exemption of the Bar from ordinary professional liability; it wanted a change in the convention that as the fee was theoretically payable when the brief was delivered the barrister was entitled to be paid even if the case was settled before he had looked at the papers; it asked for the abolition of the 'two-thirds' rule; it proposed that where the barrister who had been briefed found himself unable to appear there should be a right to an adjournment so that the client was not left with no alternative but to accept a substitute who might be and probably was quite unfamiliar with the case. The memorandum was to have been published in the Society's Annual Report for 1964 but at the request of the Bar Council it was held back. It was, however, 'leaked' to the *Guardian* newspaper and the Bar Council was forced to take some public action.[90] Incidentally the identity of the 'leaker' was never established, but the Bar for a time treated the incident as an act of bad faith. The Bar in 1966 at any rate conceded the abandonment of the 'two-thirds' rule,[91] and the only other positive result of the memorandum was the establishment in November 1965 of a Joint Committee of the Bar Council and The Law Society, originally to consider its contents but continued afterwards in order to provide a regular forum for the consideration of matters of common interest and dispute.

Since this episode relations between the two branches have been generally amicable, although they were again disturbed during the discussions

[90] *Law Society's Gazette*, May 1965.

[91] *The Times*, 23rd July 1966; *Law Society's Gazette*, vol 63, p 330.

on the eligibility of solicitors for appointments as recorders and circuit judges. From the mid-1960s onwards both branches have experienced exceptional prosperity. There has been more than enough work to go round, most of it properly paid, and that was a great soother. The old social distances were shortened. After the 1945 war Sir Hartley Shawcross as Attorney-General had uttered cautionary words about barristers not being on too close social terms with solicitors, but that was even then an anachronism. The Law Society recorded in its Annual Report for 1964 the historic event of the Treasurer and Benchers of Gray's Inn having invited the President and members of the Council to dinner in their Hall, and that was followed by invitations from the other Inns. The Bar relaxed its rule about barristers not attending local law society dinners. In 1973 on the suggestion of the Lord Chancellor the President wore a scarlet robe at the Opening of the Legal Year and in the procession then and since has walked *pari passu* with the Chairman of the Bar Council. At the end of 1975 there was a formal statement that the two branches were of equal status if of differing functions.[92] It is not in human nature that there will not be disputes in the future, but by and large both branches have in the twentieth century realised that disputes within the profession are not likely to advantage the profession as a whole.

[92] *Guardian-Gazette*, 17th December 1975, p 1245.

CHAPTER 10

Public Life

It would be possible to read every popular political history of England down to the end of the nineteenth century without finding a mention of any attorney or solicitor other than Robert Aske, who led the Pilgrimage of Grace in 1536. The political stage has for five hundred years been the House of Commons, and there were ample reasons why attorneys and solicitors found it difficult to mount it. Until the introduction of the ballot box for the 1874 elections and the corrupt practices legislation of 1883 a seat in the Commons depended on birth, favour or wealth except in the comparatively few towns where the franchise was liberal. Attorneys were rarely if ever connected by birth with families who had seats at their disposal. They were not likely to be of sufficient importance to command the favour of those able to nominate them, though a few sat as nominees for landlord-clients. In the period 1750–1790 for instance there were six attorneys who sat in that capacity, and two of them, Marshe Duckinson and John Paterson, were of sufficient standing to be successive Chairmen of Ways and Means from 1761 to 1768. There were also a few who were elected for boroughs where they had a local interest and following. But they were a small band. For those without patronage wealth was the normal means of entry. Membership of the House of Commons was highly prized and those who had seats at their disposal charged accordingly. At the beginning of the nineteenth century Lady Irwin usually asked £5,000 at each election for each of the two seats she had at Horsham, and Peel was said to have spent £132,000 on Tamworth. A vote at High Wycombe at the end of the eighteenth century cost £1,000 or so, and Lord Townshend spent £50,000 to buy enough votes to win Westminster. No attorneys could enter this sort of competition. In any event the financial burden of living in London was heavy even though the sessions were short. In 1895 a solicitor who had contested a county constituency four times was said to have spent £20,000 on the elections and his other parliamentary expenses. Moreover the House of Commons was not an attractive career for an attorney still in practice. Whereas for the Bar a seat in the Commons opened up the possibilities of the highest preferment, even of the Woolsack, and failing that of innumerable lesser jobs, the attorney had nothing to hope for in the way of professional advancement. Accordingly even after the Reform Act in 1832 the position did not materially change.

In 1847 the *Law Times* asked: 'When since the Parliament of the Revolution did the House of Commons see three practising attorneys sitting as members?'[1] and it was a matter of congratulation in the next year that the attorneys could boast five of their number as members. These tiny figures contrast with the strength of the Bar. In Elizabeth I's time there were generally between seventy and eighty barrister members and this persisted. Dod's Parliamentary Pocket Companion, published from 1832 onwards, makes sad reading for a solicitor. Every page in the biographical section has its quota of barristers, but it is a labour of love to find a single attorney. In 1892 there were 150 or more barristers, albeit not all practising, and there were only seventeen solicitors. It was not until the 1906 Parliament that the solicitors were reasonably represented with thirty-four members: that was the highest number ever achieved and in 1974 there were but twenty.

The consequences of this state of affairs have been serious. By and large the House of Commons has always been hostile to the attorneys and solicitors. Before the nineteenth century it was never reluctant to approve measures to limit their numbers or impose special taxation on them or to consider proposals for their abolition or to record its disapproval of their conduct. In the nineteenth and even in the twentieth century nothing is so remarkable as the persistence with which the House has rejected or postponed legislation promoted by The Law Society even where the object has been primarily the public benefit. Improvements in legal education were repeatedly blocked; even so uncontroversial a measure as excluding undischarged bankrupts from practice took four years to reach the statute-book; it took thirty years and the intervention of the Attorney-General to set up a Disciplinary Committee; and in 1970 when The Law Society needed further powers to put its finances on a proper footing (including power to make higher levies on the profession for the Compensation Fund) it was blocked for four years and had to concede lay representation in disciplinary matters as the price. The atmosphere was summed up in 1850 by a solicitor who was a member: 'They are perfectly rabid against us.'[2] In the nineteenth century the profession undoubtedly suffered because of its opposition to land registration; from its association with corrupt practices at elections; and from the frauds by solicitors which seemed to come in intense spasms—in the 1860s, the 1890s, the 1900s and so on. But the real cause was the small number of solicitors in the House, and it is difficult to avoid the conclusion that the comparative immunity of the Bar from unfriendly action and comment in the House was largely due to the fact that about twenty-five per cent of its members were barristers. An attempt to organise the solicitor-members into an effective group was made in 1956 by the formation of an all-party group of solicitor-members of the Commons and the House of Lords, which has certainly been of help.

Yet the attorneys and solicitors behind the scenes exercised a powerful

[1] Vol 9, p 506.

[2] *Law Times*, vol 17, p 182.

influence. As soon as the party political system emerged in the latter part of the seventeenth century the organisation of elections and the management of constituencies in the widest sense was entrusted to them. Country attorneys were already acting as agents managing the estates of those who were interested in controlling elections; they were by virtue of their businesses in close touch with the affairs and people of the constituencies; and because votes often depended on tenure and title to land they were in the best position to substantiate the title of their master's supporters and to defeat that of his opponent's. After the Restoration old Somers, the father of the future Lord Chancellor, managed the parliamentary elections of the county and city of Worcester and the boroughs of Evesham, Droitwich and Bewdley, and to his great house Whiteladies came the candidates and their representatives to consult him on their election plans, to be followed in due course by those who came to claim their rewards.[3] In the next century in little Appleby the local attorney, John Robinson, was made agent for the future Earl of Lonsdale, who ascribed to him almost all the virtues to which an attorney could aspire: 'steady, sober-minded, industrious, clever man of business'. He managed the elections well enough for his master, before he quarrelled with him, to find him a seat in the House, and he then married a rich wife so that he could devote himself to politics. He became the first attorney minister as Lord North's Secretary of the Treasury, and was the channel through which government patronage and bribery were distributed; in other words he manipulated the House of Commons on behalf of the King and his ministers. He knew the House better than any man of his time and though large sums of money passed through his hands he took none for himself. As a member he spoke but little; his work was in the corridors of power. He was the go-between through whom George III and others communicated with Lord North, and his own letters and memoranda are full of a worldly wisdom reminiscent of Wellington. The King regarded him as a personal friend and when he retired in 1778 (refusing a peerage) he went down to Windsor as Surveyor General of Woods and Forests. He planted twenty thousand oaks and millions of acorns, but he is chiefly remembered now as the butt of Sheridan's wit. Sheridan was challenged in the House to name those whom he accused of bribery and he looked Robinson straight in the eyes and said: 'I could do that just as soon as say Jack Robinson.' Of the same calibre was Thomas Nuthall, the Earl of Chatham's solicitor. His main function was also the manipulation of elections, but he was also engaged on high political business when need arose, as in 1766 when his client was trying to form a government and he was the go-between.[4]

[3] Campbell, Lives of the Chancellors, vol 4, p 68.

[4] As so often happens, public business led to errors in private matters: Lord Temple wrote to Pitt that Nuthall was 'a facetious man of business ... witness your marriage settlements not witnessed'. Nuthall died giving details of an attempted highway robbery in which he had driven off the highwayman.

By the end of the eighteenth century the attorneys and solicitors were effectively in charge of this highly technical business, and for them an election was a golden harvest. Golden it certainly was, because they had the handling of the vast sums which were spent by candidates who wished to have as little to do with the wholesale bribery as possible. The profession practised then the whole repertoire of bribery and chicanery which in a later period was to expose it to so much criticism, but until then they could not be and were not blamed for the part they played. They were expressly employed to do this work for men of the highest repute who regarded bribery at all levels as an essential instrument of government. The Reform Act 1832 did not alter the situation. In 1858 the *Law Times* said that 'solicitors are the real Parliament makers'[5] and in 1871 that the 'management of elections throughout the country is practically committed' to solicitors.[6] In fact the reform legislation, because of the technicalities it introduced into the voting system, made the hold of the profession still stronger. Election law and practice occupied a substantial space in all the legal papers. The standard work was Cox and Gray's New Law and Practice of Elections, first published in 1843 and going to thirteen editions by 1880.[7] The editors had no doubt about the position. After the 1867 Reform Act they wrote that 'with the increased constituencies more than ever before is the assistance of the solicitor necessary to success at an election. More depends on management than formerly. To watch the registration, to keep up the interest of the candidate among the electors, and to determine the order of battle is a business to be learned only by experience and requiring a clear head and a firm hand. Only the solicitor who combines a knowledge of the law with the training which forms the legal mind can master this business.'[8] The special knowledge brought continuity. 'In many counties the whole of the election organisation from the solicitor principal-agent at the top to the solicitors' clerks and their hired roughs at the bottom was almost entirely hereditary.'[9] So complete was the dominance of the profession that in 1852 Disraeli put the central organisation of the Tory party into the hands of his friend and solicitor Sir Philip Rose, and in 1874 there were only fifty-two English constituencies where the Tory agent was not a solicitor and these were practically all in Yorkshire and Lancashire. Of the power which this dominance gave the profession in public life *The Times* had no doubt. In 1853 it referred to the 'immensely potential agency of the attorneys in British society ... We are a people ridden by attorneys. ... England is a fifteen thousand attorney power machine for the performance or observance of the law'.[10]

[5] Vol 21, p 197.
[6] Vol 50, p 332.
[7] The first edition was by Mr Cox alone and had a mere 135 pages; the thirteenth had 772 pages.
[8] Op cit (1868 ed), p clvii.
[9] Hanham, Elections and Electioneering, p 236.
[10] 11th March.

There were some solicitors with exceptional knowledge and skill in this field. In the events which led to the Reform Act of 1832 one of the most important men was Joseph Parkes, a Birmingham attorney (he was the author of A History of the Court of Chancery, published in 1827) and the head and front of the powerful Birmingham Political Union. He was made secretary of the Royal Commission on Municipal Corporations because of his special experience of municipal affairs, and when he died in 1865 *The Times* said of him that 'perhaps no man was better acquainted with the secret history of politics during the last thirty or fifty years'. When Disraeli was corresponding with Queen Victoria in 1864 about the prospects of the Conservative Party at the General Election he quoted the opinion of a Mr Sudlow of Manchester, whom he described as a 'very eminent solicitor and reputed to have the most accurate and extensive electioneering experience in England'.[11] For the majority, however, it was simply a matter of money. It was for that purpose essential to ensure that there was a contest, and in this respect the Bridgwater Bribery Commission in 1867 uncovered a typical situation. According to the mayor's memory 'the candidates were always introduced by members of the legal profession', and when he was asked by the commissioners whether 'these gentlemen have contrived an election on each occasion' he replied that 'some of us have been uncharitable enough to put it down to the source you have named'. The commission found that the elections were worked by 'a knot of attorneys' and that 'the candidates were originally employed by the attorneys and not the attorneys by the candidates'. Bribery was on a vast scale, perhaps even vaster than before the Reform Act because the old tightly controlled constituencies had become more accessible to outside influences and because men with money wanted to get into the House with all its social and economic advantages. For the solicitors who had to distribute the money and protect their clients from personal risk the dangers were considerable. In 1880 at Macclesfield the two solicitor agents agreed, as had been their custom not only there but in many other places, that their respective outlay on bribes would not exceed a certain sum and that provided this was done neither would petition to unseat the other on the ground of bribery. The Conservative complained that the Liberal had spent too much, and a petition followed. Sir Edward Clark QC, who appeared on the petition, estimated that between them they had bribed 3,500 out of an electorate of 5,000; Macclesfield was disfranchised and the two solicitors were sent to prison.[12] There is no evidence that they were also struck off the roll.

The optimism of the profession that the more extensive the electorate the greater would be the demand for their services proved to be unfounded. The sordid revelations after every general election at the hearings of election petitions became nauseous to a public which adopted a much higher

[11] Quoted in Blake, Disraeli, p 512.
[12] Story of My Life, p 182.

standard of morality than that of the previous generation or two. At each hearing it was the local solicitors who had to bear the brunt of the attack, and the profession was inextricably involved and identified with election corruption. In 1860, in order to exclude them or at any rate to discourage them from undertaking election business, it was proposed in the Commons that solicitors should be prohibited from accepting any fees in respect of it. Sir Henry Bruce, who was Home Secretary in Gladstone's 1868 ministry, mounted a particularly virulent attack on the evil influence which he considered the profession had on election practices. When the 1871 Bill was promoted it was said that 'one of the foremost arguments preferred by the promoters is that it would destroy the influence of the solicitors in the elections'.[13] The President of The Law Society in 1878 appealed to solicitors 'not to do dirty work' in the forthcoming election. His appeal and the first attempts to eradicate corrupt practices failed; in 1880 Sir Edward Clark found briefs to appear on election petitions pouring on to his desk and he appeared on no fewer than thirteen.[14] Baron de Ferrieres reckoned that at that election a million pounds was spent. But that finally exhausted the patience of all decent men. 'The desire to wipe out the tribe of electioneering parasites, the Walshes and Wreghitts, the Hughes and the Lovibonds, proved to be a common goal transcending party differences.'[15] The Corrupt Practices Act 1883 arose from a desire on all sides of politics and in all walks of life to put an end to the whole sordid business, which in any event fewer and fewer candidates, particularly among the new men, could pay for. The loss in terms of money must have been substantial, but whereas the loss of any other part of its business caused a torrent of protest from the profession this one hardly raised a whimper.[16] The change did not mean that the local party organisations ceased to employ solicitors as their agents. Not a few who were big enough to require a full-time man recruited him from the ranks of the solicitors with small practices, who found that the salaries, which ranged from £150 to £400, did not compare unfavourably with their professional incomes. A good many others were part-time agents. Right down to 1939 and perhaps beyond some party organisations, particularly the Conservative ones, employed local solicitors in this way, but the palmy days were over.

Naturally the poor showing of the profession at the polls was reflected in its role in government itself. The first practising solicitor to become a cabinet minister was Sir Henry Fowler, who in 1892 became President of the Local Government Board in Gladstone's ministry, and it was not until 1905 that there were two solicitors in the cabinet at the same time.

[13] *Law Times*, vol 50, p 332.

[14] Op cit, p 174.

[15] O'Leary, Elimination of Corrupt Practices, p 229.

[16] It was reckoned that a contested election was worth £400 in fees to the solicitor agent in the mid-nineteenth century. In 1871 the *Law Times* referred to the 1871 Bill as threatening 'a loss to the profession of a sum whose magnitude would astound those who have never tried to compute the product of a general election to the lawyers' (vol 50, p 332).

This is all the more surprising when it is related to the dominant part played by lawyers—and provincial lawyers at that—in the United States of America and France during the same period. One of the problems was that solicitors had generally to establish themselves first in practice before they could afford the time and money to embark on a political career and by then they were behind in the race. The average age at which they were elected was forty-eight, by which time some barristers had been twenty-five years in the House.[17] Fowler was sixty-two when he entered the cabinet. That is late by present-day standards and it was even more so in the nineteenth century. Palmerston had been offered the Chancellorship of the Exchequer at twenty-five and Gladstone was only thirty-four when he became a cabinet minister. Yet Fowler was a man of outstanding ability and was one of the successes of Gladstone's 1892 ministry[18] and 'one of the best speakers in the House'.[19] In 1895 he saved the government from defeat by his single effort. When he rose to speak it was tottering and when he sat down it was saved with a majority of ninety-five. Modestly he said afterwards: 'The best part of my speech was never spoken; I saw that I had the House with me and I sat down.' He was one of the Queen's favourites, not only because he always agreed with her but because he understood her character.[20] In 1908 he became Lord President of the Council and but for his age he might have become leader of the Liberal Party. The Dictionary of National Biography says of his achievement: 'It was a remarkable position to have been won by a man who aided by no adventitious circumstances did not enter Parliament until he was fifty and owed everything to intellect, resolution and character.' He was the son of a poor Wesleyan minister and he died Viscount Wolverhampton. Not only that, he never forgot his profession. He was President of The Law Society in 1900 and for many years a member of the Council. The Council reports and minutes of those years show what great service he rendered to the profession. His portrait hangs in the Society's Hall.[21]

The next cabinet minister was David Lloyd George, who started his professional career in Wales. At the comparatively early age of twenty-seven he was elected—in 1890—as member of Caernarvon Boroughs and was President of the Board of Trade in 1905; Chancellor of the Exchequer in 1908; and Prime Minister in December 1916. Although the events immediately after the end of the 1914–1918 war have not adorned his memory, it is not disputed that his energy, eloquence and determination vastly contributed to a victory which seemed very remote when he took office. He is the only solicitor to have held the highest office, but after him came

[17] Judd, Members of Parliament 1734–1832. Lloyd George was a notable exception and was elected when he was twenty-seven.

[18] Magnus, Gladstone, p 402.

[19] Morley, Gladstone, vol 2, p 432.

[20] Ponsonby, Recollections of Three Reigns, p 41.

[21] His daughter wrote a biography of him published by Hutchinson in 1912.

a largish number of solicitors who reached the cabinet or at any rate ministerial rank, the best known perhaps being Sir William Joynson Hicks (afterwards Lord Brentford), who was much beloved of the cartoonists when he was Home Secretary, and Sir Howard Kingsley Wood, who in 1940 was Chancellor of the Exchequer.[22] In 1906 Mr Henry Attlee, then President of The Law Society, said: 'Better at once to tell them that, if they desire public fame and honours beyond, they must be sought in other walks of life, that in rare and exceptional cases these rewards perchance may come, but they are the accidents, not the usual or expected results of the practice of a solicitor.'[23] His son in 1945 became Prime Minister, but he had gone to the Bar.

At Westminster two men who made a noteworthy mark in the latter part of the nineteenth century had been articled clerks. Benjamin Disraeli was articled to Messrs Swanes, Stevens, Maples, Pearce and Hunt of Frederick's Place, Old Jewry, at a premium of 400 guineas in 1821. According to Mr Maples's son 'he served nearly four years' articles in 6 Frederick's Place but at the end of that period my father represented to Mr Isaac Disraeli that his talents were too great for a solicitor's office ... and suggested that he should go to the Bar'.[24] But that was written in the light of subsequent success and Disraeli himself said: 'My life was not in harmony with this practice and business.' Like other attorneys-*manqué* he had nevertheless found that his time in the office had given him 'great facility with his pen and not inconsiderable knowledge of human nature'.[25] Perhaps if he had made a match with Miss Maples, as was originally contemplated, he would have stayed the course. Charles Bradlaugh had a very different start in life. At the age of twelve he became an office boy to Mr Rogers, a solicitor in Fenchurch Street who also employed his father as a clerk. He did not stay there long and joined the army. When he was bought out he went as a clerk to another solicitor, a Mr Leverson, who in 1862 gave him his articles and agreed to pay him £150 during the first three years and £200 in the last two. He stayed only two years, but his subsequent career shows that he had been an apt pupil. He was a man of fine character. At the third attempt he was elected to the House of

[22] A list of the solicitors who have held the more important posts is:

Sir Howard Kingsley Wood (1881–1943): admitted 1903; Postmaster-General 1931; Health 1935; Air 1938; Exchequer 1940.

William Joynson Hicks (Viscount Brentford) (1865–1932): admitted 1887; Postmaster-General 1923; Home Secretary 1924–1929.

Sir Laming Worthington Evans (1868–1931): admitted 1890; Postmaster-General 1923; War 1921–1922 and 1924–1929.

Sir Donald Maclean (1864–1932): admitted 1887; Education 1931.

Isaac Foot (1880–1960): admitted 1902; Mines 1931.

Lewis Silkin (Lord Silkin) (1889–1972): admitted 1920; Town and Country Planning 1945.

Edward Leslie Burgin (1887–1945): admitted 1909; Transport 1937; Supply 1939–1940.

[23] *Solicitors' Journal*, vol 50, p 778.

[24] Blake, Disraeli, p 18.

[25] Ibid, p 19.

Commons in 1880 and then repeatedly excluded for refusing to take the oath and just as often re-elected. He persisted single-handed until in 1886 the Speaker insisted on admitting him. Ironically enough he rapidly became the most popular man in the House and just before he died it was unanimously resolved to delete from the House Journals the resolutions which had excluded him. Bradlaugh put through a remarkable number of Bills although he had no party behind him. He concerned himself particularly with the law of evidence, and the Oaths Act 1888 was passed on his initiative. Until then men of conscience who felt unable to take the oath had suffered the injustice of not being able to give evidence.

In local government the role of the profession was much more important. From the time when King John granted the status of *liber burgus* to Dunwich in 1199, self-government was acquired to a material extent by a large number of cities and towns throughout the country, and in these places the attorneys as among the most important local residents played their part as mayors and councillors. In the country districts local government was from Tudor times in the hands of the justices assembled in quarter sessions, and attorneys were excluded from the commission until 1906. But whether in town or country the actual administration was primarily in the hands of the local attorneys. They were the only men with the necessary knowledge and facilities to provide any sort of continuous administration of the policy decisions which the councils or quarter sessions might make. As the need arose for the creation of a vast number of committees and bodies each with a function to perform in relation to highways or poor law or health inevitably a clerk was required, and almost as inevitably a local attorney was appointed. The situation, already well developed in the eighteenth century, continued well into the nineteenth. The vast programme of legislation starting with the Municipal Corporations Act 1835 and ending with the Local Government Act 1888, coupled with the vast increase in population, gradually changed this situation. Towns particularly began to appoint full-time staff, though when they did the chief man was generally a solicitor. But the process was slow. As large an authority as the Dorset County Council had a Sherborne solicitor as its clerk as late as 1925. It remained common enough for some firms to specialise in providing this sort of service and for one or more partners to hold a number of so-called public appointments as town clerks, clerks to rural and urban district councils, to commissioners of Inland Revenue, to old-age pension committees, to rating committees and to literally a dozen more of one statutory body or another, each of them not large enough to justify the appointment of full-time staff. These appointments were much sought after because they gave their holders an improved professional status and, even though the salaries paid were not over-generous, they were a useful and regular addition to ordinary professional earnings.[26] As local govern-

[26] The Dorset County Council paid its clerk (who was also clerk of the peace) £2,000 a year in 1890 and he reckoned that after paying the staff he would have £1,000 profit; in

ment was tidied up the part-time solicitor appointment became a rarity and generally when a holder died or retired the new man was a full-time official. The profession still maintained its hold.[27] In 1956 eighty per cent of all local authorities with populations of 5,000 or more had solicitors as their 'clerks', as the chief executive was then invariably called. In the 1960s a tendency started for some important towns[28] to appoint men thought to have more practical business experience to the chief posts and to support them with a legal department. But in 1967 530 authorities had a solicitor as chief executive.

When local government was reformed in the nineteenth century it might have been expected that attorneys and solicitors would be active on the district, town and county councils which the reforms created. It was noted that they were much more active than barristers.[29] The professional papers for a time tried to encourage their readers' ambitions by printing the names of solicitors who had been elected mayors. In 1876 there were twelve; in 1882 thirteen; in 1885 twelve; and in one year (1901) there were four solicitors elected mayors of London boroughs and eleven elected as aldermen. There have been seven who became Lord Mayor of London.[30] On the whole solicitors have not made much of a showing; they are generally too busy when they are young and when they might have time they are too old.

But public life is not all politics or government and its other aspects can be dark and light. The dark aspect has been war and threat of war. The Gentlemen Practisers encouraged volunteers to meet the possibility of an invasion by Napoleon.[31] Solicitors and their clerks were involved in the volunteer movement of the later nineteenth century and Sir Albert Rollitt, President in 1903, could claim that he had been as a young man one of the first to join in 1859. But except for a few adventurous spirits the profession's military ambitions were mainly limited to defence of the mother country. The Boer War was hardly mentioned in the legal press, but at the end of it a dinner was given to the hundred and fifty or so solicitors and articled clerks who had served in South Africa and the President and Vice-President caused a medal to be struck and presented to them. The 1914 war was a very different matter. By the end of 1915, 2,427 solicitors

---

1939 Mr Tilney Barton reckoned he had £360 pa from his part-time official receivership (A Country Solicitor in War and Peace).

[27] A few authorities appointed barristers and this was resented by solicitors as an intrusion on what they considered their territory (see pp 181–185, *supra*).

[28] Eg Newcastle-upon-Tyne and Bournemouth.

[29] *Law Journal*, vol 35 (1901), p 609.

[30] Claudius Hunter in 1811 (he revived the Lord Mayor's Show); Anthony Brown in 1825; David William Line in 1858; David Henry Stone in 1874; William Waterlow in 1929; Phenie Neal in 1930 (he had an unconquerable aversion to public speaking and on one occasion made a speech of fifteen words); and Cullum Welch in 1956 (he was at the time a member of the Council): see *Law Society's Gazette*, vol 54 (1957), pp 16–17.

[31] Minutes, p 189

and 1,265 articled clerks had volunteered for active service, and in the war 5,610 in all served. Six hundred and sixty-nine solicitors and 458 articled clerks were killed and it was estimated that between four and five thousand were wounded. In 1915 a solicitor's clerk, Lance-Corporal Keysworth, was awarded the Victoria Cross, and during the war about a thousand decorations were won, including five hundred Military Crosses. A War Memorial was placed in the Society's Hall and unveiled on 4th March 1921 by Lord Birkenhead as Lord Chancellor; in addition a War Memorial Fund was set up to help those who had suffered and a total of £45,060 19s was subscribed. In the 1930s solicitors and articled clerks strongly supported the volunteer sections of all three services, and when the 1939 war started they were a large reservoir of future officers, particularly in the Army. In all 6,124 solicitors and 2,490 articled clerks served in that war and sixty-nine per cent of them held commissions. Mr Jack Maynard Cholmondeley Easton was awarded the George Cross in 1941 and there were fifteen Distinguished Service Orders and numerous other decorations gained. Three hundred and fourteen solicitors and 223 articled clerks were killed or missing.

On the light side there has been sport, and the profession has distinguished itself over a very wide field. Perhaps pride of place should be given to Mr D R Jardine, who captained the MCC with conspicuous success and determination in the 1930s; to Mr W P Dutton, who won the Grand National at odds of 100 to 1 on Tiny Tim in 1928 but gave up the law immediately afterwards; and to Mr Anthony Neary, who captained England at Rugby football in 1975 and 1976. There have also been Mr Sydney Wooderson, who in 1938 set up a world record for the mile in 4 minutes 6·4 seconds and won the world title at the same distance in 1946; Mr A N L Jay, who won gold medals in fencing at the Olympic Games in 1952, 1956 and 1960; and Mr Ian Macdonald-Smith, then an articled clerk, who won a gold medal in the yachting events in the 1968 Olympic Games. Mr J B Carslake won the Queen's Prize at Bisley in 1868 and Mr D L Birney, then an articled clerk, won the King's Prize in 1937. Mr R J White represented England at golf and Mr Michael Pinner repeatedly at Association football. No doubt there have been others equally distinguished.

In literature and the arts generally there have been no really outstanding figures, at any rate among those who stayed the course and were admitted as attorneys or solicitors. It is customary in this connection to mention Mr Alexander Broome, who lived from 1620 to 1666 and was a poet of some merit, though only those who take a special interest in the literature of his time will know of him. He does not appear in the Oxford Companion to English Literature but the Oxford Dictionary of Quotations gives two entries. There is nobody else to match him among the admitted men, but there is a wide variety of writers who spent some part of their early life in an attorney's or solicitor's office, sometimes under articles and sometimes not. William Cowper spent three years articled to a Mr Chapman near Bedford Row and spent the time giggling with his fellow clerk, who later became Lord Chancellor Thurlow. He recorded the fact that 'there I might have lived and died without hearing or seeing anything that reminded me of a single Christian duty'.[32] William Cobbett (1762–1835), famous for his Rural Rides and *Weekly Political Register*, also spent some time in an attorney's office, but of his experience was not more complimentary than Cowper: 'Gracious Heavens, if I am doomed to be wretched bury me beneath Iceland snows and let me feed on blubber ... but save me from the desk of an attorney.'[33] Three Victorian novelists started their adult life in attorneys' offices and the experience of one of them at least was turned to good effect. Charles Dickens was first employed for a couple of weeks by Mr Molloy in New Square, Lincoln's Inn, and then for eighteen months by Mr Blackmore in Gray's Inn at a starting salary of 13s 6d rising to 15s per week. When Arnold Bennett was twenty-one in 1888 he left his home in Stafford to take a job as a clerk with Messrs Le Brasseur and Oakley at 25s per week, but he did not stay long. Benjamin Disraeli, known in his early years better for his novels than his politics, served four years as an articled clerk in Frederick's Place. In more recent times Mr John van Druten, the playwright, was an articled clerk and Mr Roy Fuller, Professor of Poetry at Oxford, was a building society solicitor. It is not a very long list. Perhaps a solicitor's office is not really conducive to literary production, though it might have been thought that it would have provided a good deal of the raw material of which literature is made. Perhaps solicitors have been inhibited by the fear that writing non-technical books might be reckoned a form of advertising and as such a professional offence. That inhibition at least has been removed since 1968 by a Council statement.[34] But there has been no sign that a flood of literature was waiting to be released.

[32] Cowper, Memoirs (1816), p 25.
[33] Browne, Law and Lawyers in Literature, p 403.
[34] *Law Society's Gazette*, vol 65 (1968), p 405.

CHAPTER 11

Status and Reputation

The recurring themes of the legal press and of speakers at meetings of attorneys and solicitors in the nineteenth century were the causes of the inferior status and reputation of the profession, the means by which they could be improved, and the extent to which the profession's efforts to that end had been successful. No one doubted that the problem existed or questioned the importance of its solution. It was as old as the profession itself. No sooner had the attorney passed out of the stage of the voluntary helper into that of the paid representative than criticism began. The mercenary and the professional have generally been suspected of insincerity for the cause in which they are being paid to take part, and this was particularly so in the case of the attorney, who represented a new concept in English jurisprudence. Moreover, he made his money out of other men's misfortunes and disputes, and to make matters worse he did so not by honest toil as a craftsman did but by pen and paper and the use of his wits.[1] It was then as later believed that to increase his business he encouraged quarrels and therefore unrest. If it had been possible Parliament would gladly have abolished him just as Jack Cade in 1450 wanted to hang him. Yet the charge of avarice was probably ill-founded;[2] the charge of fomenting trouble and litigation was certainly unjust, for there was little need to do so in fourteenth- and fifteenth-century England; in an age of widespread bribery and corruption at all levels in the English legal system the attorney was no more guilty of those crimes than his superiors, some of them in the highest places. He was, however, made the butt and target of critics partly because he was the least able to defend himself and partly because he was the man through whom the ordinary citizen had immediate contact with a corrupt legal administration. The misfortune was that too many attorneys were men who had taken up the work having failed at everything else, and they were ready to do anything provided that they were paid. Anybody could become an attorney, or at any rate act as one, and this meant that for most the work was underpaid and insufficient to make it a full-time occupation or provide a living or status much, if at all, above that of a small tradesman.

[1] 'Attourneis in cuntre theih geten silver for noht': Political Songs, p 339.

[2] Ives, The Reputation of the Common Lawyer in English Society 1455–1550, in *Birmingham Historical Journal*, vol 7, *passim*.

The popular image of the attorney had crystallised in the sixteenth century. The Elizabethan slang-name for a highwayman or a foot-pad was a 'high lawyer'. Sir Thomas Overbury[3] in his Characters applied to the attorney the description of a mere pettifogger which stuck to him for another three hundred years or more, and Webster in A Cure for a Cuckold[4] adopted Pettifog and Dodge as appropriate names for the two attorneys who appeared in it. In 1614 the Inns of Court described attorneys as ministerial persons of an inferior nature;[5] 'attorneys and their subordinates no less than solicitors were not really men of a profession as members of the Inns of Court and Doctors' Commons would understand it with their superior and ancient traditions'.[6] In 1628 or thereabouts Bishop Earle wrote of 'An Attorney ... he talks statutes as fiercely as if he had mooted seven years in the Inns of Court when all his skill is stuck in his girdle or his office window. Strife and wrangling make him rich and he is thankful to his benefactor and nourishes it.... His business gives him not leave to think of his conscience and when the time or term of life is going out, for domesday he is secure for he hopes he hath a tricke to reverse judgement.'[7] The profession had an apologist, albeit one of themselves. In West's Symboleography, published in 1590, it was described in words which ring true because they are ageless: 'Attornies at the Common Law, men verrie honest and learned, yea, and also very necessarie for the civil businesses; insomuch that by no means their labour and services may want. And yet such is the unthankfulness of this age that even their own clyents (of whom they are best deserved) when they have served their turns so that they see no present occasion to use them any longer for the fault of some few will not afford the best of them one good word for many good deeds. Nay, which is worse, they will generally slander and condemn them all as covetous persons and disturbers of the common peace and quietnesse of all men by unnecessary suits. Where, in verie truth, the most part of the said attornies being verie peaceable do oftentymes dissuade their clients from the same so much as they can, by means whereof they greatly offend their minds insomuch they will for that only cause suspect them of affection towards the adverse parties and threaten earnestly that if they will not intermeddle therewith others will.'

Altogether the latter end of the seventeenth century saw the status and reputation of the profession at its lowest, whatever might be the merits of Mr West's arguments. The solicitor had by that time made his mark and that did not help. He was variously described as a caterpillar, a grasshopper, or a dunghill rampant, starting another long tradition of using the lower and more repulsive and slithery animals as similes in anti-

[3] 1581–1613.

[4] *Circa* 1624.

[5] Chapter 9, p 168, *supra*.

[6] Jones, Elizabethan Court of Chancery, p 125.

[7] In his Microcosmographie.

attorney propaganda. The law as a profession was one of the main targets of the radicals in the Civil War and Protectorate period and many of the New Model Army thought that the reform of the law and lawyers was one of the things for which they had fought the King.[8] In 1650 Cromwell himself said that 'the law as it is now constituted serves only to maintain the lawyers and to encourage the rich to oppress the poor'. Some of the reformers of the Protectorate period would have been content merely with reformation of the lawyers. In 1659 an Order in Council was introduced with the object among other things of reforming the abuses and of limiting their fees, but the lawyers raised £100,000 for the Army and the matter was dropped.[9] The Levellers on the other hand did not distinguish one type of lawyer from another. All from the judges downwards should be abolished. If the ordinary man were left to decide disputes according to basic moral principles justice would be done and lawyers would cease to make fortunes out of oppressing the poor and plundering the rich. There had always been in England a feeling that lay tribunals unencumbered by lawyers were the best vehicles on the road to absolute justice. The facility with which the lawyers like other professions switched their allegiance at the right moment did not improve their image; it merely lent additional proof to the charge that they would take on any case which would pay them best. The attorney in Queen Anne's time was described in the *London Spy* as 'an amphibious monster that partakes of two natures and those contrary. He is a great lawyer of both peace and enmity and has no sooner set people together by the ears but is soliciting the law to make an end of the difference ... His affection to the law proceeds from the litigiousness of his ancestors who brought the family to beggary. Therefore there is nothing he abhors more than poverty in a client ... He gets money in term by sitting in a tavern for every client that comes in he makes pay sixpence a glass till he has sold a quart or two at that rate and puts the surplus in his pocket ... He concerns himself with no justice but the justice of a cause and for making out an unconscionable bill he outdoes a tailor ... His learning is all experience and his library is in his pocket',[10] which was exactly what Bishop Earle had written in his Microcosmographie. Allowing for all the prejudice and the exaggeration of such accounts and of all the other lampoons and pamphlets of the period, the picture was not one of which the profession could be proud. Meeting one's clients at a tavern was of course a commonplace and there was nothing wrong with it; but waiting for business there and having one's entire office equipment on one's person conjures up an image of a man who was little better than a tout. The public estimate was that the condition of the profession was nothing short of a scandal and the 1729 Act 'for the better regulation of Attornies and Solicitors' and the formation of the Society of Gentle-

[8] Veall, Popular Movement for Law Reform 1640–1660, p 73.
[9] Ludlow, Memoirs, p 246, and vol 2, p 161.
[10] Quoted Jeafferson, A Book about Lawyers, vol 2 (1867 ed), p 324.

men Practisers in 1739 were reactions to that view. So also were the handful of local law societies founded in the eighteenth century. In terms of improving the status and reputation of the profession these things in themselves probably achieved very little. But the societies by their very exclusiveness and their clublike character introduced for the first time the concept of the gentleman as the standard at which the profession should aim. It was a period when the status of gentility and of a gentleman were vitally important. 'The high standards and traditions of professional conduct derive from the eighteenth century concept of gentility.'[11]

The attainment of that standard was at the beginning of the eighteenth century only a distant prospect. The profession continued to be the butt of almost everybody who put pen to paper for publication, and the opportunity of quotation is unlimited.[12] It is only necessary to refer to Dr Johnson's dictum that 'he did not wish to speak ill of any man behind his back but he thought that the gentleman was an attorney' or Horace Walpole's that the attorney was a 'pest of Society'. Being an attorney, far from being a sign of respectability, was something to be ashamed of: Tom Clarke in Smollett's Humphrey Clinker 'never owned himself an attorney without blushing'. 'Mr Latitat[13] was the rogue of every farce—the knave of every novel.' The correspondence of the times better reflects the opinion of the general public than any novel, play or *bon mot*: 'My aunt mentioned to me a desire of employing Mr Trollop as your Solicitor in this business. I have been applied to by Mr Adams who transacted some Affairs for me last year, but leave it to your pleasure to appoint whom you please. He is I believe as Honest as an Attorney can be and intelligent in his business.'[14] The bitterest attack of all was mounted by the Earl of Abingdon in the House of Lords. Considering himself badly used by an attorney, he compared the 'pettifogging attornies of this country' to the 'locusts in Africa'; he warned the House against the profession: 'The greater, the higher, the richer you are the more prone you are to its consequences and the surer of becoming sooner or later the victims of its all-devouring avarice'; of those who had acted as attorneys for his former lawyer he said 'he is not half so black as those rotten limbs of the law' who had aided him by every 'pettifogging artifice'.[15] Of course, the pictures were caricatures rather than portraits, but when at the beginning of the nineteenth century men inside the profession were writing about the matter they did

[11] Hughes, *Durham University Journal*, vol 14 (NS), p 55.

[12] There is a short anthology in the *Law Times*, vol 104 (1897), at pp 204–205.

[13] Stephens, Adventures of an Attorney, p 199. The term was obsolete by about 1860 but previously was slang for an attorney and was first common about 1560. It derived from *lateo*—I lurk—and the first word of the writ addressed to the sheriff to arrest an absconder.

[14] Thomas Noel, second Viscount Wentworth, to his sister Judith, 31st October 1775—Elwin, The Noels and the Milbankes, p 47.

[15] Hansard, Parliamentary History, vol 31, cols 931–935. Lord Abingdon published the speech as a broadsheet, so his attorney was able to prosecute him for criminal libel; he was convicted and fined £100 and sentenced to three months' imprisonment.

not altogether disagree with the likeness. In general terms the title of the attorney to be ranked even among the middle classes was doubtful. The standard of general education in the profession was abysmally low, and even among the better sort there were hardly any with a university education.[16] But there was a strong ground swell which was carrying the profession forward. This was the period which saw the rise of Methodism and the slow beginnings of a movement towards higher standards of conduct in public and business life. A man was no longer for ever excluded from gentility by the accident of birth; it was a status which could be earned. There was of course nothing new about a gentleman being also an attorney (Thomas Fane, a Bristol attorney, became heir to the Earl of Westmorland in 1757), but that was something which was apart from and possibly despite his profession. The meaning of 'gentleman' was changing, too. For the profession it meant above all the acceptance of moral as well as legal obligations; it meant fair dealing with friend and foe; it meant a 'liberal' outlook and education. Now it is a commonplace that it is much easier to meet these standards if one is not faced with the immediate problem of making ends meet. 'The most unpleasant and unamiable result of professional etiquette is the production of a class of men who enforce against others rules which they put themselves into a position to enforce by disregarding them during the earlier period of their career.'[17] If the rules of gentlemanly professional conduct—*aliter* etiquette—had not been much observed in the past, the growth in the profession's prosperity during the eighteenth century meant that there was in London and possibly even more in the provinces a growing body of men who were in a financial position to abandon or indeed never to take up the malpractices which had given the profession so evil a reputation.

The type of business which the profession was doing on a wide scale greatly enhanced its standing. Obviously the financial success of a goodly number made its impact if only because it permitted a higher standard of living. In addition the nobility and gentry were finding it convenient and pleasant to leave their affairs in the hands of their legal men of business whilst they themselves spent more and more time in London or at English and continental spas. 'Did a landowner find the personal management of his farms irksome and difficult? He made a solicitor his agent and put all his business in his hands. Or did he find difficulty in performing his duties as a magistrate? He made a solicitor his salaried clerk who prompted him and did all the work. Or again was he moved by political ambition to stand for a borough or a county? A solicitor was indispensable to watch over his interests, take part in local intrigues and distribute money

[16] One of the very few was Oliver Edwards, who had known Dr Johnson at Oxford and was responsible for the saying that 'I have tried too in my time to become a philosopher but I don't know how. Cheerfulness was always breaking in.'

[17] *Cornhill Magazine*, vol 8 (1863), p 104.

in his client's interest.'[18] Then, as a century later, it was true that solicitors 'stood in the place which is or rather was occupied by the Father Confessors in Roman Catholic countries and scarcely any important step can be taken without their advice and assistance'.[19] Probably there never had been a time when matrimonial and family matters were so complicated, because estates were built up by judicious marriages in which the interests of the two families had to be most carefully adjusted. Sir Ralph Milbanke, one of the great North Country magnates of the period, wrote to his beloved Miss Noel, daughter of Viscount Wentworth, *à propos* of their marriage settlement, of 'Mr Hartley who by the way is our *sine qua non*'[20] and who, an attorney in little Richmond in Yorkshire, was nevertheless entrusted with this important matter. The ardent bridegroom had to wait for six months whilst Mr Hartley, grown fat and therefore slow, settled the terms with Mr Adams of Chancery Lane, acting for the bride, and reduced them to 30,000 words.[21] The upper class, themselves largely recruited two or fewer generations back from men who had made their way through their brains, did not despise education or those who earned their living by using their wits, nor did they as their earlier counterparts had done regard such men as nothing more than tradesmen. In 1637 Camden wrote of a nobleman of Tudor times who said it was for 'noble mens sonnes ... to leave study and learning to the children of meane men', to which, significantly in the light of future events, Richard Pace replied: 'Then you ... must be content ... while the children of meane men manage the matters of Estate';[22] and in 1729 Daniel Defoe in his Compleat English Gentleman[23] asked: 'What occasion has a gentleman to trouble himself with books and to spend his time poring over old hystoryes?' But in 1819 things had altered: the jingle went: 'Kings may make titles, heralds scutcheons plan, But Education forms the Gentleman.'[24] All these changes had been pushing the profession up the social ladder. In London there were men like Mr Boehm, solicitor to the Palmerstons, who went hunting and with whom the second viscount was on social visiting terms.[25] In the North of England 'next to the country gentlemen in brilliance was the legal constellation.... In the first quarter of the century [ie the eighteenth] these all pointed as to a polar star to Charles Sanderson who seemed to be cousin to everybody.'[26] The father of Lord Brampton (as Sir Henry Hawkins QC eventually became) was towards the end of the century a country attorney in Hitchin, and according to his son was not only agent to many of the

[18] Halévy, History of the English People, p 21.
[19] Johnston, England As It Is, p 170.
[20] Elwin, The Noels and the Milbankes (1967), p 48.
[21] Ibid, p 57.
[22] Remaines Concerning Britaine, p 273.
[23] Ed Bulbring, p 38.
[24] Rhodes, The Gentleman, vol 1, p 630.
[25] Connell, Portrait of a Whig Peer, pp 63–64 and 196.
[26] Hughes, North Country Life in the Eighteenth Century, p 77.

country families but also on terms of friendly intercourse with them.[27] The partners in his firm (perhaps the oldest in the country) had in the previous century 'thought it politic to belong to the Royston Club where most of the Jacobite magistrates foregathered'[28] and no doubt equally politic to leave it in 1688; in the eighteenth century they were members of the Welwin Club, no doubt a centre of the social life of the district. In the Midlands 'a fellow called Peniston Lamb' had started in very humble circumstances the career which was to found the family of Lord Melbourne, who so described his forbear to his admiring Queen; and in remote Appleby in the 1750s John Robinson was starting on the course which, assisted by matrimony, was to lead him to the management of the House of Commons and the friendship of George III.

There was a marked difference beteen the status of London and country practitioners. 'With comparatively few exceptions the mind of the London practitioner was uninstructed and narrow ... and it can cause no surprise that his social and moral standing was what it was' and the 'social position and moral worth of these gentlemen [ie the country attorneys and solicitors] would be decidedly superior to the majority of those who practised in the metropolis'.[29] But whether in town or country there was much to be done before the profession was rid of the stigma which attached to it. At the end of the century 'although scarcely a day passes during any term without complaint to some of the courts against one or more attornies; the censures passed and the punishments inflicted neither tend to prevent a continuance of the numerous and serious evils with which the lower and unprincipled members of the profession torment society nor in the smallest degree diminish the vast load of obloquy that has long attached to the general body of practitioners'.[30] It was the heyday of the Wapping lawyer willing to do or say anything for the price of a drink. The general repute was such that at Kingston Assizes in 1813 counsel invited the jury to reject the evidence of one witness simply because he was an attorney.[31] This was the period when many attorneys were calling themselves solicitors, though the more conservative did not like it. All the legislation and all the orders of the judges had been of little use. 'It is obvious that howmuchsoever may have been affected by legislative provisions the complete reform of abuse and the accomplishment of all further improvement must originate within the profession itself',[32] and in spite of the flood of legislation in the nineteenth century designed to achieve these ends, the leaders of the profession always realised that 'social estimation cannot be

[27] The Reminiscences of Sir Henry Hawkins QC (Collins ed), p 13.

[28] Hine, Relics of an Uncommon Attorney, p 47.

[29] Mr Devonshire's paper at the 1899 Provincial Meeting.

[30] Day, An Address to the Attorneys at Law and to the Public, pp 11–12.

[31] Maugham, Treatise on the Law of Attorneys and Solicitors, p xii: he was rebuked by Chief Baron MacDonald, who said that there were not only good but to his own knowledge some of the best and most honourable men in that branch of the profession.

[32] Maugham, op cit.

conferred by Act of Parliament' and that if the profession wanted 'consideration the simplest way of getting it was to do something to deserve it'.[33]

The nineteenth century found the profession in the mood for self-improvement and determined to reverse the old presumption that an attorney was not a gentleman in fact even if he was one by law. The objective was frankly acknowledged. 'The qualification we desire to secure is that the attorney should be a gentleman';[34] the attorney's properly recognised rank should be that of a gentleman.[35] It appears in every context. The admission of university graduates was made easier because that would bring gentlemen into the profession; the preliminary examination was to be of such a standard as would entitle the man who passed it 'to be, as he will be called, a gentleman and to assume the social status of a gentleman';[36] local law societies were urged because it was 'difficult for the most impudent to exhibit the character of a knave in the presence of gentlemen';[37] premiums and stamp duties on articles were considered to have advantages in excluding the poor and therefore ungentlemanly. The idea that an attorney was a gentleman by statute was probably of long standing,[38] but it was immortalised and popularised by the statement of Mr Sampson Brass in Dickens's The Old Curiosity Shop, first published in 1841: 'I am of the Law, I am styled gentleman by Act of Parliament, I maintain the title by the annual payment of twelve pounds sterling for a certificate.'[39] There is no statute which expressly so provides, but it has been suggested that it is implied in the Attornies and Solicitors Act of 1729, which confirmed the status of attorneys and solicitors as officers of the court. As early as 1534 court officers were sometimes given the title of 'generoso' and Camden[40] refers to a fifth grade of esquire arising from status as an official and which he traces back to the reign of Richard II. According to him they were men whom valour or fortune had 'raised out of the dregs of mankind'. On a similar tack is Coke's statement of the rule at common law that 'a man may have an addition of gentleman within this statute [ie 1 Hen 5 c 5] if he be a gentleman by office (though he be not by birth) as many of the King's Household and of other Lords are; and clerks being officers in the King's Court of Record ... so long as they continue in their office they ought to be named gentleman as their due

[33] Annual Provincial Meeting, 1885, p 95.

[34] *Legal Observer*, vol 1, p 132: the fact that the owner and editor was the secretary of the Incorporated Law Society makes this almost an official statement of policy.

[35] *Law Times*, vol 1, p 217.

[36] Ibid, vol 35, p 333: see also Chapter 3, pp 48–49, *supra*.

[37] Ibid, vol 1, p 217.

[38] It is mentioned as already accepted in Adventures of an Attorney in search of a Practice (p 195) in 1839; and in the *Law Times* in 1843: 'Vainly is the title of gentleman bestowed by law if such be the practical illustrations of it' (vol 1, p 326).

[39] Chapter 60.

[40] 1551–1623.

addition'.[41] Whatever the explanation might be, it was completely irrelevant to the object which the profession had set for itself, which was that its members should act and be recognised as English gentlemen. In 1881 the profession was exhorted: 'Let us cultivate in the discharge of our daily duties the spirit of English gentlemen',[42] and the rules of professional conduct and etiquette were developed on the basis and to the standard of the conduct of a gentleman.[43]

The times were ripe for reform. A young Queen in 1837 seemed to symbolise the end of all the degradations and scandals of the previous seventy years and to cleanse the air of public and private life. Particularly the middle classes, from which the better elements in the profession were mainly recruited, were emerging as the most powerful element in the State and bringing with them their standards of probity and decency. Their wealth, said Brougham, if set against all the broad acres of the aristocracy, would make the balance kick. The Court after Queen Victoria's marriage to Prince Albert became 'middle-class' because the aristocracy did not like Prince Albert and he reciprocated. Lord Carlingford noted in his diary in November 1857 that Prince Albert 'likes the professional classes'; and another observer of the social scene also noted that 'in some favoured instances chemists and solicitors and bank managers form the phalanx from which so to speak Prince Albert drew his personal bodyguard'.[44] Naturally solicitors had a close connection with and a strong influence on this powerful element. 'Amongst those classes of the nation who, raised above the struggle for existence, are especially the subjects of moral influence solicitors enjoy a power seldom if at all rivalled.'[45] It was this overall and national trend which changed the profession's status and reputation for the better, rather than anything which the profession had done as a matter of deliberate policy. In 1839 the *Law Magazine and Review* commented: 'Within the last half century the educated classes have gradually succeeded in emancipating themselves from the undue preponderance of rank and wealth; a feeling of self-respect has been communicated to all; and it seems to us more logical to attribute the elevation of solicitors to the general diffusion of property and education than to any change peculiar to themselves';[46] and sixty years later it was acknowledged that 'if to-day our profession occupies a more honourable and more responsible position than it did a hundred years ago this may be entirely accounted for by the great political and moral development which has taken place in every class and in every department of the State'.[47] The improvement in moral standards

[41] This theory is set out in an entertaining and ingenious article by Sir Thomas Lund in the *Law Society's Gazette* (1956), pp 53–59; see also *Notes and Queries*, 12th July 1884, p 28, and 19th December 1885, p 493, and *Law Notes*, 23rd December 1935, p 356.

[42] Annual Provincial Meeting, Proceedings, p 145.

[43] Lund, Guide to Professional Conduct and Etiquette of Solicitors, p 1.

[44] G W E Russell, Collections and Recollections, 2nd series, p 140.

[45] *Legal Observer*, vol 2 (1831), p 40. [46] Page 382.

[47] Annual Provincial Meeting: Mr Devonshire's paper.

meant on the one hand that practices which had not seemed to be particularly obnoxious or which had even been acceptable were gradually rejected as unethical; and on the other hand it meant that there were more and more solicitors who recognised the need for improvement and who with a professional organisation in being in both town and country were able to persuade the profession generally to accept that need and meet it. Whereas previously criticism of the profession had come almost entirely from outside it, in the nineteenth century the profession was if anything more critical of itself than were those outside it.

But even in these generally favourable conditions the climb from the depths of the seventeenth and even eighteenth century was slow and hard. The problem was that the profession covered such a wide range, as wide as the population it had to serve. 'There are various grades from the low rapacious pettifogger who grabs at 3s 6d fees and is something between the common cur and the bull-dog of the law up to the finished gentleman who has in his hands the most important affairs and is professionally acquainted with the most delicate secret histories of the first families of the land.'[48] So long as the large part of the profession was drawn from the uneducated classes[49] the status of the others suffered. In 1843 the *Law Times* thought that 'undoubtedly the attornies of this country enjoy and deserve a high social position but not so high as they might and ought to enjoy'[50] because so many were 'wanting in the good breeding and education required to constitute a gentleman and for the absence of which no other qualifications can compensate'.[51] A correspondent in the *Legal Observer* in 1839 said that attorneys were 'not looked upon as honourable and useful members of the public belonging to a gentlemanly and learned profession',[52] because men without financial backing or decent education were admitted. The exclusion of the poor (who were therefore presumably illiterate and also lacking in proper standards of conduct) was a popular suggestion for improving the status of the profession. It was for this reason that the profession was never whole-heartedly behind the campaign to reduce the expense of admission, though it did not mind a reduction in the charges on those already admitted.[53] Indeed when the Stamp Acts were originally passed their purpose was 'generally understood to be to increase the respectability of the profession by excluding the uneducated and necessitous' as well as to raise revenue.[54] Naturally this view did not go unchallenged by those at whom it was aimed. Their side was taken by the *Westminster Review*: 'Besides a premium of some two or three hundred

[48] Johnston, England As It Is, vol 1 (1851), p 169. William Johnston was a barrister.
[49] *Supra*, p 48.
[50] Vol 1, p 93.
[51] Ibid, p 131.
[52] Vol 20, p 102.
[53] *Supra*, p 132 et seq. Mr Joseph Day welcomed the increased tax imposed in 1795 by 34 Geo 3 c 14 as 'a means of excluding unworthy members from the profession' (op cit, p 15).
[54] Maugham, op cit, p 22.

pounds an attorney is taxed at the outset with a duty of £120 upon the Articles of Clerkship for the maintenance of the respectability of the profession.... This is respectability of the gig order.'[55] For the socially sensitive it could be embarrassing. A Leeds attorney—Amicus Verus—found that it was not 'considered etiquette to ask a solicitor to meet a party of gentlemen at dinner. By gentlemen I mean the clergy, barristers, military and naval men, and squires or gentlemen living on their means.'[56] Sir George Stephens said in 1846 that in the course of thirty-two years he had only once been asked to dine at a barrister's table.[57] *The Times* considered that at this period 'the University of Oxford would hardly have thought of entertaining "the lower branch" of the profession'.[58]

The going was certainly slow. Mr Pleydell Bouverie, a barrister and Chairman of Committees in the House of Commons, said in 1854 that the 'two great evils of the country were taxes and attornies' and that an attorney was a man who did nothing for six and eightpence and something for thirteen and fourpence. In 1863 what progress had been made could be judged from the comment that 'there are among attornies and solicitors a large proportion of men as well educated, possessed of as high principles of honour and as much entitled in all respects to every sort of social consideration as any members of the community; but there are also a considerable number of persons of whom not one of these assertions is true ... Men are always judged by the standard of their profession and as long as attornies are viewed with prejudice the less respectable members of the profession will always be able to say, I am only an attorney, you do not expect me to act up to the standard of what in other walks of life would be considered honourable.'[59] At this very time William Gilbert was writing his two-volume novel The Country Attorney. 'Our hero', as he called the central character, was a man of both wealth and taste as well as solicitor and agent to the two local noblemen—the continual absence of one was a particularly fortunate circumstance—clerk to the local justices and of course solicitor to the better-off private residents of Coombe Bissett in Wiltshire, where he lived in style. The novel, written with a considerable knowledge of legal practice, turns on the hero's efforts to swindle his widowed sister-in-law, in which he is helped by another local attorney who advises the sister-in-law. That advice is affected by the obligation which the one attorney owes to the other, and taken by and large the novel presents as unpleasant a story of professional chicanery and Victorian hypocrisy as one would expect to find. Mrs Gaskell found a plot at the same period in the story of an attorney who sent his son to Eton and Oxford; the son found that when his father decided that he should become

[55] 1833, p 68.
[56] *Legal Observer*, vol 36, p 522.
[57] Select Committee on Education, 1846, Report, p 366.
[58] 9th October 1901, *à propos* of the Provincial Meeting at Oxford.
[59] *Cornhill Magazine*, 1863, p 108.

an attorney too instead of going to the Bar all his friends cut him; this so enraged the son that he struck his father down and buried the body in the flower garden at home. Quite rightly this did not avail him, because when a railway was built through the garden the body was found and justice was done. Of social aspirations that keen observer of the scene at that time or a little later, G W E Russell, wrote: 'In vain did the solicitor build himself a French chateau a hundred yards off the high road and give tennis parties in the dusty garden. The baronets and their belongings held aloof and the clergy though they attended the parties apologised to their squires for doing so.'[60] Aiming at catching a baronet was perhaps setting one's sights too high when the whole profession could boast not more than four[61] and the President was knighted only in special cases or on special occasions such as the opening of the new Law Courts. Down in the country in the middle of the century the directories still listed the attorneys, with one or two exceptions, amongst the tradesmen. 'The solicitors, the bank managers, one or two brewers (wholesale, nothing retail), large corn factors or coal merchants who kept a carriage of some kind—these formed the select society next under ... the clergy and the gentry.'[62] Trollope put his finger on one of the perpetual ironies: 'Is it not remarkable that the common repute which we all give to attorneys in general is exactly the opposite to that which every man gives to his own attorney in particular? Whom does anybody trust so implicitly as he trusts his own attorney? And yet is it not the case that the body of attorneys is supposed to be the most roguish body in existence?'[63]

It is not easy to reconcile all the statements made at the time by lawyers and others who clearly found the topic of inexhaustible interest and vital importance. The fact was that, in a profession so large, generalisations were bound to be inaccurate in relation to quite large sections. As early as 1840 Sir George Stephens, who had some hard things to say about the profession and its personnel to the Select Committee on Education in 1846 and was certainly an acute observer, said that 'attornies in the higher walks of the profession have in many instances established for themselves an acknowledged title to rank with the first circles'.[64] In 1849 the *Law Review* wrote about the attorneys in the middle walks of life: 'It is now some years since the élite of the Attornies took measures to secure the respectability of their profession by requiring of its members a good professional education which has already produced a marked improvement among them; while as we are all aware, the improvement of education generally, especially among the middle classes, has conferred advantages upon the middle

[60] Londoner's Log-book, p 72.

[61] Until the life peerage system was introduced there were never more than four solicitor-peers.

[62] Jefferies, Hodge and His Masters, 1880.

[63] Miss Mackenzie (1865).

[64] Adventures of an Attorney in Search of a Practice, 2nd ed (1840), pp 201–202: the book was published anonymously, but Sir George later acknowledged he was the author.

classes, advantages which the public schools and universities have not always accorded to the higher classes. ... The Attorney is no longer (if he ever was) the creeping servile thing which it delighted the authors of older plays and novels, and some of their modern plagiarists, to describe the scrivener of former days to be. He holds his head with the best and bends it only with the courtesy which every gentleman will accord to others.'[65] Acceptance in society is one of the important sub-themes, and by 1869 it seemed that the fears of Amicus Verus of Leeds were less justified: 'The foolish and thoroughly vulgar prejudice against attornies is altogether a thing of the past. Even in the dullest and dingiest coteries of new-made wealth its last whispers have utterly died out; and in any company of English gentlemen the man would be unanimously rated as a snob who would venture to hint that an attorney simply because he was an attorney could not claim to associate with gentlemen as their equal.'[66] In the mid-century people might still feel that the profession did 'not form one of the few callings between which a young man had to choose after completing that sort of education at a public school and university on which English parents (not unjustly) set so high a value'.[67] That was the acid test. What was the status of the profession in the eyes of the Victorian parent in comfortable circumstances; not the man on the Clapham omnibus but the man with his own carriage? In the next two decades he had decided that the profession was a respectable and honourable, not to say profitable, one into which his son might properly be entered. By 1881, when it was claimed that 'no profession has risen so much in public estimation during the last fifty years as our own',[68] the principal reason was said to have been that the profession was being recruited from the public schools and the universities. Parents were sending their sons to be articled instead of entering them in the Inns of Court. Why send one's son to starve at the Bar when he could expect to make a comfortable living as an equally respected family solicitor?[69] It was Education which had turned the scale. So long as the public felt that the main body of the profession consisted of uneducated men and so long as there was no system of examination or education the status and reputation of the profession could not improve. 'There were two main causes for the improvement in the status of attornies and solicitors. The first was the work of the Incorporated Law Society ... The second ... is the provision of a system of legal education and as part of that system the institution of a system of compulsory examinations.'[70] Although there were discordant notes to be heard later, opinion and comment after the 1860s was much more optimistic. In 1869 the *Law Magazine and Review*

[65] Vol 10, p 151.
[66] Jeafferson, A Book about Lawyers, vol 2, p 328—Jeafferson was a barrister.
[67] *Cornhill Magazine*, 1863, p 105.
[68] Annual Provincial Meeting, Proceedings, p 137.
[69] See Harding, Social History of English Law (1969), p 289.
[70] Holdsworth, History of English Law, vol 15, pp 230–231.

said that 'in social respects the change in the status of the attorney has been remarkable' and that the profession had grown enormously in social importance.[71] In 1880 a Mr Gray told the Annual Provincial Meeting that there had been a 'great improvement in his generation'[72] and in 1882 the Meeting heard that 'we are all proud that during the past few years the position of the solicitor has greatly advanced. Socially solicitors take much higher rank than formerly and the mean and pettifogging practitioner of fiction and I fear in olden times too often of fact is now known only as an antiquarian relic.'[73] On the stage, where the attorney had never cut a fine figure, the solicitor in the late nineties 'begins to attend quite respectable dinner parties and is usually attired in evening dress with a large buttonhole'.[74] The profession was being far better treated in works of fiction[75] and in real life in the country 'the upper ten basked themselves in the Sun Assembly Rooms at Hitchin and again the lawyers and their wives were there'.[76] When Galsworthy was later selecting the central character of his Forsyte Saga set in the eighties he chose a solicitor; not perhaps a very attractive man, but one of cultivated tastes with an income allowing him to gratify them and by every contemporary criterion a gentleman.

It was at this period that the profession decided it had had enough of the name of attorney. The Supreme Court of Judicature Act 1873 finally extinguished the title and on 1st January 1875 the members of the profession were all simply Solicitors of the Supreme Court. On the face of it, it was remarkable that the profession should have chosen a title which in its origin was much more recent and in its meaning much humbler than that of attorney, and it was a plea of guilty to all that had been alleged against the attorney in the past. The suggestion has been made that the title of solicitor was preferred because practically all London attorneys were also solicitors and accordingly the humbler men preferred to take on the same title as the more eminent. But the reason given at the Annual Provincial Meeting in 1880 when the matter was fresh in the minds of the speaker and his audience is more likely to be the true one: it was 'the relegation to the region of the obsolete of the opprobrious term of the attorney'. The use of the title of solicitor had been more and more common over the previous hundred years or more. For the man in the street the two titles were interchangeable, but he tended to use the title of attorney when he wished to be critical or even offensive. In her novel Patronage written in 1800 Maria Edgeworth has one of her characters say in reply to a question whether there was such a thing as an honest attorney: 'There are no such things as attorneys now in England, they are all turned solici-

[71] Vol 26, p 285.
[72] Proceedings, p 61.
[73] Proceedings, p 129.
[74] Haynes, Concerning Solicitors, p 42.
[75] *Law Times*, vol 71, p 102.
[76] Hine, Relics of an Uncommon Attorney, p 47.

tors.'[77] The Stamp Act 1804 set out the legal pecking order of the time, and just as serjeants at law preceded barristers so solicitors preceded attorneys. Mr Maugham, who was probably in the best position to know, wrote in 1825 that attorneys had recently 'adopted the term solicitor in preference to that of attorney'.[78] The Act only confirmed what had become the general practice. As always there were some who did not like the change. To a man complaining he could not get to his counsel Lord Tenterden asked who he was and was told he was the plaintiff's solicitor. His lordship replied: 'We know nothing of solicitors here. Had you been of the respectable rank of attorney I would have ordered room to be made for you.' And Mortimer Collins, continuing the custom of resorting to animal similes when describing the profession, said: 'A crocodile is not improved by calling him an alligator. Still the attorney is gone. He used to call himself a solicitor; now he can do it with a clear conscience if he has such a thing.'[79]

Ironically just when the profession seemed to have achieved its objective it had to meet the very adverse publicity arising from the substantial frauds and defalcations which were disclosed from about 1880 right through to the end of the century. These cases were all the more damaging because some of them involved leading firms of family solicitors, the class which had been the leaders in the improvement in the status of the profession. The situation was further aggravated by the allegations made in Parliament and in the press at the same period that solicitors were opposing land registration simply for their own financial benefit and thereby preventing the public from having the advantages of a cheap and efficient system of land transfer such as was said to operate in many other countries. The happy phrases of earlier years were no longer heard. 'I confidently assert that there is no profession which has had in the past and alas still has to endure more attacks and obloquy and kicks both covert and overt than our own', said a speaker at the 1893 Provincial Meeting.[80] In 1896 Mr Christian thought that the solicitors' 'unpopularity deserved or undeserved is undoubtedly declining',[81] but in 1903 it was said that public opinion amounted to 'an indictment of the profession as a clique of outlaws'.[82] There was another bad patch in the 1960s. The profession was heavily criticised for its conveyancing fees, said to be particularly a burden on young married couples starting out in life. The efforts of The Law Society to provide a solution to the problem produced something

[77] Chapter 22.
[78] Op cit, p 4.
[79] Hine, Confessions, p 108.
[80] Proceedings, p 196.
[81] Solicitors, An Outline of Their History, p 235.
[82] Annual Provincial Meeting, p 192. How hard the old reputation died can be seen in such statements as that of Lady Dorothy Nevill in her Reminiscences in 1906 that 'I may add that in defiance of well-known prejudice and tradition this man was a lawyer' (p 106). The solicitor in question had just paid Lady Dorothy a debt owed by his father for an amount more than she had thought was owing.

approaching a split in the profession and altogether 1965 was described as 'a bad year for solicitors'.[83] But apart from these perhaps inevitable crises the general trend of the nineteenth century had continued. It is natural that the profession should be somewhat introspective, and from time to time it had asked the question why it was so disliked without much proof that the question had in fact arisen.[84] The answers varied, but on the whole the problem of status and reputation which had been so important to the Victorian solicitor receded into the background in the twentieth century. Whereas it had been raised in countless letters to editors, articles in the legal and general press, and speeches it was now hardly referred to. Significantly, whereas in the past success in the profession had been regarded as a means of getting away from it, now more and more sons were following fathers into a profession to which they were proud to belong. Since 1945 changes in practice conditions have brought the solicitor into daily touch with a far larger number of people from a far wider cross-section of society than ever before; innumerable influences, social, financial and educational, have taken away from the solicitor and his office the stuffiness and unworldliness which made him seem remote; more and more people have discovered that their solicitor is the one person to whom they can confidently go with their problems. The solicitor has largely replaced the doctor and the parson in this respect, and the closer he has got to the general public the higher has become his status and reputation.

[83] *Solicitors' Journal*, vol 110, p 1.

[84] Eg *Law Society's Gazette*, 1959, p 689: 'The fall in the standing of our profession expressed in terms of social esteem and remuneration caused much heart-searching.'

INDEX

INDEX

INDEX